George Henry Napheys, M. L. Holbrook

The Physical Life of Woman

Advice to the Maiden, Wife and Mother

George Henry Napheys, M. L. Holbrook

The Physical Life of Woman
Advice to the Maiden, Wife and Mother

ISBN/EAN: 9783744738897

Printed in Europe, USA, Canada, Australia, Japan

Cover: Foto ©Lupo / pixelio.de

More available books at **www.hansebooks.com**

THE
PHYSICAL LIFE OF WOMAN

ADVICE TO THE

MAIDEN, WIFE, AND MOTHER.

BY

GEO. H. NAPHEYS, A.M., M.D.,

Member of Philadelphia County Medical Society;
Corresponding Member of the Gynæcological Society of Boston;
Author of "Compendium of Modern Therapeutics," &c., &c.

"Je veux qu'une femme ait des clartés de tout."
MOLIÈRE.

SYNOPSIS OF THE BOOK.

It treats in detail three particular phases of woman's life, viz: maidenhood, matrimony and maternity. Under the first head, the subject of puberty, its dangers and hygiene, and of love, are discussed from a medical stand-point. Valuable advice is given on the marriage of cousins, on the effects of marriage on woman and man, on "choosing a husband," on "the engagement," on the right time of the year to marry, on the wedding tour, and on many kindred topics. The physiology of the marriage relation is then considered. In the second part of the book, "the wife." It commences with some salutary hints on the "wedding night." Such inquiries of universal hygienic interest as, Shall husband and wife occupy the same room and bed? What kind of bed is most healthful? the dignity and propriety of the sexual instinct, its indulgence, restraint, and physiological laws, &c., are decorously but plainly treated. Well-considered views are advanced in regard to over-production and the limitation of offspring. The author also gives much useful advice to sterile wives who desire to have children, and he answers the question, Can the sexes be produced at will? in the light of the most recent scientific research. Many pages are devoted to the discussion of inheritance, how to have beautiful children, twin bearing, &c. The information in regard to the signs of pregnancy and the avoid-

ance of its diseases and discomforts, the prevention of "mothe
marks" and of miscarriage, is of incalculable value to every woma
Minute, practical, and careful directions are laid down as to the pr
per preparations for confinement, how to preserve the form aft
childbirth, etc. Under the head of "the mother" the rules f
nursing, weaning and bringing up by hand, are copious, and wou
benefit every mother to know. The volume closes with a conside
ation of "The Perils of Maternity," and of the dangers and hygie
of "The change of life."

TESTIMONIALS.

The following, among others, have been received, indicating t
scientific value and moral worth of this book :—

SIR WM. STERLING MAXWELL,
Recently elected Lord Rector of Edinburgh University,

gave the usual address on being installed in that office. Amo
other things he referred to the medical education of women, and sa
he was in favour of teaching women everything that they desired
learn, and for opening to them the doors of the highest oral i
struction as wide as the doors of book learning. So long, he sai
as women would administer to their sick children and husbands,
must hear some argument more convincing than he had yet hea
why they were to be debarred from learning the scientific groun
of the art of which they were so often the empirical practitioners
the docile and intelligent instruments.

FROM PROFESSOR JOHN S. HART, LL.D.

STATE NORMAL SCHOOL, TRENTON, N. J.

GEO. H. NAPHEYS, M. D.—

Dear Sir: I have read with attention the advance sheets of yo
book, "The Physical Life of Woman," and take pleasure in sayi
that you have handled a most difficult and important subject wi
equal delicacy and ability.

Yours truly,
JOHN S. HAR

OPINION OF MARK HOPKINS, D.D., LL.D.,
President of Williams College.

"Your book is conscientiously written, and will be likely to
good."

PHYSICAL LIFE OF WOMAN.

FROM THE N.Y. EVANGELIST, NOV. 18, 1869.

This is a plain and practical treatise prepared by a physician of skill and experience, in which he aims to furnish information to women, in their peculiar conditions and relations, married and single, so as to enable them to preserve their own health, and perform their duties to themselves and their children. The most delicate subjects are treated in language so chaste as not to offend any pure mind.

EDITORIAL FROM PHILADELPHIA MEDICAL AND SURGICAL REPORTER.

It is a singular fact, that in this country most of the works on medical hygienic matters have been written by irregular practitioners in order to help on its legs some ism or pathy of their own. The public is really desirous of information about the great questions of life and health. It buys whatever is offered it, and cannot tell, of course, the tares from the wheat. In fact, as we have said, there has been very little wheat offered it. Scientific physicians do not seem to have taken the pains in this country, as in Germany, to spread sound medical information among the people.

We, therefore, welcome all the more warmly a work which, under any circumstances, would command our praise, advance sheets of which are now before us. The author is Dr. George H. Napheys, of this city, well known to all the readers of the "Reporter" as a constant contributor to its pages for a number of years, a close student of therapeutics, and a pleasing writer. The title of the book is "The Physical Life of Woman; advice to the Maiden, Wife and Mother." It is a complete manual of information for women, in their peculiar conditions and relations, married and single.

The style is simple, agreeable, and eminently proper and delicate, conspicuously so when treating of such difficult topics to handle in a popular book, yet so necessary to be handled, as the marital relations of husband and wife, the consummation of marriage, etc.

We do not doubt that this work will find as large a sale both in and out of the profession in this country, as the works of Bockh and Klencke in Germany, and of Tilt and Chavasse in England.

FROM REV. HORACE BUSHNELL, D.D.

HARTFORD, CON., Sept., 1869.

GEO. H. NAPHEYS, M.D.—

Dear Sir: I have read a large part of your book with interest. I shrink from expressing any estimate of it, as respects its physiological merit, but it seems to be a book well studied, and it is written with much delicacy and a careful respect, at all points, to the great interests of morality. It will certainly be a great help to intelligence on the subject, and ought, therefore, to be correspondingly useful.

Very respectfully yours,
HORACE BUSHNELL.

FROM HARVEY L. BYRD, M.D.,
Professor of Obstetrics in the Medical Department of Washington U
versity of Baltimore, Maryland.

BALTIMORE, Sept., 1869

DR. GEO. H. NAPHEYS, Philadelphia,—

Dear Sir: I have examined with much pleasure and satisfact
your work on "The Physical Life of Woman," and do not hesit
to commend it most warmly to our countrywomen, for whose be
fit it is intended. I congratulate you on the felicitous manner
which you have treated so difficult a subject, and would recomm
it to the public as supplying a want that has long been felt in
country.

Omne verum utile dictu, and what can be more proper, or m
useful, than that woman should be made acquainted with the g
laws of her being, and the duties for which she was created?

Very respectfully, your obed't servant,

HARVEY L. BYRD

EXTRACTS FROM LETTER RECEIVED FROM EDWARD M. SNOW, M.D.,
PROVIDENCE, RHODE ISLAND.

PROVIDENCE, Sept., 1869

DR. NAPHEYS,—

Dear Sir: I have examined with much interest the adva
sheets of your book, "The Physical Life of Woman;" I
highly pleased with it. The advice given seems to me to
generally correct and judiciously expressed; and, in my opini
the wide circulation of the book would be a benefit to
community.

Truly yours,

EDWARD M. SNOW

OPINION OF LLOYD P. SMITH,
Librarian Philadelphia Library.

LIBRARY CO. OF PHILADELPHIA, FIFTH ST. BEL. CHESNUT,
PHILADELPHIA, Sept., 1869

It is an open question whether books *de secretis mulier*
should be written for the general public, but there is
doubt that when they are written, it should be done by
regular medical faculty and not by ignorant quacks.
Napheys' "Physical Life of Woman" shows not only
scientific attainments of the author, but also a wide range
miscellaneous reading. The delicate subjects treated of
handled with a seriousness and earnestness becoming tl
importance, and the author's views are expressed in excell
English.

LLOYD P. SMITH

OPINION OF S. W. BUTLER, M.D.,
Editor of the Philadelphia "Medical and Surgical Reporter."

I have carefully examined "The Physical Life of Woman," and find it a work at once thoroughly representing modern science, and eminently adapted for family instruction. It is well suited to female readers, to whom it is specially addressed, both in the matter it contains and in the delicacy with which points relating to their physiological life are mentioned. W. BUTLER.

FROM REV. GEORGE ALEX. COOKE, D.D., D.C.L.

PHILADELPHIA, Sept., 1869.

DR. GEO. H. NAPHEYS,—

Dear Sir: I have carefully read your work entitled "The Physical Life of Woman," and as the result, I must candidly say that I believe the information it contains is well calculated to lessen suffering and greatly benefit the human race. I know there are some falsely fastidious persons who would object to any work of the kind, but "to the pure all things are pure." You have done your part fearlessly and well, and in a popular manner, and I trust that your work may be productive of all the good you design by its publication. Very faithfully,
GEO. ALEX. COOKE.

LETTER RECEIVED FROM REV. GEO. BRINGHURST,
Rector of the P. E. Church of the Messiah, Philadelphia.

PHILADELPHIA, Sept., 1869.

DR. GEO. H. NAPHEYS,—

My Dear Sir: I have perused with considerable care and pleasure the work on the "Physical Life of Woman," and feel no hesitation in pronouncing it admirably composed, honest, succinct, refined and worthy the companionship of every lady of this age. I hail its appearance with gratitude, and look upon it as a valuable contribution to those efforts which are making in various directions to elevate the tone of morals of the nineteenth century, and to enable mothers to discharge faithfully the duties they owe to their children.

Sincerely yours,
GEORGE BRINGHURST.

FROM THE NEW YORK MEDICAL GAZETTE, JAN. 8, 1870.

Though professedly written for popular instruction, this book will not fail to instruct, as well the professional reader. We cordially recommend the perusal of Dr. Napheys' book to every woman seeking a fuller acquaintance with her physical organism.

FROM THE MEDICAL RECORD, NEW YORK, JAN. 15, 1870.

Doctor Napheys, in his work on "The Physical Life of Woman," has acquitted himself with infinite credit. The subject which for a work of its size takes a very wide range, is treated in choice, nay elegant language, and we have not noticed a single expression upon the most delicate matter, that could offend the most refined taste. There are, too, a great many interesting historical facts connected with the general topic, both in an ethical and physiological point of view, which show much discrimination in their production, and a good amount of sterling scholarship. To the medical reader there are many points in the book that are worthy of attention, prominent among which are remarks bearing upon the right of limitation of offspring. We sincerely hope that for the real benefit of women, it may meet with a hearty reception, and be productive of great good in preventing many of those disorders, now so rife in the community, which are solely the result of ignorance of the ordinary laws of female hygiene.

No one, however scrupulous, need fear to admit the work within the pale of his family circle, and place it with confidence in the hands of his daughters.

FROM H. N. EASTMAN, M.D.,
Professor of Practical Medicine in Geneva Medical College.

GENEVA, Sept., 1869.

GEO. H. NAPHEYS, M.D.,—

Dear Sir: I have just completed a careful reading of your advance sheets of "The Physical Life of Woman," and I unhesitatingly pronounce it an admirable work, and one especially needed at this time.

The book is written in a chaste, elevated, and vigorous style, is replete with instructions indispensable to the welfare and happiness of women, and should be placed in the hands of every mature maiden and matron in our land.

H. N. EASTMAN.

FROM THE BOSTON MEDICAL AND SURGICAL JOURNAL, NOV. 25, 1869.

Most valuable for the perusal of mothers, and of those fathers who may be equal to the task of advising sons liable to commit matrimony. The style—of the text—is unexceptionable. Words are not wasted, and those used are to the point. The volume is not a mere *resumé* of others' opinions; but the author has made the topics of which he treats his own.

FROM THE NASHVILLE JOURNAL OF MEDICINE AND SURGERY FOR NOVEMBER, 1869.

The outside of this book is more stylish and artistic than any the market has owed to the press this season. The type and paper of the inside are in keeping with the elegant exterior. The work contains much valuable matter, in a style peculiarly attractive. It is intended to treat woman as a rational being, to let her know much about herself as a woman, that from this knowledge she may prevent and therefore escape much of the suffering endured by her sex.

And who can do this but a physician? This may be regarded as the first attempt of the kind in this country.

FROM THE CHICAGO MEDICAL EXAMINER OF NOVEMBER 19, 1869.

This work is written in a plain and pleasing style well calculated both to please and instruct. There is nothing of the *sensational* or imaginative character in it. On the contrary, its teachings are in strict accordance with scientific facts and good sense. Though designed specially for females, yet a careful perusal would be productive of much benefit to both sexes.

FROM THE NATIONAL BAPTIST,—PHILADELPHIA, DEC. 30, 1869.

We join in the cordial welcome which this book has received. There is no other work which tells so well just what every woman,—and every considerate man also,—ought to know. Maternity is the one great function of woman, according to God's ordinance, and for this marvellous and holy mission, her physical, intellectual, and moral constitution has been designed. Dr. Napheys, in his wise "advice to maiden, wife, and mother," passes in review the cardinal facts respecting woman's physical life. The book is written in a very clear and simple style, so that no one can misunderstand it, while there is nothing to disturb or offend the most sensitive. A judicious mother would do her maturing daughters great service by first carefully reading this volume herself, and then have them read it under her guidance.

OPINION OF DR. R. SHELTON MACKENZIE.

PHILADELPHIA, Oct., 1869.

Believing that such a work as Dr. Napheys' "Physical Life of Woman," giving a great deal of valuable information, explicitly and delicately, is likely to be of very essential importance to the fair sex, I cannot hesitate to express my favourable opinion of its object and execution.

OPINION OF MRS. R. B. GLEASON, M.D.

ELMIRA, N. Y., Sept. 1869.

The advanced sheets of "The Physical Life of Woma[n] have been read with much interest. In this book Dr. Naphe[ys] has well met a real need of the age. There are many thin[gs] incident to woman's physical organization which she needs [to] know, and concerning which she still does not want to ask [a] physician, and may not have one at hand when she most desi[res] the information. This book can be easily read and perfec[tly] understood by those not familiar with medical terms. [All] matters of delicacy are treated with freedom, and still wit[h] purity of thought and expression which is above criticism.

For many years we have been often asked for just such [a] book, and shall gladly commend it to the many wives a[nd] mothers who want for themselves and grown up daught[ers] such a book of helps and hints for home life.

MRS. R. B. GLEASON.

FROM THE NEW YORK CHRISTIAN UNION, JAN. 8, 1870.

Society owes a debt of gratitude to this brave and scientific p[hy]sician for the unexceptional way in which he has performed a wo[rk] that has, up to the publication of this book, been a paramount ne[ed] not to be satisfied anywhere in the English language. If t[he] volume contained only the chapter on the influence of the mothe[r's] mind upon her unborn child, we would recommend its purchase [in] every family in the land.

FROM REV. HENRY CLAY TRUMBULL,

Secretary of New England Department of Missions of the Americ[an] Sunday-school Union.

HARTFORD, CT., Oct., 1869.

GEO. H. NAPHEYS, M.D.—

My Dear Sir: Understanding, from my long acquaintance with yo[u,] your thoroughness of mental culture, your delicacy of sentime[nt] and your sound good sense, I was prepared to approve heartily t[he] tone and style of your new work—"The Physical Life of Woman" when its advanced sheets were first placed in my hands.

A close examination of it convinces me that it is a book which c[an] be read by every woman to her instruction and advantage.] manner is unexceptionable. Its style is remarkably simple.] substance evidences your professional knowledge and your exte[n]sive study, I believe it needs only to be brought to notice to co[m]mend itself widely. I think you have done an excellent work [in] its preparation. Sincerely your friend,

H. CLAY TRUMBULL.

THE
PHYSICAL·LIFE OF WOMAN:

Advice to the
MAIDEN, WIFE, AND MOTHER.

BY
GEO. H. NAPHEYS, A.M., M.D.,

MEMBER OF PHILADELPHIA COUNTY MEDICAL SOCIETY; CORRESPONDING MEMBER OF THE
GYNÆCOLOGICAL SOCIETY OF BOSTON; AUTHOR OF "COMPENDIUM
OF MODERN THERAPEUTICS," ETC., ETC.

TO WHICH IS ADDED
PARTURITION WITHOUT PAIN.
BY M. L. HOLBROOK, M. D.

"Je veux qu'une femme ait des clartés de tout.
MOLIÈRE.

Toronto:
ROSE PUBLISHING COMPANY.

PREFACE.

It seems well to offer, at the outset, a few words explanatory of the nature and object of this book. The author feels that its aim is novel, is daring, and will perhaps subject him to criticism. He therefore makes his plea, *pro domo suâ*, in advance.

The researches of scientific men within the last few years have brought to light very many facts relating to the physiology of woman, the diseases to which she is subject, and the proper means to prevent those diseases. Such information, if universally possessed, cannot but result in great benefit to the individual and the commonwealth. The difficulty is to express one's self clearly and popularly on topics never referred to in ordinary social intercourse. But as the physician is obliged daily to speak in plain yet decorous language of such matters, the author felt that the difficulty was not insurmountable.

He is aware that a respectable though diminishing class in the community maintain that nothing which relates exclusively to either sex should become the subject of popular medical instruction. With every inclination to do this class justice, he feels sure that such an opinion is radically erroneous. Ignorance is no more the mother of purity than she is of religion. The men and women who study and practise medicine are not

PREFACE.

the worse but the better, for their knowledge of such mat[ters]. So it would be with the community. Had every person a s[ound] understanding of the relations of the sexes, one of the [most] fertile sources of crime would be removed.

A brief appendix has been added, directed more espec[ially] to the professional reader, who may desire to consult son[e of] the original authorities upon whom the author has dr[awn]. And here he would ask from his fellow-members of the me[dical] profession their countenance and assistance in his attem[pt to] distribute sound information of this character among the pe[ople]. None but physicians can know what sad consequences are [con]stantly occurring from the want of it.

This book but follows the precedent set by Dr. Bo[ck,] Professor of Pathology in Leipzic; Ernest Legouvé, of [the] French Academy; Dr. Edward John Tilt, M.R.C.P., Lo[nd.;] Dr. Henry Pye Chavasse, F.R.C.S., Eng.; and others [who] stand in the front rank of the profession abroad.

In concluding, the auth[or] desires to express his thanks [and] acknowledge his obligatio[n]s [to] a medical friend, whose na[me is] well known in the literature of the profession as that of [one] alike distinguished for his general culture and scientific at[tain]ments. It is to his very material assistance in the prepar[ation] of the manuscript, and in the passage of the book throug[h the] press, that any merit which this work may possess is in a [great] measure owing.

PREFACE
TO
THE THIRD CANADIAN EDITION.

IN bringing out a new Canadian Edition of Dr. Naphey's invaluable Work, little need be said by way of Preface. No one can read the book without profiting by it; and no one need expect to find in its pages a single word to offend any mind rightly constituted. In the words of the NEW YORK EVANGELIST, "the most delicate subjects are treated in language so chaste as not to offend any pure mind; and the highest authority we acknowledge declares, that 'to the pure all things are pure.'"

The work covers the whole ground embraced in the Table of Contents: And on the great engrossing subject which lately called forth such emphatic deliverances by the Right Rev BISHOP COXE, Right Rev. PRIMATE SPAULDING, the old and new school PRESBYTERIAN GENERAL ASSEMBLIES, &c., &c., it utters no uncertain sound.

The facts, references, &c., are mainly applied to the United States, where the book was first published, but they all tell with equal force in our own country.

That the Work is highly appreciated where it is best known, a sale of over one hundred thousand copies in a few months amply proves.

TORONTO, February, 1889.

CONTENTS.

INTRODUCTORY 17

    Knowledge is safety— The distinction of the sexes—Persons of both sexes and of neither sex—The sphere of woman.

THE MAIDEN. PUBERTY 22

    What is the age of puberty?—What hastens and what retards puberty?—The changes it works—The dangers of puberty—Green sickness—Hysterics—Secret bad habits—The hygiene of puberty—The age of nubility.

LOVE 40

    Its power on humanity—What is love?—Love a necessity—Love is eternal—What of flirtation?—Second Marriages—Of divorce—Of a plurality of wives or husbands—Courtships—Love at first sight—How to choose a husband—Shall Cousins Marry?—The mixture of races—Shall Americans marry foreigners?—The age of a husband—His temperament—His character—The symbolism of the human body—The engagement—Concerning long engagements—The right time of the year and month to marry—The wedding tour.

THE WIFE 71

    The wedding night—Shall husband and wife occupy the same room and bed?—What kind of a bed is most healthful?—The dignity and propriety of the sexual instinct—The indulgence and the restraint of sexual desire—Times when marital relations should be suspended or are painful—Sterility—Advice to wives who desire to have children—On the limitation of offspring—The crime of abortion—Nature of conception—The signs of fruitful conjunction—How to retain the affections of a husband—Inheritance—How to have beautiful children—Inheritance of talent and genius—Transmission of disease—Why are women redundant?—How to have boys or girls—Twin-bearing—More than two at a birth.

CONTENTS.

PREGNANCY..

Signs of pregnancy—Miscarriage—Mothers' marks—Education of the child in the womb—Double pregnancies—Is it a son or daughter?—How to foretell twins—Length of pregnancy—How to calculate the time of the confinement—Care of health during pregnancy—Food—Clothing—Exercise—Bathing—Ventilation—Sleep—Relation of husband and wife during pregnancy—Diseases of pregnancy.

CONFINEMENT..

Preparations for confinement—Signs of approaching labour—Symptoms of labour—The confinement—Hints to attendants—Attention to the mother—Attention to the child—To have labour without pain—Mortality of child-bed—Weight and length of new-born children—Duration of labour—Still-births—Imprudence after child-birth—How to preserve the form after child-birth.

THE MOTHER..

Nursing—When the mother should not nurse—Rules for nursing—Influences of diet on the milk—Of pregnancy on the milk—Of the mother's mind on the child—Quantity of milk required by the infant—Over-abundance of milk—Scantiness of milk—Wet-nursing by virgins, aged women, and men—Care of health while nursing—Relations of husband and wife during nursing—Signs of over-nursing—Directions for mothers who cannot nurse their own children—How to select a wet-nurse—Bringing up by hand—Weaning—The care of infancy—Is the race degenerating?—The perils of maternity.

THE SINGLE LIFE..

THE CHANGE OF LIFE..

Its dangers, diseases, and hygiene.

NOTES..

INDEX..

THE
PHYSICAL LIFE OF WOMAN.

KNOWLEDGE IS SAFETY.

"KNOWLEDGE is power," said the philosopher. The maxim is true; but here is a greater truth: "Knowledge is safety,"—safety amid the physical ills that beset us, safety amid the moral pitfalls that environ us.

Filled with this thought, we write this book. It is the Revelation of Science to Woman. It tells her, in language which aims at nothing but simplicity, the results which the study of her nature, as distinct from that of man, has attained. We may call it her physical biography.

It is high time that such a book were written. The most absorbing question of the day is the "woman question." The social problems of chiefest interest concern her. And nowhere are those problems more zealously studied than in this new land of ours, which has thrown aside the trammels of tradition, and is training its free muscles with intent to grapple the untried possibilities of social life. Who can guide us in these experiments? What master, speaking as one having authority, can advise us? There is such a guide, such a master. The laws of woman's physical life shape her destiny and reveal her future. Within these laws all things are possible; beyond them, nothing is of avail.

Especially should woman herself understand her own nature. How many women are there, with health, beauty,

merriment, ay, morality, too, all gone, lost forever, throu
ignorance of themselves? What spurious delicacy is t
which would hide from woman that which beyond
else it behoves her to know? We repudiate it, and
plain but decorous language—truth is always decorou
we purpose to divulge those secrets hidden hitherto un
the technical jargon of science.

THE DISTINCTION OF THE SEXES.

The distinction of the sexes belongs neither to the hi
est nor to the lowest forms of existence. Animals
vegetables of the humblest character have no sex. S
is with spirits. Revelation implies that beyond this
sexual characteristics cease. On one occasion the Sad
cees put this question to Christ: There was a woman v
lawfully had seven husbands, one after the other; now
the resurrection, which of these shall be her husband;
shall they all have her to wife? He replied that herea
there shall be neither marrying nor giving in marri
but that all shall be "as the angels which are in heav
Sexuality implies reproduction, and that is something
do not associate with spiritual life.

It further implies imperfection, which is equally
from our hopes of happiness beyond the grave. The po
which reproduces by a division of itself, is in one se
more complete than we are. The man is in some resp
inferior to the woman; the woman in others is subo
nate to man. A happy marriage, a perfect union, t
twain one flesh, is the type of the independent, comple
being. Without the other, either is defective. "N
riage," said Napoleon, "is strictly indispensable to l
piness"

There is in fact a less difference between the sexes t
is generally believed. They are but slight variations f
one original plan. Anatomists maintain, with plaus
arguments, that there is no part or organ in the one
but has an analogous part or organ in the other, sin

in structure, similar in position. Just as the right side resembles the left, so does man resemble woman.

Let us see what differences there really are:

The frame of woman is shorter and slighter. In the United States the men average five feet eight inches in height and one hundred and forty five pounds in weight; the women five feet two and a half inches in height, and one hundred and twenty-five pounds in weight. Man has broad shoulders and narrow hips; woman has narrow shoulders and broad hips. Her skull is formed of thinner bones, and is in shape more like that of a child. Its capacity, in proportion to her height, is a very little less than in man; about one-fiftieth, it is said, which, so far as brain-power is concerned, may readily be made up by its finer texture. Her shoulders are set farther back than in the other sex, giving her greater breadth of chest in front. This is brought about by the increased length of her collar bone, and this is the reason why she can never throw a ball or stone with the accuracy of a man. Graceful in other exercises, here she is awkward.

Her contour is more rounded, her neck is longer, her skin smoother, her voice softer, her hair less generally distributed over the body, but stronger in growth than in man. She breathes with the muscles of her chest—he with those of his abdomen. He has greater muscular force—she more power of endurance. Beyond all else she has the attributes of maternity—she is provided with organs to nourish and protect the child before and after birth.

PERSONS OF BOTH SEXES AND OF NEITHER SEX.

Nature is very sedulous in maintaining these differences. It is the rarest thing in the world to find a human being of doubtful sex. Many a physician disbelieves that there ever has been a person of both sexes—a true hermaphrodite. They are very scarce, but they do exist. There is

one now living in Germany. It bears a female n
Catherine Hohman. She was baptized and brougl
a female; but Catherine is as much man as woman.
learned professor of anatomy, Rokitansky, of Vie
asserts most positively that this is a real hermaphre
Her history is sad. Born in humble circumstances,
of marriageable age she loved a man, who wished h
emigrate with him to America. But when she disc
to him her deformity, he broke off the engagement
deserted her. Then her affections became fixed
young girl; but how could she make her suit to on
parently of her own sex? With passions that promp
to seek both sexes, she belongs to neither. "What sl
do here on earth?" she exclaimed, in tears, to a m
science who recently visited her. "What am I? I
life an object of scientific experiment, and after my o
an anatomical curiosity."

There are also persons—very few indeed—who hav
sex at all. They are without organs and without pass
Such creatures seem to have been formed merely to
us that this much-talked-of-difference of sex is, afte
nothing inherent in the constitution of things, and
individuals may be born, live and thrive, of both sex
of neither.

THE SPHERE OF WOMAN.

Our province lies within the physical sphere of wc
But we will here allow ourselves a momentary digre
It will be seen that while these differences are not r
yet they are peculiarly permanent. They hint to v
mental and intellectual character of woman. What op
should we hold on this much-vexed question?

To this effect: The mental faculties of man and w
are unlike, but not unequal. Any argument to the
trary, drawn from the somewhat less weight of the
of woman, is met by the fact that the most able me
often undersized, with small heads. The subord

place which woman occupies in most states arises partly from the fact that the part she plays in reproduction prevents her from devoting her whole time and energies to the acquisition of power, and partly from the fact that those faculties in which she is superior to man have been obscured and oppressed by the animal vigour and selfishness of the male. As civilization advances, the natural rights of woman will be more and more freely conceded, until the sexes become absolutely equal before the law; and finally, her superiority in many respects will be granted, and she will reap the benefits of all the advantages it brings, without desiring to encroach on those avocations for which masculine energy and strength are imperatively needed.

The most peculiar feature of woman's life are hers for a limited period only. Man is man for a longer time than woman is woman. With him it is a lifetime matter; with her it is but a score of years or so. Her child-bearing period is less than half her life. Within this time, she passes through all the phases of that experience which is peculiarly her own.

And these phases, what are they? Nature herself defines them. They are three in number—the Maiden, the Wife, and the Mother. In one and then another of this triad, her life passes. Each has its own duties and dangers; each demands its own precautions; each must be studied by itself.

Let us at once commence this important study, and proceed in the order of time.

THE MAIDEN.

PUBERTY.

AT a certain period in the life of the
to be a girl, and becomes a *woman*.
felt no distinction between herself and t
mates. But now a crisis takes place,
after to hedge her round with a mysteri
most real barrier from all *mankind*.

This period is called *the age of pube*
flow of blood recurring every month;
the female has entered upon that portio
peculiar obligations are to the whole r
herself alone. The second part of her
opened. Why is it that on her, the wea
burden is laid? Why this weakness,
recurring loss of vital fluid?

Perhaps it is a wise provision that she
of her lowly duty, lest man should mak
ject of his worship, or lest the pride
obscure the sense of shame. But this
rather the moralist than the physician,
ing *why* it is, and shall only inquire *wh*

To this, science returns a clear reply.
of woman there are two small bodies,
like large almonds, called the ovaries. T
side of the womb, and are connected wit
four inches in length. These bodies are
a great number of diminutive vesicles
mysterious law of nature, mature one
thirty days. for thirty years of wom

mature, the vesicle separates from the ovary, traverses the tube into the womb, and is thence expelled and lost or becomes, by contact with the other sex, the germ of a living being. This process is accompanied by a disturbance of the whole system. Wandering pains are felt; a sense of languor steals over the mind; the blood rushes with increased violence through the vessels, and more or less of it escapes from the veins, causing that change which we term *menstruation*.

The ancients had a tradition that in the beginning of things the world was made from an egg; the naturalists of past generations had this maxim: Everything living comes from an egg; and science to-day says the same. For this vesicle we have mentioned is in fact an *egg*, similar in structure to those which birds, fish, and turtles deposit. The only differences are that the one is developed out of the body, and the other within; the one has a shell, the other has none.

Therefore, physiologists give this definition; menstruation is ovulation—it is the laying of an egg.

WHAT IS THE AGE OF PUBERTY?

This has been a matter of careful study by physicians. They have collected great numbers of observations, and have reached this conclusion: In the middle portion of the temperate zone, the average age when the first period appears in healthy girls is fourteen years and six months. If it occurs more than six months later or earlier than this, then it is likely that something is wrong, or, at least, the case is exceptional.

Exceptional cases, where this average is widely departed from in apparently perfect health are rare. But they do occur. We have known instances where the solicitude of parents has been excited by the long delay of this constitutional change, and others in which it has taken place at an almost tender age, without causing any perceptible injury to the general health.

There is an instance recorded, on g(
a French child but three years old un
.sical changes incident to puberty, and
woman. But what children can sur
cocity ? This French child-woman
shade by one described in a recent n
medical journal, who *from her birth*
changes, and the full physical develo
the perfect woman!

Thus sometimes, a wide deviation f
we have stated occurs, without havir
ing. Yet at no time is such a devia
In nine out of ten instances it is ow
the constitution, the health, or format
ascertained and corrected. Otherw
health and mental misery may be the
teachers, it is with you this respor
thousands of wretched wives who
ness to a neglect of proper attention
of their lives warn you how serious

The foundation of old age, says a c
is laid in childhood; but the health o
upon puberty. Never was there a
two years which change the girl to t
for ever the happiness or the hopeles
life. They decide whether she is
hopeful, cheerful wife and mother, or
ing invalid, to whom marriage is a cu
tion, and life itself a burden.

We reiterate our warning. Motl
whom children are confided at this
look well to it that you appreciate,
serve the duties you have assumed.
prevent you from learning and enforc
so necessary at this period of life

WHAT HASTENS AND WHAT RETARDS PUBERTY.

As a rule, we find that those who develop early, fade early. A short childhood portends a premature old age. It often forshadows also feeble middle life.

Having ascertained, therefore, what is the average age at which puberty takes place with us, let us see what conditions anticipate or retard this age.

The most important is *climate*.

In hot climates, man, like the vegetation, has a surprising rapidity of growth. Marriages are usual at twelve and fourteen years of age. Puberty comes to both sexes as early as at ten and eleven years. We even read in the Life of Mahomet, that one of his wives bore him a son when but ten years of age. Let another dozen years pass, and these blooming maidens have been metamorphosed into wrinkled, faded old women. The beauty of their precocious youth has withered almost literally like a flower which is plucked.

Very different is it in the cold and barren regions of the far north. The man, once more partaking of the nature of his surroundings, yields as slowly to the impulses of his passions, as does the ice-bound earth to the slanting rays of the summer sun. Maturity, so quick to come, so swift to leave in the torrid heats, chilled by the long winters, arrives to the girls of Lapland, Norway, and Siberia, only when they are eighteen and nineteen years of age. But, in return for this, they retain their vigour and good looks to a green old age.

Between these extremes, including as they do the whole second decade of existence, this important change takes place normally in different latitudes. We have said that in the middle temperate zone the proper age is fourteen years and six months. Let us now see what conditions ead to deviations from this age in our climate.

First on the list is that sacred fire handed down to us from our ancestors, which we call in our material language the *constitution*.

The females of certain races, cert[ain]
noticed, mature earlier than their r[...]
for example, are always precocious, [...]
years. So are coloured girls, and t[...]
We can guess the reasons here. N[...]
still retain in their blood the tropic[...]
ratively recent periods, their foref[athers]
vertical rays of the torrid zone.

Nor is this all. It is well ascert[ained,]
observations, that brunettes devel[op...]
blonde sisters; that those who will [...]
men are slower than those whose [...]
that the dark-haired and black eye[d...]
in this respect than the light-haire[d...]
the fat, sluggish girl is more tardy t[han...]
one; that, in general, what is know[n...]
temperament is ever ahead of tha[t...]
or phlegmatic.

It is a familiar fact, that it is not [...]
change before the usual average [...]
weakly, excitable, diminutive frame [...]
ous, regular muscular exertion,—p[...]
words, never tend to anticipate thi[s...]
retard it.

With this warning fresh in our ea[rs...]
what causes constantly incline und[...]
and thus to forestall Nature in her [...]
beauty. They are of two kinds, ph[...]

Idleness of body, highly-seasoned [...]
ages such as, beer, wine, liquors, and, [...]
and tea, irregular habits of sleep—[...]
causes of premature development. [...]
are still more potent.

Whatever *stimulates the emotion[s...]*
rally early sexual life. Late hours, [...]
sational novels, "flashy" papers, lo[...]
the ball-room talk of beaux, love a[...]

mosphere of riper years which is so often and so injudiciously thrown around children in the United States—all hasten the event which transforms the girl into the woman. A particular emphasis has been laid by some physicians on the power of music to awaken the dormant susceptibilities to passion, and on this account its too general or earnest cultivation by children has been objected to. Educators would do well to bear this caution in mind.

How powerfully these causes work is evident when we compare the average age of puberty in large cities and in country districts. The females in the former mature from six to eight months sooner than those in the latter. This is unquestionably owing to their mode of life, physically indolent, mentally over-stimulated. The result, too, is seen with painful plainness in comparing the sturdy, well-preserved farm-wife of thirty with the languid, pale, faded city lady of the same age.

THE CHANGES IT WORKS.

Two short years change the awkward and angular girl of fourteen into the trim and graceful maiden of sweet sixteen. Wonderful metamorphosis! The magic wand of the fairy has touched her, and she comes forth a new being, a vision of beauty to bewitch the world.

Let us analyze this change.

The earliest sign of approaching puberty is a deposit of fat in the loose cellular tissue under the skin. This gives roundness to the form, and grace to the movements. According to the distinguished naturalist (Buffon), it is first observable by a slight swelling of the groins. Thence it extends over the whole body. The breasts especially receive additions, and develop to form the perfect bust.

Parts of the body previously free from hair become covered with a soft growth, and that which covers the head acquires more vigour and gloss, usually becoming one or two shades darker. The eyes brighten and acquire un-

THE MAIDEN.

wonted significance. These windows
to the close observer the novel emotion
in the mind within,

The voice, too, shares in the transfo
ing, slender articulation of the child gi
melodious, soft voice of woman, the
ever hears. To the student of humani
physician, nothing is more symbolical
than the voice. Would you witness a
Watch how a person born blind unerr
the character of those he meets by thi

Beyond all external modifications, w
indicate how profound is the alteratio
The internal organs of the body assum
new powers. The taste for food chang
system has demands hitherto unknown
have adverted to, called the ovaries, in
does the uterus. The very frame-wo
does not escape. The bones increase i
around the hips expand, and give the
tive form, upon the perfection of whi
of her children depend.

MENTAL CHANGES.

Such are the changes which strike
are others which are not less significant
far more urgently our watchful hee
strange desires, are invading the soul
is assumed to the world. It is vague,
disturbing all the same.

The once light-hearted girl inclin
seeks solitude; her mother surprises he
her teacher discovers an unwonted
studies, a less retentive memory, a disi
labour; her father misses her accustom
perhaps, is annoyed by her listlessness
does it all mean? What is the matte

Mother, teacher, father, it is for you to know the answer to these questions. You have guarded this girl through years of helpless infancy and thoughtless childhood. At the peril of her life, and of what is of more value than life, do not now relax your vigilance. Every day the reaper Death reaps with his keen sickle the flower of our land. The mothers weep, indeed, but little do they realize that it is because they have neglected to cherish them, as was their duty, that the Lord of Paradise has taken them back to Himself.

THE COMPLETION OF PUBERTY.

The symptoms increase until at length the system has acquired the necessary strength, and furnished itself with reserve forces enough to complete its transformation. Then the monthly flow commences.

In thoroughly healthy girls it continues to recur at regular intervals, from twenty-five to thirty days apart. This is true of about three out of four. In others a long interval, sometimes six months, occur between the first and second sickness. If the general health is not *in the least* impaired, this need cause no anxiety. Irregularities are found in the first year or two, which often right themselves afterwards. But whenever they are associated with the *slightest* signs of mental or bodily disorder, they demand instant and intelligent attention.

It used to be supposed that the periods of the monthly sickness were in some way connected with the phases of the moon. So general is this belief even yet in France, that a learned academician not long since thought it worth while carefully to compare over four thousand observations, to see whether they did bear any relations to the lunar phases. It is hardly worth while to add that he found none.

We have known perfectly healthy young women who were ill every sixteen days, and others in whom a period of thirty-five or thirty-six days would elapse. The rea-

sons of such differences are not clear. Some inheri[t]
peculiarity of constitution is doubtless at work. [C]
mate is of primary importance. Travellers in Lapla[nd]
and other countries in the far north, say that the wo[men]
there are not regulated more frequently than three or f[our]
times a year. Hard labour and phlegmatic temperam[ent]
usually prolong the interval between the periodical
nesses.

An equal diversity prevails in reference to the *len[gth]*
of time the discharge continues. The average of a la[rge]
number of cases observed in healthy women in this co[un]try, between the ages of fifteen and thirty-five, is f[our]
days and a fraction. In a more general way, we may
from two to six days is the proper duration. Shoul[d it]
diverge widely from this, then it is likely some miscl[ief]
is at work.

In relation to the *amount* of the discharge, every
man is a law unto herself. Usually it is four or
ounces in all. Habits of life are apt to modify it mat[eri]ally. Here, again, those exposed to p[r]olonged cold
inured to severe labour escape more easily than their
ters petted in the lap of luxury. Delicate, feeble, nerv[ous]
women, those, in other words who can least [a]fford the
of blood, are precisely those who lose the most. Nat[ure]
who is no tender mother, but a stern step-mother, t[hat]
punishes them for disregarding her laws. Soft couches
dolent ease, highly spiced food, warm rooms, weak mus[cles]
—these are the infractions of her rules which she reve[nges]
with vigorous, ay, merciless severity.

It is well-known, too, that excitement of the emoti[ons]
whether of anger, joy, grief, hatred, or love, increases
discharge. Even the vulgar are aware of this, and, mi[s]terpreting it, as half knowledge always does, suppose
sign of stronger animal passions. It bears no such m[ean]ing. But the fact reads us a lesson how important it i[s to]
cultivate a placid mind, free from strong desire or [fear]
and to hold our emotions in the firm leash of reason.

Physicians attach great importance to the *character of* the discharge. It should be thin, dark, watery coloured. and never clot. If it clots, it is an indication that something is wrong.

THE DANGERS OF PUBERTY.

We have shown that there are constantly individual deviations, quite consistent with health, from any given standard. They only become significant of disease when they depart decidedly from the average, either in the frequency of the illness, its duration, the amount of the discharge, or the character. More or less pain, more or less prostration, and general disturbance at these epochs, are universal and inevitable. They are part of the sentence which at the outset He pronounced upon the woman, when He said unto her: "I will greatly multiply thy sorrow and thy conception." Yet with merciful kindness He has provided means by which the pain may be greatly lessened, and the sorrow avoided; and that we may learn and observe these means, their neglect often increases a hundred-fold the natural suffering.

At this critical period, the seeds of hereditary and constitutional disease manifest themselves. They draw fresh malignancy from the new activity of the system. The first symptoms of tubercular consumption, of scrofula, of obstinate and disfiguring skin diseases, of hereditary insanity, of congenital epilepsy, of a hundred terrible maladies, which from birth have lurked in the child, biding the opportunity of attack, suddenly spring from their lairs and hurry her to the grave or the madhouse. If we ask why so many fair girls of eighteen or twenty are followed by weeping friends to an early tomb, the answer is, 'chiefly from diseases which had their origin at the period of puberty.

It is impossible for us to rehearse here all the minute symptoms, each almost trifling in itself, which warn the practised physician of the approach of one of these fearful

foes in time to allow him to make a c
little more than reiterate the warning
this momentous epoch, any disquietin
it physical or mental, let not a day b
skilled competent medical advice.

There is, however, a train of symp
insidious, fruitful with agony of min
shall mention them particularly. Th
how all-important is close observation
to the wise physician are trifles seem

If you notice a girl of fourteen or si
ing always gives one arm in prefere
her companion; if, in sleeping, she m
side; if, in sitting, she is apt to pre
back, and throws one arm over its b
that she always sits with one foot a
the other; if she, on inquiry, confesses
pains in one side of her chest, do not
wardness. These are ominous por
spinal disease, than which a more fea
known to medicine.

Not less stealthy is the approach
joint, of white swelling of the knee,
curable if taken at the very first, al
when they have once unmasked thei

Apart from these general dangers
thoroughly sound constitutions are n
disorders called functional, to which

GREEN SICKNESS.

When we speak of "green sicknes
haps the most common of all, and
mother has heard. Doctors call it
means *greenness*; for one of its most
symptoms is a pale complexion with

It never occurs except at or near
and was long supposed to be merely

of the blood. Now, however, we have learned that it is a disease of the nervous system, and one very often confounded by physicians with other complaints.

Its attack is insidious. A distaste for exertion and society, a fitful appetite, low spirits—these are all the symptoms noticed at first. Then, one by one, come palpitation of the heart, an unhealthy complexion, irregularity, dyspepsia, depraved tastes,—such as a desire to eat slate-pencil dust, chalk, or clay—vague pains in body and limbs, a bad temper; until the girl, after several months, is a peevish, wretched, troublesome invalid.

Then if a physician is called in, and gives her iron, and tells her there is nothing the matter, or is himself alarmed and imagines she has heart disease or consumption, it is a chance if she does not rapidly sink, out of mere fright, and over-much dosing, into some fatal complaint. Let it be well understood chlorosis, though often obstinate and obscure, is always curable if properly and promptly treated. The remedies must be addressed to the nervous system, and can be administered with intelligence only by a competent medical adviser. It can be prevented by a hygienic mode of life; and as its most common causes are anxiety, home-sickness, want of exercise, or over-work at school, nothing is so salutary in its early stages as a change of air and scene, cheerful company, a tour to the mountains or some watering-place, and regular exercise.

Many young women suffer considerable pain during their monthly illness. This may arise from many different causes, such as congestion, inflammation, malformation, or a wrong position of the parts, or over-sensitive nerves. They can only be successfully treated when the cause is known; and they must rest assured that this suffering, in nearly every case, can be removed.

Sometimes a girl grows to the age of eighteen or twenty without having her periodical changes. We have already said that this is not unusual in some climates, and in some families; so, as long as the general health is good, and the spirits cheerful—always an important point needs cause no anxiety. But if the health grows [poor] and especially if there are pains and weakness recur[ring] monthly without discharge, then something is wrong. the doctor should be consulted.

HYSTERICS.

There is a disease of the nerves to which girls about [the] age of puberty are very subject, particularly in the hi[gh] circles of society, where their emotions are over-educ[ated] and their organization delicate. It is called hysteria, more commonly *hysterics*. Frequently it deceives [the] doctor and friends, and is supposed to be some dange[rous] complaint. Often it puts on the symptoms of epile[psy] or heart disease, or consumption. We have witnessed most frightful convulsions in girls of fourteen, which [were] brought on by this complaint. Sometimes it injures [the] mind, and it should always receive prompt and effic[ient] attention, as it is always curable.

This disease is apt to produce a similar affection in o[ther] girls of the same age who see the attacks. For this [rea]son, hysterical girls should not be sent to large sc[hools] but cured at home. Often a strong mental impres[sion] restores them. The anecdote is told of a celebrated [sur]geon (Boerhave), who was called to a female seminary w[here] there was a number of hysterical girls. He summo[ned] them together, heated a number of iron instrument[s be]fore their eyes, and told them that the first one who [had] a fit should be cauterized down the spine. They al[l re]covered immediately.

SECRET BAD HABITS.

We now approach a part of our subject which we w[ould] gladly omit, did not constant experience admonish u[s of] our duty to speak of it in no uncertain tone. We ref[er to] the disastrous consequences on soul and body to w[hich] young girls expose themselves by exciting and indul[ging] morbid passions. Years ago, Miss Catherine E. Beecher sounded a note of warning to the mothers of America on this secret vice, which leads their daughters to the grave, the madhouse, or, worse yet, the brothel.

Gladly would we believe that her timely admonition had done away with the necessity for its repetition. But though we believe such a habit is more rare than many physicians suppose, it certainly exists to a degree that demands attention. Surgeons have recently been forced to devise painful operations to hinder young girls from thus ruining themselves; and we must confess that, in its worst form, it is absolutely incurable.

The results of the constant nervous excitement which this habit produces are bodily weakness, loss of memory, low spirits, distressing nervousness, a capricious appetite, dislike of company and of study, and, finally, paralysis, imbecility, or insanity. Let it not be supposed that there are many who suffer thus severely; but on the other hand let it be clearly understood that any indulgence whatever in these evil courses is attended with bad effects, especially because they create impure desires and thoughts which will prepare the girl to be a willing victim to the arts of profligacy. There is no more solemn duty resting on those who have the charge of young females than to protect them against this vice.

But, it is exclaimed, is it not dangerous to tell them anything about it? Such a course is unneccessary. Teach them that any handling of the parts, any indecent language, and impure thought, is degrading and hurtful. See that the servants, nurses, and companions with whom they associate are not debased; and recommend scrupulous cleanliness.

If the habit is discovered, do not scold nor whip the child. It is *often* a result of disease, and induced by a disagreeable local itching. Sometimes this is connected with a disorder of the womb, and very frequently with worms in the bowels. Let the case be submitted to a

judicious skilful medical adviser, and the girl will yet
saved. But do not shut your eyes, and refuse to see th
fact when it exists. Mothers are too often unwilling
entertain for a moment the thought that their daughte
are addicted to such a vice, when it is only too plain
the physician.

THE HYGIENE OF PUBERTY.

Concerning the maladies of puberty, we may broad
say, that if we are obliged to have recourse to medicir
it is because we have neglected hygiene. That the peri
requires assiduous care, we grant; but, given that ca
drugs will be needless.

In a general way, we have already emphasized the da
ger of indolence and the benefits of exercise or labou
the perils of exciting the emotions, and the advantag
of a placid disposition; the impropriety of prematu
development, and the wisdom of simplicity and moderatio
This is an old story—a thrice-told tale. Let us go mo
into minutiæ.

One of the most frequent causes of disease, about tl
age of puberty, is *starvation*. Many a girl is starved
death. Food is given her, but not of the right qualit
or in sufficient quantity, or at improper hours. Tl
system is not nourished: and, becoming feeble, it is la
open to the attacks of disease, and to no form of disea
more readily than to consumption.

To correct this, let the food be varied, simply prepare
and abundant. Good fresh milk should be used dail
while tea and coffee should be withheld. Fat meats ar
vegetable oils, generally disliked by girls of this age, a
exactly what they need; and were they partaken of mo
freely, there would be less inquiry at the drug-stores f
cod-liver oil.

A modern writer of eminence lays it down as one of tl
most common causes of consumption in young people th
just at the age when their physical system is undergoi

such important changes, that invaluable article of diet, *milk*, is generally dropped, and nothing equally rich in nitrogen substituted in its place.

Exercise, whether as games, the skipping rope, croquet, walking, dancing, riding, and calisthenics, or as regular labour, is highly beneficial, especially when it leads one into the fresh air, the sunshine, and the country. A particular kind of exercise is to be recommended for those whose chests are narrow, whose shoulders stoop, and who have a hereditary predisposition to consumption. If it is systematically practised along with other means of health, we would guarantee any child, no matter how many relatives have died of this disease, against its invasion. It is voluntary inspiration. Nothing is more simple. Let her stand erect, throw the shoulders well back and the hands behind; then let her slowly inhale pure air to the full capacity of the lungs, and retain it a few seconds *by an increased effort*; then it may be slowly exhaled. After one or two natural inspirations, let her repeat the act, and so on for ten or fifteen minutes, twice daily. Not only is this simple procedure a safeguard against consumption, but, in the opinion of some learned physicians, it can even cure it when it has already commenced.

At first the monthly loss of blood exhausts the system. Therefore plenty of food, plenty of rest, plenty of sleep are required. That ancient prejudice in favour of early rising should be discarded now, and the girl should retire early, and, if she will, should sleep late. Hard study, care, or anxiety should be spared her. This is not the time for rigid discipline.

Clothing is a matter of importance, and if we were at all sure of attention, there is much we would say of it. The thought seriously troubles us, that so long as American women consent to deform themselves and sacrifice their health to false ideas of beauty, it is almost hopeless to urge their fitness for, and their right to, a higher life than they now enjoy. No educated painter or sculptor is

ignorant of what the model of female beauty is; n[o]
fashionable woman in America is content unless she de[-]
parts from it as far as possible.

Now beauty implies health, and ugliness of form is at[-]
tained not only at the expense of æsthetics, but of com[-]
fort. The custom of fastening growing girls in tigh[t]
corsets, or flattening their breasts with pads, or distortin[g]
their feet in small high-heeled shoes, and of teaching them
to stoop and mince in gait, is calculated to disgust ever[y]
observer of good sense and taste, and what is of more con[-]
sequence, to render these girls, when they become women
more liable to every species of suffering connected wit[h]
child-bearing.

Some young women suffer more, some less, during thei[r]
periodical illnesses. Both classes should be equally cau[-]
tious to *do less than usual* at that time. Over-exertio[n]
is a most fruitful cause of disease. Long-walks, shop[-]
ping, dancing, riding, labour, should be avoided, or dimin[-]
ished. Iced drinks, exposure to dampness or to grea[t]
heat, are likewise perilous. If there is much pain or de[-]
bility, or an abundant discharge, they should rest on th[e]
sofa or bed. If the discharge is delayed, soaking the fee[t]
in hot water, a tumbler of hot ginger tea, a brisk walk o[r]
a gentle laxative will often bring it on. But under n[o]
circumstances should more violent means than these b[e]
used. Properly, there is no great suffering connected wit[h]
this function, and when such is present, the physicia[n]
should be consulted.

THE AGE OF NUBILITY.

It does not follow because a girl is capable of marriag[e]
that she is fit for it. Science teaches us many valid objec[-]
tions to too early unions. It goes farther, and fixes [a]
certain age at which it is wisest for woman to marry[.]
This age is between twenty and twenty-five years.

Anatomists have learned that after puberty the bone[s]
of a woman's body undergo important modifications to fi[t]

her for child-bearing. This requires time, and before twenty the process is not completed. Until the woman is perfect herself, until her full stature and completed form are attained, she is not qualified to assist in perpetuating the species.

We might urge that up to this moment neither does her self-knowledge qualify her to choose a life-companion, nor can her education be finished, nor is her experience sufficient for her to enter on the duties of a matron. But we do not appeal to these arguments. There are others still more forcible. If her own health, life, and good looks are of value to her, if she has any wish for healthy, sound-minded children, she will refrain from premature nuptials.

A too-youthful wife finds marriage not a pleasure but a pain. Her nervous system is prostrated by it, she is more liable to weakness and diseases of the womb, and, if of a consumptive family, she runs great risk of finding that fatal malady manifest itself after a year or two of wedded life. It is very common for those who marry young to die young.

From statistics which have been carefully compiled, it is proven that the first labours of very young mothers are much more painful, tedious, and dangerous to life than others. As wives, they are frequently visited either with absolute sterility, and all their lives must bear the reproach of barren women, or what to many is hardly less distasteful, they have an excessively numerous family.

What adds to their sufferings in the latter event is that the children of such marriages are rarely healthy. They are feeble, sickly, undersized, often with some fault of mind or body, which is a cross to them and their parents all their lives. They inherit more readily the defects of their ancestors, and, as a rule, die at earlier years than the progeny of better-timed unions.

These considerations are formidable enough, it would

seem, to prevent young girls from marrying, without [
need of a law, as exists in some countries. Moreover, th
are not imaginary but real, as many a woman finds out
her cost.

The objections to marriage after the age of twenty-f
are less cogent. They extend only to the woman hers
She should know that the first labours of wives over thi
are nearly *twice* as fatal as those between twenty a
twenty-five. Undoubtedly, nature points to the per
between the twentieth and twenty-fifth year as the fitt
one for marriage in the woman.

LOVE.

ITS POWER ON HUMANITY.

LOVE, pure, true love, what can we say of it? 1
dream of youth; the cherished reminiscence of age; ce
brated in the songs of poets; that which impels the w
rior to his most daring deeds; in which the inspired prop
chooses to typify the holiest sentiments—what new thi
is it possible to say about this theme?

Think for a moment on the history or the literature
the world. Ask the naturalist to reveal the mysteries
life; let the mythologist explain the origin and meani
of all unrevealed religions: look within at the prompti
of your own spirit, and this whole life of ours will app
to you as one grand epithalamium.

The profoundest of English poets has said—

> " All thoughts, all passions, all delights,
> Whatever stirs the mortal frame
> All are but ministers of Love,
> And feel his sacred flame."

That life which is devoid of love is incomplete, sterile, unsatisfactory. It fails of its chiefest end. Nature, in anger, blots it out sooner, and it passes like the shadow of a cloud, leaving no trace behind. Admirable as it may be in other respects, to the eye of the statesman, the physician, the lover of his species, it remains but a fragment, a torso.

Love is one thing to a woman, another to a man. To him, said Madame de Stael, it is an episode; to her, it is the whole history of life. A thousand distractions divert man. Fame, riches, power, pleasure, all struggle in his bosom to displace the sentiment of love. They are its rivals, not rarely its masters. But woman knows no such distractions. One passion only sits enthroned in her bosom; one only idol is enshrined in her heart, knowing no rival, no successor. This passion is love! This idol is its object.

This is not fancy, nor rhetoric; it is the language of cool and exact science, pronounced from the chair of history, from the bureau of the statistician, from the dissecting table of the anatomist. We shall gather up their well-weighed words, and present them not as fancy sketches but as facts.

This deep, all-absorbing, single, wondrous, love of woman is something that man cannot understand. This sea of unfathomed depth is to him a mystery. The shallow mind sees of it nothing but the rippling waves, the unstable foam crests dashing hither and thither, the playful ripples of the surface, and blind to the still and measureless waters beneath, calls women capricious, uncertain—*varium et mutabile*. But the thinker and seer, undeceived by such externals, knows that beneath this seeming change is stability unequalled in the stronger sex; a power of will to which man is a stranger; a devotion and purpose which strike him with undefined awe.

Therefore in the myths and legends which the early men framed to express their notions of divine things,

the Fates who spin and snip the thread of life, the No[r]
who
> Lay down laws,
> And select life
> For the children of time—
> The destinies of men,

are always females. The seeresses and interpreters
oracles, those who, like the witch of Endor, could summ[on]
from the grave the shades of the departed, were wome[n]

Therefore, also, modern infidelity, going back as it e[ver]
does, to the ignorance of the past, and holding it up
something new, makes woman the only deity. Comte a[nd]
his disciples having reasoned away all gods, angels, a[nd]
spirits and unable to still the craving for something
adore, agree to meet once a week to worship—wom[an.]
The French revolutionists, having shut up the church[es]
and abolished God by a decree of the Convention, set
in His stead—a woman.

We could never exhaust this phase of world histo[ry.]
Everywhere we see the unexpected hand of Love mouldi[ng]
fashioning all things. The fortunes of the individual,
fate of nations, the destinies of races are guided by t[his]
invisible thread. Let us push our enquiries as to
nature of this all-powerful agent.

WHAT IS LOVE?

It has a divided nature. As we have an immortal s[oul]
but a body of clay; as the plant roots itself in decay
earth, but spreads its flowers in glorious sunlight; so l[ove]
has a physiological and a moral nature. It is rooted
that unconscious law of life which bids us perpetuate
kind; which guards over the conservation of life; wh[ich]
enforces, with ceaseless admonition, that first prec[ept]
which God gave to man before the gates of Eden [had]
been closed upon him: "Be thou fruitful, and multi[ply]
and replenish the earth." Nothing but a spurious delic[acy]
or an ignorance of facts can prevent our full recognit[ion]

that love looks to marriage, and marriage to offspring, as a natural sequence.

Do we ask proofs of this? We have them in abundance. those unfortunate beings who are chosen by oriental custom to guard the seraglios, undergo a mutilation which disqualifies them from becoming parents. Soon all traces of passion, all regard for the other sex, all sentiments of love, totally disappear. The records of medicine contain not a few cases where disease had rendered it necessary to remove the ovaries from women. At once a change took place in voice, appearance, and mind. They spoke like men, a slender beard commenced on their faces, a masculine manner was conspicuous in all their motions, and every thought of sexual love passed away forever. These are the results in every case. What do they signify? Undoubtedly that the passion of love is dependent upon the capacity of having offspring, and such was the intention of nature in implanting in our bosom this all-powerful sentiment.

But this is not all. Nature, as beneficent to those who obey her precepts as she is merciless to those who disregard them, has added to this sentiment of love a physical pleasure in its gratification; an honourable and proper pleasure, which none but the hypocrite or the ascetic will affect to contemn, none but the coarse or the lewd will regard as the object of love. There is indeed a passion which is the love of the body. We call it by its proper name of *lust*. There is another emotion for which the rich tongue of the ancient Greeks had a word to which we have nothing to correspond. Call it, if you will, Platonic love, and define it to be an exalted friendship. But understand that neither the one nor the other is love, in the true sense of the word, and that both are inferior to it.

Does the father, watching, with moistened eyes, his child at its mother's breast; does the husband, bending with solicitude over the sick bed of his wife; does the wife, clinging to her husband through evil report and

good report, through broken fortunes and failing h[ealth]
indicate no loftier emotion than *lust*, no warmer senti[ment]
than *friendship*? What ignorance, what perversi[ty]
so gross as not to perceive something here nobler [than]
either? Do you say that such scenes are, alas, [rare?]
We deny it. We see them daily in the streets; we [see]
them daily in our rounds. Admitted by our calli[ng to]
the sacred precincts of many houses in the trying hou[rs of]
sickness and death, we speak advisedly, and know [that]
this is the prevailing meaning of love in American li[fe.]

A warm, rich affection blesses the one who give[s and]
the one who receives. Character develops under it a[s a]
plant beneath the sunlight. Happiness is an unk[nown]
word without it. Love and marriage are the only n[ormal]
conditions of life. Without them, both man and w[oman]
forever miss the best part of themselves. They [ail]
more, they sin more, they perish sooner. These ar[e no]
hasty assertions. As a social law, let it be well u[nder-]
stood that science pronounces that

LOVE IS A NECESSITY.

The single life is forced upon many of both sex[es in]
our present social condition. Many choose it [from]
motives of economy, from timidity, or as a religious [duty]
pleasing to God. The latter is a notion which pro[bably]
arose from a belief that, somehow, celibacy, strictl[y ob-]
served, means chastity. It simply means contin[ence.]
The chastest persons have been, and are, not the vi[rgins]
and celibates, but the married. When this truth is k[nown]
better, we shall have fewer sects and more religion.

We know women who refrain from marrying to [keep]
out of trouble. The old saying is that every sigh [is]
a nail in one's coffin. They are not going to worry t[hem-]
selves to death bearing children and nursing them. [It is]
too great a risk, too much suffering. How often ha[ve we]
been told this? Yet how false the reasoning is!

carefully prepared statistics show that between the ages of twenty and forty-five years, more unmarried women die than married, and but one instance of remarkable longevity in an old maid is known. The celebrated Dr. Hufeland, therefore, in his treatise on the "Art of Prolonging Life," lays it down as a rule, that to obtain a great age one must be married.

As for happiness, those who think they can best attain it outside the gentle yoke of matrimony, are quite as wide of the mark. Their selfish and solitary pleasures do not gratify them. With all the resources of clubs, billiard-rooms, saloons, narcotics and stimulants, single men make but a mock show of satisfaction. At heart every one of them envies his married friends. How much more monotonous and more readily exhausted are the resources of woman's single life! No matter what "sphere" she is in, no matter in what "circle" she moves, no matter what "mission" she invents, it will soon pall on her. Would you see the result? We invoke once more those dry volumes, full of lines and figures, on vital statistics. Stupid as they look, they are full of the strangest stories, and, what is more, the stories are all true. Some of them are sad stories, and this is one of the saddest:—Of those unfortunates who, out of despair and disgust of the world, jump from bridges, or take arsenic, or hang themselves, or in other ways rush unbidden and unprepared before the great Judge of all, *nearly two-thirds* are unmarried, and in some years nearly *three-fourths*. And of those other sad cases—dead, yet living—who people the mad-houses and asylums, what of them? Driven crazy by their brutal husbands, do you suggest? Not at all. In France, Bavaria, Prussia, and Hanover, four out of every five are unmarried, and throughout the civilized world there are everywhere three or four single to one married woman in the establishments for the insane, in proportion to the whole number of the two classes above twenty-one years of age.

Other women decline to marry because they have, forsooth, a "life work" to accomplish. Some great project fills their mind. Perchance they emulate Madame de Stael, and would electrify the country by their novel views in politics; or they have a literary vein they fain would explore; or they feel called upon to teach the freedmen, or to keep their position as leaders of fashion. A husband would trammel them. If they did marry, they would take the very foolish advice of a contemporary, and go through life with an indignant protest at its littleness. Let such women know that they underrate the married state, its powers and its opportunities. There are no loftier missions than can be carried out, no nobler games than can there be played. When we think of these objections, coming, as they have to us, from high-spirited, earnest girls, the queens of their sex, our memory runs back to the famous women of history, the brightest jewels in the coronet of time, and we find as many, ay more, married women than single who pursued to their ends, mighty achievements.

If you speak of Judith and Joan of Arc, who delivered their fatherlands from the enemy, by a daring no man can equal, we shall recall the peaceful victories of her wife of the barbarian Chlodwig, who taught the rude Franks the mild religion of Nazareth, and of her who extended from Byzantium the holy symbol of the cross over the wilds of Russia. The really great women of this age, are they mostly married or single? They are mostly married, and they are good wives and tender mothers.

What we have just written, we read to an amiable woman.

"But," she exclaimed, "what have you to say to her whom high duties or a hard fate condemns to a single life, and the name of an old maid?"

Alas! what can we say to such? We feel that

> 'Earthlier happy is the rose distilled,
> Than that which, withering on the virgin thorn,
> Grows, lives, and dies in single blessedness."

Yet there is ever a blessing in store for those who suffer here, and the hope of the future must teach them to bear the present.

LOVE IS ETERNAL.

We have said love is a necessity in the life of either man or woman to complete their nature. Its effects, therefore, are eternal. We do not intend this as a figure of speech. It is a sober statement of physiology.

From the day of marriage the woman undergoes a change in her whole structure. She is similar to her former self, but not the same. It is often noticed that the children of a woman in her second marriage bear a marked resemblance to her first husband. In the inferior races and lower animals this obscure metamorphosis is still apparent. A negress, who has borne her first child to a white man, will ever after have children of a lighter colour than her own. Count Strzelewski, in his "Travels in Australia," narrates this curious circumstance:—A native who has once had offspring by a white man, can never more have children by a male of her own race. Dr. Darwin relates that a male zebra was once brought to England, and a hybrid race, marked with the zebra's stripes, was produced from certain mares. Always after, the colts of these mares bore the marks of the zebra on their skins. In some way the female is profoundly altered throughout her whole formation, and entirely independent of her will, by the act of marriage and the alteration is never effaced.

If the body is thus influenced, shall not the far more susceptible mind and spirit be equally impressed?

Another common observation supports what we say, and extends it farther. Not the woman alone; the man also undergoes a change, and loses a portion of his personality in his mate. They two are one, not merely in a moral sense. We constantly notice a decided resemblance in old couples, who have passed, say, two score years together. They have grown to look alike in form, feature, and expression. That for so long a time they have breathed the same air, eaten the same fare, and been subjected to the same surroundings, explains this to some extent. But the greater part of the change flows from mental sources. They have laughed and wept together; they have shared the same joys and pleasures; a smile or a tear on the face of one evoked a corresponding emotion and expression on the face of the other. Their co-partnership has become a unity. Even without speaking, they sympathize. Their souls are constantly *en rapport*. The man is as different as the woman from his former self.

WHAT IS FLIRTATION?

Flirtation is an American word. They have neither the word nor the thing in foreign countries. It results from the freedom and the daring of our women. They use as playthings those edged tools which in other lands are locked up from them. Love, engagements, and beaux, are their pastimes.

In view of what we have said of the nature of love, its necessity and eternity, is this wise?

We are not moralists, and speak as physicians merely. To us the coquette is as bad as the rake. Both waste their nature in dalliance with passion. They both suffer in body and soul, and by every new indulgence unfit themselves the more for a happy marriage. Look at the woman of thirty, who has passed her youth encouraging men to offer her the most a man can offer—all he has—in order to enjoy the vanity of refusing him. If she is married, you will see a discontented, nervous invalid; if unmarried, a cross, faded, neglected spinster.

OF SECOND MARRIAGES.

Science, therefore, seems to say to woman, "your first husband is your eternal husband." How, then, about second marriages? Are we to say that they are not advisable?

Let us not answer hastily. It is yet to be seen whether ill-assorted marriages produce those impressions we have mentioned. They may indeed, on the body, while the mind is free. One must remember, also, that the exigencies of social life must be consulted. If a woman cannot love two men equally—and she cannot—other motives, worthy of all respect, justify her in entering the marriage life the second time. Then, the higher refinements of the emotions are not given to all alike, nor do they come at the same age to all. True love may first dawn upon a woman after one or two husbands have left her a widow. Orphan children, widowhood, want of property, or the care of property,—these are sad afflictions to the lonely woman. Do not blame her if she accepts a husband as a guardian, a protector, whom she can no longer receive to her arms as a lover. She is right.

We cherish the memory of a lady of strong character, who died past eighty. She had survived three husbands. "The first," she said "I married for love; the second, for position; the third, for friendship. I was happy with them all." But when in her mortal illness this venerable friend sank into the delirium which preceded death, she constantly called out the name of her first husband only. More than half a century had not effaced the memory of those few years of early love. This is fidelity indeed.

OF DIVORCE.

He of Nazareth laid down the law that whoever puts away his wife for any cause except adultery, and marries again, commits adultery, and that whatever woman puts away her husband for any cause save adultery, a[nd mar]ries again, herself commits adultery.

This has been found a hard saying.

John Milton wrote a book to show that the L[ord] did not mean what he said, but something quite d[ifferent.] Modern sects, calling themselves *Christians*, af[ter the] Lawgiver, dodge the difficulty, and refer it to Stat[e Legis]latures. State Legislatures, not troubling thems[elves] all about any previous law or lawgiver, allow d[ozen] causes, scores of them, as perfectly valid to put [asunder] those whom God has joined together.

Science, which never finds occasion to disagre[e with] that Lawgiver of Nazareth, here makes His wo[rds her] own.

Whether we look at it as a question in social morals, or in physiology, the American plan of g[ranting] absolute divorces is dangerous, and destructive to [the] best in life. It leads to hasty, ill-assorted matche[s, to] unwillingness to yield to each other's peculiarit[ies, to] weakening of the family ties, to a lax morality. [Push] it a trifle farther than it now is in some States, a[nd mar]riage will lose all its sacredness, and degenerat[e to a] physical union not nobler than the crossing of flie[s in the] air.

Separation of bed and board should always be p[rovided] for by law, and whether single, married, or separa[ted, a] woman should retain entire control of her own p[erson.] But in the eyes of God and Nature, a woman o[r man] with two faithful spouses living, to each of whom [conju]nal fidelity has been plighted, is a monster.

OF A PLURALITY OF WIVES OR HUSBANDS.

What has been said of divorce applies with tenfo[ld force] to the custom of a woman living as a wife to seve[ral men,] or of a man as husband to several women. We [need] not speak of these customs, but that we know bo[th exist] in this country, no[t] among the notoriously wic[ked] among those who claim to be the peculiarly good—the very elect of God. They prevail, not as lustful excesses, but as religious observances. Every reader of the daily press know what sects we mean.

It is worth while to state that such practices lead to physical degradation. The woman who acknowledges more than one husband is generally sterile; the man who has several wives has usually a weakly offspring, principally males. Nature attempts to check polygamy by reducing the number of females, and failing in this, by enervating the whole stock. The Mormons of Utah would soon sink into a state of Asiatic effeminacy were they left to themselves.

COURTSHIP

A wise provision of nature orders that *woman shall be sought*. She flees, and man pursues. The folly of modern reformers who would annul this provision is evident. Were it done away with, man, ever prone to yield to woman's solicitations, and then most prone when yielding is most dangerous, would fritter away his powers at an early age, and those very impulses which nature has given to perpetuate the race would bring about its destruction.

To prevent such a disaster, woman is endowed with a sense of shame, an invincible modesty, her greatest protection and her greatest charm. Let her never forget it, never disregard it, for without it she becomes the scorn of her own sex and the jest of the other.

The urgency of man and the timidity of woman are tempered by the period of courtship.

This, as it exists with us, is something almost peculiar to Americans. On the continent of Europe, girls are shut up in convents or in seminaries, or are kept strictly under the eyes of their parents until marriage, or, at any rate, betrothal. The liberty used in this country is something unheard of and inconceivable there. In Spain a duenna, in France some aunt or elderly cousin, in Germany some similar person, makes it her business to be present at every interview which a young lady has with an admirer. He never dreams of walking, driving, or going out of an evening with her alone. It is taken for granted that should he invite her for such a purpose, the mother or aunt is included in the party. They would look on the innocent freedom of American girls as simply scandalous.

We have had opportunities to see society in these various countries, and have failed to perceive that the morality of either sex is at all superior to what it is with us, while the effect of this cloister-like education on young women is to weaken their self-reliance, and often prepare them for greater extravagances when marriage gives them liberty.

With us, the young woman is free until her wedding day. After that epoch, she looks forward to withdrawing more or less from society, and confining her thoughts to family matters. In France, Spain, or Italy, in the wealthier classes, precisely the contrary is the rule. Marriage brings deliverance from an irksome espionage and numberless fetters; it is the avenue to a life in public, and independent action. How injurious to domestic happiness this is can readily be imagined.

It is true that the liberty of American girls occasionally leads to improprieties. But, except in certain great cities, such instances are rare. The safeguards of virtue are knowledge and self-command, not duennas and *jalousies*. Let mothers properly instruct their daughters, and they need have no apprehensions about their conduct.

The period of courtship is one full of importance. A young woman of unripe experience must decide from what she can see of a man during the intercourse of a few months whether he will suit her for a life companion. She has no knowledge of human nature; and what would it avail her if she had, when at such a time a suitor is care im to show only his eligible traits? "Go a-courting." says old Dr. Franklin, in his homely language, "in your every-day clothes." Not one man out of a thousand is honest enough to take his advice.

It is useless for her to ask aid of another. She must judge for herself. What, then, is she to do?

There is a mysterious instinct in a pure-minded woman which is beyond all analysis—a tact which men do not possess, and do not readily believe in. At such a crisis this instinct saves her. She feels in a moment the presence of a base, unworthy nature. An unconscious repulsion is manifest in her eye, her voice. Where a suitor is not a man of low motive, but merely quite incongruous in temper and disposition, this same instinct acts, and the man, without being able to say just why, feels that he is labouring in vain. If he blindly insists in his wooing, he has no one to chide but himself when he is finally discarded.

But if the man is worthy and suitable, does this blessed instinct whisper the happy news with like promptness to the maiden's soul? Ah! that raises another issue. It brings us face to face with that difficult question of

LOVE AT FIRST SIGHT.

Jung Stilling, a German author of note, a religious enthusiast, and full of strange fancies, was, when young, a tutor in a private family. On one occasion his employer took him to a strange house, and introduced him to a roomful of company. Stilling had not contemplated marriage; but, in the company, he saw, for the first time, a young woman whom he felt was his destined wife. Walking across the room, he addressed her with the utmost simplicity, telling her that an inward monitor advised him that she of all womankind was his predestined helpmeet. She blushed, was confused, but presently confessed that she had experienced the same conviction on first beholding him. They married, and the most curious part of the tale remains to tell. It is, that they proved a happy, well-matched couple.

We do not advise others to follow their example. Not many souls are capable of such reciprocity. Choosing an associate for life is too serious a business to be made the affair of a moment. Reason, reflection, thought, prayer—these are aids in such a momentous question not to be lightly thrown aside. Many a passing fancy, many an evanescent preference catches for a moment the new-fledged affection. But for the long and tedious journey of life we want a love rooted in knowledge.

We are not blind to the fact, that often from the first interview the maiden feels an undefined spell thrown around her by him who will become her husband. She feels differently in his presence; she watches him with other eyes than she has for the rest of men. She renders no account to herself of this emotion; she attempts no analysis of it; she does not acknowledge to herself that it exists. No matter. Sooner or later, if true to herself she will learn what it is, and it will be a guide in that moment, looked forward to with mingled hopes and fears, when she is asked to decide on the destiny, the temporal and eternal destiny of two human lives.

That she may then decide aright, and live free from the regrets of a false step at this crisis of life, we shall now rehearse what medical science has to say about

HOW TO CHOOSE A HUSBAND.

*"Choose well. Your choice is
Brief but endless."*

Woman holds as an inalienable right in this country the privilege of choice. It is not left to notaries, or parents, to select for her, as in the societies of Europe.

First comes the question of relationship. A school-girl is apt to see more of her cousin than of other young men

Often some of them seek at an early hour to institute a far closer tie than that of blood. Is she wise to accept it?

SHALL COUSINS MARRY?

Hardly any point has been more warmly debated by medical men. It has been said that in such marriages the woman is more apt to be sterile; that if she has children they are peculiarly liable to be born with some defect of body or mind—deafness, blindness, idiocy, or lameness; that they die early, and that they are subject, beyond others, to fatal hereditary diseases, as cancer, consumption, scrofula, etc.

An ardent physician persuaded himself so thoroughly of these evils, resulting from marriage of relatives, that he induced the Legislature of Kentucky to pass a law prohibiting it within certain degrees of consanguinity. Many a married couple have been rendered miserable by the information that they have unwittingly violated one of nature's most positive laws. Though their children may be numerous and blooming, they live in constant dread of some terrible outbreak of disease. Many a young and loving couple have sadly severed an engagement, which would have been a prelude to a happy marriage, when they were informed of these disastrous results.

For all such we have a word of consolation. We speak it authoritatively, and not without a full knowledge of the responsibility we assume.

The fear of marrying a cousin, even a first cousin, is entirely groundless, provided there is no decided hereditary taint in the family. And when such hereditary taint does exist the danger is not greater than in marrying into any other family where it is also found. On the contrary, a German author has urged the propriety of such unions, where the family has traits of mental or physical excellence, as a means of preserving and developing them.

So far as sterility is concerned, an examination of records shows that whereas in the average of unions one woman in *eight* is barren, in those between relatives but one in *ten* is so. And as for the early deaths of children, while, on an average, fifteen children in a hundred die under seven years, in the families of nearly-related parents but twelve in a hundred is the mortality.

The investigations about idiotic and defective children are by no means satisfactory, and are considered by some of the most careful writers as not at all proving a greater tendency to such misfortunes in the offspring of cousins. Among a thousand idiotic children recently examined in Paris, not one was descended from a healthy consanguinity.

But as few families are wholly without some lurking predisposition to disease, it is not well, as a rule, to run the risk of developing this by too repeated unions. Stockbreeders find that the best specimens of the lower animals are produced by crossing nearly-related individuals a certain number of times; but that, carried beyond this, such unions lead to degeneracy and sterility. Such, also, has been the experience of many human families.

How slight a cause even of that most insidious disease, consumption, such marriages are, may be judged from the fact, that of a thousand cases inquired into by Dr. Edward Smith, of London, in only six was there consanguinity of parents.

THE MIXTURE OF RACES.

Mankind, say the school geographies, is divided into five races, each distinguished by its own colour. They are the white, the black, the red, the yellow, and the brown races. In this country we have to do with but the white and black races. Shall we approve of marriages between them? Shall a white woman choose a black man to be her husband?

We are at the more pains to answer this, because recently a writer,—and this writer a woman, and this woman one of the most widely known in our land—has written a novel intended to advocate the affirmative of this question. Moreover, it is constantly mooted in certain political circles, and is one of the social problems of the day.

The very fact that it is so much discussed shows that such a union runs counter to a strong prejudice. Such aversions are often voices of nature, warning us against acts injurious to the species. In this instance, it is not of modern origin, created by our institutions. Three centuries ago, Shakspeare, who had probably never seen a score of negroes in his life, with the divination of genius, felt the repugnance which a refined woman would feel to accepting one as her husband. The plot of one of his plays turns on it. He makes Iago say of Desdemona:

> "Not to affect many proposed matches,
> Of her own clime, complexion, and degree,
> Whereto we see in all things nature tends:
> Foh! one may smell, in such, a will most rank,
> Foul disproportion, thoughts unnatural."

It is, indeed, "nature erring from itself" which prompts to these marriages. They are not sterile, but the children are sickly and short-lived. Very few mulattoes reach an old age.

Then, it is well known that the black race cannot survive a northern climate. Dr. Snow, of Providence, R.I., who has given great attention to the study of statistics, says emphatically that in New England the coloured population inevitably perish in a few generations, if left to themselves. This debility no woman should wish to give to her children.

A mental inferiority is likewise apparent. Friends of the negro are ready to confess this but attribute it to his long and recent period of servitude. We deal with facts only. The inferiority is there, whatever be its cause; and she who would willingly curse her offspring with it, manifests, indeed, "thoughts unnatural."

The children born of a union of the black and red race,

negroes and Indians, are, on the contrary, remarkable for their physical vigour and mental acuteness; though, of course, the latter is limited to the demands of a semi-barbarous life.

SHALL AMERICAN WOMEN MARRY FOREIGNERS!

When we narrow the question of race to that of nationality, quite new elements come in.

In speaking of the intermarriage of relatives, we showed that a certain number of such unions in healthy stocks was advantageous rather than otherwise, but that too many of them lead to deterioration. This law can be applied to nations. Historians have often observed that the most powerful states in the world arose from an amalgamation of different tribes. Rome, Greece, and England are examples of this. On the other hand, Russia, China, Persia, which have suffered no such crosses of blood, are either stationary or depend for their progress on foreigners.

Physicians have contributed other curious testimony on this point, the bearing of which they themselves have not understood. Marriages between nationalities of the same race are more fertile, and the children are more vigorous, than those between descendants of the same nation. For instance, it has been proved that if two descendants of the "Pilgrim Fathers" in Massachusetts marry, they will probably have but three children; while if one of them marries a foreigner, the children will number five or six.

So it is well ascertained that in the old and stationary communes of France, where the same families have possessed their small farms for generation after generation, the marriages have become gradually less and less productive, until it has seriously interfered with the quota those districts send to the army.

American women have suffered many hard words because they do not have more children. Several New

England writers have accused them of very bad practices, which we shall mention hereafter. But the effect of the law of production just now laid down has been quite overlooked.

As it is best that there should be four or five children in a family in ordinary circumstances, the union of American and foreign blood is very desirable. We need to fuse in one the diverse colonies of the white race annually reaching our shores. A century should efface every trace of the German, the Irish, the Frenchman, the English, the Norwegian, and leave nothing but the American. To bring about this happy result, free intermarriage should be furthered in every possible way.

THE AGE OF THE HUSBAND.

The epoch of puberty comes to a boy at about the same age it does to a girl—fourteen or fifteen years. And an even greater period passes between this epoch and the age it is proper for a man to marry—his age of nubility.

Not only has he a more complete education to obtain, not only a profession or trade to learn, and some property to accumulate, some position to acquire, ere he is ready to take a wife, but his physical powers ripen more slowly than those of a woman. He is more tardy in completing his growth, and early indulgence more readily saps his constitution.

We have placed the best age for woman to marry at between twenty and twenty-five years; for similar reasons, man is best qualified to become a husband between twenty-three and thirty-three years.

Previous to the twenty-third year, many a man is incapable of producing healthy children. If he does not destroy his health by premature indulgence, he may destroy his happiness by witnessing his children the prey of debility and deformity. An old German proverb says, 've a boy a wife, a child, and a bird, and death will knock at the door." Even an author so old as Aristotle warns young men against early marriage, under penalty of disease and puny offspring.

From the age of thirty-three to fifty years, men who carefully observe the laws of health do not feel any weight of years. Nevertheless they are past their prime. Then, also, with advancing years the chances of life diminish, and the probability increases that they will leave a young family with no natural protector. The half century once turned, their vigour rapidly diminishes. The marriages they then contract are either sterile, or yield but few and sickly children. Many an old man has shortened his life by late nuptials, and the records of medicine contain accounts of several who perished on the very night of marriage.

The relative ages of man and wife is next to be considered. Nature fits woman earlier for marriage, and hints thereby that she should, as a rule, be younger than her husband. So, too, the bard of nature speaks:

> "Let still the woman take
> An elder than herself: so wears she to him,
> So sways the level in her husband's heart.

The woman who risks her happiness with a man many years younger than herself, violates a precept of life and when her husband grows indifferent, or taunts her with her years, or seeks companions of more suitable age, she is reaping a harvest sown by her own hand.

So commonly do such matches turn out badly, that in 1828 the kingdom of Wurtemburg prohibited unions where the woman was more than twelve years the senior, except by special dispensation.

After forty-five years most women cannot hope for children. A marriage subsequent to this period can at best be regarded as a close friendship. Marriage in its full meaning has no longer an existence.

The relative age of man and wife has another influence and quite a curious one. It influences the sex of the children. But this point we reserve for discussion on a later page.

The folly of joining a young girl to an old man is happily not so common in this country as in Europe. It would be hard to devise any step more certain to bring the laws of nature and morality into conflict.

"What can a young lassie do wi' an auld man?"

What advice can we give to a woman who barters her youthful charms for the fortunes of an aged husband? Shall we be cynical enough to agree with "auld auntie Katie?"

"My auld auntie Katie upon me takes pity,
I'll do my endeavour to follow her plan;
I'll cross him and rack him, until I heart-break him;
And then his auld brass will buy me a new pan."

No! she has willingly accepted a responsibility. It is her duty to bear it loyally, faithfully, uncomplainingly to the end.

Let us sum up with the maxim that the husband should be the senior, but that the difference of age should not be more than ten years.

WHAT SHOULD BE HIS TEMPERAMENT?

It is often hard to make out what doctors mean by *temperaments*. It is supposed that our mental and physical characters depend somehow on the predominance of some organ or system—that it controls the rest. Thus a person who is quick, nervous, sensitive to impressions, is said to have a *nervous* temperament; one who is stout, full-blooded, red-faced, has a *sanguine* temperament; a thin, dark-featured, reticent person, is of a *bilious* temperament; while a pale, fat, sluggish nature is called *phlegmatic* or *lymphatic*.

In a general way these distinctions are valuable, but they will not bear very exact application. They reveal in outline the constitution of mind and body, and, what is to our present purpose, they are of more than usual importance in the question of selecting a husband.

Nature, hating incongruity, yet loves variety. She preserves the limits of species, but within those limits she seeks fidelity to one type. Therefore it is that in marriage a person inclines strongly to one of a different temperament—to a person quite unlike themselves.

So true it is, that a Frenchman of genius, Bernardin de St. Pierre, vouches for this anecdote of himself. He was in a strange city, visiting a friend whom he had not seen for years. The friend's sister was of that age when women are most susceptible. She was a blonde, deliberate in motion, with blue eyes and fair hair. In a jesting way St. Pierre, who had never seen her before, and knew nothing of her personal life, said—

"Mademoiselle, you have many admirers. Shall I describe him on whom you look with most favour?"

The lady challenged him to do so.

"He is short of stature, of dark complexion, dark hair and eyes, slight in figure, active and nervous in all his movements."

The lady blushed to the eyes, and cast a glance of anger at her brother, who she thought had betrayed her secret. But no! St. Pierre's only informant was his deep knowledge of the human heart.

This instance is founded upon the truth that the perfect temperament is that happily balanced one which holds all the organs in equilibrium, in which no one rules, where all are developed in proportion. Nature ever strives to realize the ideal. She instils in the nervous temperament a preference to the lymphatic, in the sanguine a liking for the bilious constitutions. The offspring should combine the excellencies of both, the defects of neither. We do well to heed her admonitions here, and to bear in mind that those matches are, as a rule, most fortunate which combine opposite temperaments.

THE MORAL OR MENTAL CHARACTER.

Very few words are necessary here. We have already said we speak as physicians not as moralists. But there are some false and dangerous ideas abroad which it is our duty as physicians to combat.

None is more false, none more dangerous, than that embodied in the proverb, "A reformed rake makes the best husband." What is a rake? A man who has deceived and destroyed trusting virtue,—a man who has entered the service of the devil to undermine and poison that happiness in marriage which all religion and science are at such pains to cultivate. We know him well in our capacity as physicians. He comes to us constantly the prey to loathsome diseases, the results of his vicious life, which diseases he will communicate to his wife, for they are contagious, and to his children, for they are hereditary; which no reform can purge from his system, for they are ineradicable.

Is this the man a pure woman should take into her arms? Here repentance avails nothing. We have witnessed the agony unspeakable which overwhelmed a father when he saw his children suffering under horrible and disgusting diseases, the penalty of his early sins.

Very few men of profligate lives escape these diseases. They are alarmingly prevalent among the "fast" youths of our cities. And some forms of them are incurable by any effort of skill. Even the approach of such men should be shunned—their company avoided.

A physician in central Pennsylvania lately had this experience: A young lady of unblemished character asked his advice for a troublesome affection of the skin. He examined it and to his horror recognised a form of one of the loathsome diseases which curse only the vilest or the most unfortunate of her sex. Yet he could not suspect the girl. On enquiry he found that she had a small but painful sore on her lip, which she first noticed a few days after being at a pic-nic with a young man. Just as he was bidding her good night, he had kissed her on the lips.

At once everything was clear. This young man was a patient of the physician. He was a victim to this vile disease, and even his kiss was enough to convey it.

The history of the sixteenth century contains the account of an Italian duke who on one occasion was forced by his ruler to reconcile himself with an enemy Knowing he could not escape obedience, he protested the most cheerful willingness, and in the presence of the king embraced his enemy and even kissed him on the lips. It was but another means of satisfying his hatred. For he well knew that his kiss would taint his enemy's blood with the same poison that was undermining his own life.

How cautious, therefore, should a woman be in granting the most innocent liberties? How solicitous should she be to associate with the purest men!

Would that we could say that these dangerous and loathsome diseases are rare. But alas! daily professional experience forbids us to offer this consolation. Every physician in our large cities, and even in smaller towns, knows that they are fearfully prevalent.

We have been consulted by wives, pure innocent women, for complaints, which they themselves, and sometimes their children suffered from, the nature of which we dared not tell them, but which pointed with fatal finger to the unfaithfulness of their husbands. How utterly was their domestic happiness wrecked when they discovered the cause of their constant ill-health!

Nor are such occurrences confined to the humbler walks of life. There, perhaps, less than in any other do they occur. It is in the wealthy, the luxurious, the self-indulgent class that they are found.

Are we asked how such a dreadful fate can be averted?

There are, indeed, certain signs and marks which such diseases leave, with which physicians are conversant. As if nature intended them as warnings, they are imprinted on the most visible and public parts of the body. The skin, the hair, the nose, the voice, the lines of the face, often divulge to the trained observer, more indubitably than the confessional, a lewd and sensual life.

Such signs, however, can only be properly estimated by the medical counsellor, and it were useless to rehearse them here. Those women who would have a sure guide in choosing a man to be their husband, have they not Moses and the prophets? What is more, have they not Christ and the apostles? Rest assured that the man who scoffs at Christianity, who neglects its precepts, and violates its laws, runs a terrible risk of bringing upon himself, his wife, and his children, the vengeance of nature, which knows justice but not mercy. Rest assured that the man who respects the maxims of that religion, and abstains from all uncleanness, is the only man who is worthy the full and confiding love of an honourable woman.

THE SYMBOLISM OF THE HUMAN BODY.

Philosophers say that every idle word which is spoken continues to vibrate in the air through all infinity. So it is with the passions and the thoughts. Each impresses on the body some indelible mark, and a long continuance of similar thoughts leaves a visible imprint.

Under the names phrenology, physiognomy, palmistry, and others, attempts have been made at divers times to lay down fixed principles by which we could judge of men by their outsides. But only vague results have been obtained. A learned German author, of high repute in exact science, has gone a different way to work. He has studied the body as a whole, and sought, with the eye of an anatomist, how different avocations, passions, temperaments, habits, mould and fashion the external parts of man. His results are embraced in a curious volume which he entitles

"The Symbolism of the Human Body." We shall borrow some hints from it, germane to our present theme.

As to size, large-bodied and large-boned men possess greater energy, a more masculine character, but often less persistence, and are usually devoid of the more delicate emotions. Fat people are good tempered, but indolent; thin people, full of life, but irascible.

The neck is a significant part of the body. View it from the front, and it discloses the physical constitution. There are the conduits of the food and the air; there the great blood-vessels pass to the head, and its base is modified by their form as they pass from the heart. When broad and full it denotes a vigorous physical life—a plethoric constitution. A distinguished teacher of midwifery, Professor Pagot, of Paris, says that when he sees one of those necks full in front, like that of Marie Antoinette, as shown in her portraits, he prepares himself to combat child-bed convulsions. That queen, it is well known nearly perished with them.

The back of the neck contains the vertebral column and is close to the brain. It reveals the mental constitution. The short, round neck of the prize-fighter betrays his craft. The slender, arched, and graceful neck of the well proportioned woman is the symbol of health, and a well-controlled mind. Burke, in his essay on "The Beautiful," calls it the most beautiful object in nature. It is a common observation that a sensual character is shown by the thick and coarse development of this portion of the body.

The hair, also, has a significance. Fine, whitish hair, like that of a child, goes with a simple, child-like disposition; black hair denotes a certain hardness of character; red hair has long been supposed to be associated with a sensual constitution, but it rather indicates a physical weakness—a tendency to scrofula. This is, however, a tendency merely. Thin hair is often the result of protracted mental labour, though many other causes produce it.

Every great man, says Herder, has a glance which no one can imitate. We may go farther, and say that every man of decided character reveals it in his eyes. They are the most difficult organs for the hypocrite to control. Beware of the man who cannot look you in the eyes, and of him in whose eyes there lurks an expression which allures yet makes you shudder. The one has something he dares not tell you, the other something you dare not listen to.

Symmetry, strength, grace, health, these are admirable qualities in a man. From the remotest ages they have been the marks of heroes. Secondary though they are to moral and mental qualities, they should ever be highly valued. A *manly* man! Nature designs such to be the sires of future generations. No danger that we shall fall to worshipping physical beauty again. The only fear is that in this lank, puny, scrawny generation of ours we shall, out of vanity, underrate such beauty. Let it be ever remembered that is the ideal, from which any departure is deterioration.

THE ENGAGEMENT.

In this country a young lady engages herself, and tells papa or not as she sees fit. Often it is a profound secret for months between her lover and herself, with, perhaps, a friend or two on either side.

When our grandmothers were engaged, the minister rose in his pulpit on Sunday morning, before the assembled congregation, and proclaimed the "banns," stating that if any one knew just cause or lawful impediment why the lovers should not be married, he should state it there and then. Sometimes a great hubbub was created, when some discarded suitor rose and claimed that the capricious maiden had previously promised herself to him. Perhaps it was to avoid such an uncomfortable check on the freedom of flirtation that the ancient custom was dropped.

Certain it is, that to be "engaged" sits very lightly on the minds of both young men and maidens nowadays. We know some of either sex who make it a boast how often they have made and unmade this slender tie. It is a dangerous pastime. "The hand of little use hath the daintier touch," and he or she who thus trifles with their affections will end by losing the capacity to feel any real affection at all.

Undoubtedly there occur instances where a woman has pledged herself in all seriousness, and afterwards sees her affianced in a light which warns her that she cannot be happy with him; that the vows she will be called upon to pronounce at the altar will be hollow and false. What is she to do?

We are not inditing the decrees of the Court of Love. Here is the advice of another to her hand:

"First to thine own self be true,
And then it follows, as the night the day,
That thou canst ne'er be false to any man."

CONCERNING LONG ENGAGEMENTS.

They are hurtful, and they are unnecessary. Is love so vagrant that it must be tied by such a chain? Better let it go. True love asks no oath; it casteth out fear, and believes without a promise.

There are other reasons, sound physiological reasons, which we could adduce, if need were, to show that the close personal relations which arise between persons who are engaged should not be continued too long a time. They lead to excitement and debility, sometimes to danger and disease. Especially is this true of nervous, excitable, sympathetic dispositions, such as many of us Americans have.

If we are asked to be definite, and give figures, we should say that a period not longer than a year, nor shorter than three months, should intervene between the engagement and the marriage.

THE RIGHT TIME OF YEAR TO MARRY.

Woman, when she marries, enters upon a new life, and a trying one. Every advantage should be in her favour. The season is one of those advantages. Extreme heat and extreme cold both wear severely on the human frame. Mid-winter and mid-summer are, therefore, alike objectionable, especially the latter.

Spring and fall are usually chosen in this country, as statistics show, and the preference is just. On the whole, the spring is rather to be recommended than the autumn. In case of a birth within the year, the child will have attained sufficient age to weather its period of teething more easily ere the next summer.

THE RIGHT TIME IN THE MONTH TO MARRY.

We mean the woman's own month, that which spans the time between her periodical sicknesses, be it two or five weeks. Let her choose a day about equi-distant from the two periods. The reasons for this we shall specify hereafter.

THE WEDDING TOUR.

The custom of our country prescribes a journey immediately after marriage, of a week or a month or two. It is an unwise provision. The event itself is disturbance enough for the system; and to be hurried hither and thither, stowed in berths and sleeping-cars, bothered with baggage, and annoyed with the importunities of cabmen, waiters, and hangers-on of every description, is enough, in ordinary times, to test the temper of a saint.

The foundation of many an unhappy future is laid on the wedding tour. Not only is the young wife tried beyond all her experience, and her nervous system harassed, but the husband, too, partakes of her weakness. Many men, who really love the woman they marry, are subject to a slight revulsion of feeling for a few days after marriage. "When the veil falls, and the girdle is loosed," says the German poet, Schiller, "the fair illusion vanishes." A half regret crosses their minds for the jolly bachelorhood they have renounced. The mysterious charms which gave their loved one the air of something more than human, disappear in the prosaic light of familiarity.

Let neither be alarmed or lose their self-control. Each requires indulgence, management, from the other; both should demand from themselves patience and self-command. A few weeks and this danger is over; but a mistake now is the mistake of a lifetime. More than one woman has confessed to us that her unhappiness commenced from her wedding-tour; and when we inquired more minutely, we have found that it arose from an ignorance and disregard of just such little precautions as we have been referring to.

Yet it is every way advisable that the young pair should escape the prying eyes of friends and relatives at such a moment. Let them choose some quiet resort, not too long a journey from home, where they can pass a few weeks in acquiring that more intimate knowledge of each other's character so essential to their future happiness.

THE WIFE.

THE WEDDING NIGHT.

We now enter upon the consideration of the second great period in the life of woman. The maiden becomes a Wife. She is born into a new world. She assumes new relationships, the sweetest, and, at the same time, the most natural of which she is capable.

The great object of the conjugal union is the transmission of life—a duty necessary in order to repair the constant ravages of death, and thus perpetuate the race. In the fulfilment of the sublime obligation, woman plays the more prominent part, as she is the source and depositary of the future being. It is of moment, therefore, that she should not be altogether ignorant of the nature and responsibilities of her position. Ignorance here means suffering, disease, and sometimes death. Let us then interrogate science in regard to these matters, among the most interesting of all human concerns.

The initiation into marriage, like its full fruition, maternity, is attended with more or less suffering. Much, however, may be done to avert and to lessen the pain which waits upon the first step in this new life. For this purpose regard must be had to the selection of the day. We have said that a time about midway between the monthly recurring periods is best fitted for the consummation of marriage. As this is a season of sterility, it recommends itself on this account, in the interest of both the mother and offspring. The first nuptial relations should be fruitless, in order that the indispositions possibly arising from them shall have time to subside before the appearance of the disturbances incident to pregnancy. One profound change should not too quickly succeed the other. About the tenth day after menstruation should, therefore, be chosen for the marriage ceremony.

It sometimes happens that marriage is consummated with difficulty. To overcome this, care, management, and forbearance should always be employed, and anything like precipitation and violence avoided. Only the consequences of unrestrained impetuosity are to be feared. In those rare cases in which greater resistance is experienced than can be overcome by gentle means, the existence of a condition contrary to nature may be suspected. Violence can then only be productive of injury, and is not without danger. Medical art should be appealed to, as it alone can afford assistance in such an emergency.

Although the first conjugal approaches are ordinarily accompanied by slight flooding, a loss of blood does not always occur. Its absence proves nothing. The appearance of blood was formerly regarded as a test of virginity. The Israelites, Arabs, and others carefully preserved and triumphantly exhibited the evidence of it as an infallible sign of the virtue of the bride. They were in error. Its presence is as destitute of signification as its absence, for it is now well known that widows, and wives long separated from their husbands, often have a like experience. The temperament is not without its influence. In those of lymphatic temperament, pale blondes, who often suffer from local discharge and weakness, the parts being relaxed, there is less pain and little or no hemorrhage. In brunettes, who have never had any such trouble, the case is reversed. The use of baths, unguents, etc., by the young wife, however serviceable it might prove, is obviously impracticable. This great change sometimes, also, produces swelling and inflammation of the glands of the neck.

Marital relations ordinarily continue during the first few weeks to be more or less painful. General constitutional disturbances and disorders of the nervous system often result. These troubles are all increased by the stupid custom of hurrying the bride from place to place, at a time when the bodily quiet and mental calmness and serenity so desirable to her should be the only objects in view. Too frequent indulgence at this period is a fruitful source of various inflammatory diseases, and often occasions temporary sterility and ill-health. The old custom requiring a three days' separation after the first nuptial approach, was a wise one, securing to the young wife the soothing and restoring influence of rest. Nothing was lost by it, and much gained.

In a little while, however, all irritation should subside, and no suffering or distress of any kind, whether general or local, should attend upon the performance of this important function. The presence of suffering now becomes indicative of disease. Of this we will speak hereafter.

SHALL HUSBAND AND WIFE OCCUPY THE SAME ROOM AND BED?

One third of life is passed in sleep. This period of unconsciousness and rest is necessary for the renewal of vital strength, and upon its proper management depends much of the health, not merely of the husband and wife, but of their offspring. A great deal has been written upon the effect on health and happiness of occupying separate apartments, separate beds in the same apartment, or the same bed. This vexed question it is impossible to set by absolute rules, suitable to all cases. In general it may be asserted that there are no valid physiological reasons for desiring to change the custom which now prevails in this and most other countries. When both parties are in good health, and of nearly the same age, one bed-chamber, if it is sufficiently roomy, may be used without any disadvantage to either. Such an arrangement is also to be commended because it secures closer companionship, and thus devalops and sustains mutual affection.

It is said that in Zurich, in the olden time, when a quarrelsome couple applied for a divorce, the magistrate refused to listen to them at first. He ordered that they should be shut up together in one room for three days, with one bed, one table, one plate and one cup. Their food was passed in by attendants, who neither saw nor spoke to them. On the expiration of three days it was usual to find that neither of them wanted a separation.

As before stated, there are conditions under which sleeping together is prejudicial to the health. A certain amount of fresh air during the night is required by every one. Re-breathed air is poisonous. During sleep constant exhalations take place from the lungs and from the skin, which are injurious if absorbed. A room twelve feet square is too small for two persons, unless it is so thoroughly ventilated that there is constant change of air. In fact, a sleeping apartment for two persons should contain an air-space of at least twenty-four hundred cubic feet, and the facilities for ventilation should be such that the whole amount will be changed in an hour; that is, at the rate of forty cubic feet per minute: for it has been ascertained that twenty cubic feet of fresh air a minute are required for every healthy adult.

The young and old should never occupy the same bed. When the married couple hold the relation to each other, in regard to age, of grandfather and grandaughter, separate apartments should be insisted upon.

Certain diseases can be produced by sleeping together. The bed of a consumptive, it is well known, is a powerful source of contagion. In Italy it is the custom to destroy after death the bed-clothing of consumptive patients. Tubercular disease has, within the past few years, been transferred from men to animals by inoculation. Authentic cases are upon record of young robust girls of healthy parentage, marrying men affected with consumption, acquiring the disease in a short time, and dying in some instances before their husbands. In these significant cases, the sickly emanations have apparently been communicated during sleep. When, therefore, either husband or wife is known to have consumption, it would be highly imprudent for them to pass the long hours of the night either in the same room or in the same bed.

WHAT KIND OF REST IS MOST HEALTHFUL?

Feather-beds are not conducive to the health of either sex. Mattresses made of wool, or of wool and horsehair, are much better. The bed should be opened, and its contents exposed to the air and sunlight, once every year. Beds long saturated with the night exhalations of their occupants are not wholesome. A number of ancient writers have alleged—and it has been reasserted by modern authorities—that sleeping on sponge is of service to those who desire to increase their families. The mattresses of compressed sponge recently introduced, therefore, commend themselves to married people thus situated. Hemlock boughs make a bed which has a well-established reputation for similar virtues.

The odour of cone-bearing trees has a well-known influence upon the fruitfulness of wedlock. Those who live in pine forests have ordinarily large families of children.

Excessive clothing at night is highly injurious. So, also, is a fire in the bedroom, excepting in case of sickness. If the body be too much heated during sleep, perspiration occurs, or the action of the heart is increased, and the whole economy becomes excited. Either condition prevents sound sleep and reinvigoration of the body. Wives in feeble health, and those liable to attacks of flooding, should, therefore, have a particular regard to the quantity of clothing on their beds.

THE DIGNITY AND PROPRIETY OF THE SEXUAL INSTINCT.

A distinguished medical writer has divided women into three cases in regard to the intensity of the sexual instinct. He asserts that a larger number than is generally supposed have little or no sexual feeling. A second class of women, more numerous than these, but still small as compared with the whole of their sex, are more or less subject to strong passion. Those of the first class can no more form an idea of the strength of the impulse in other women than the blind can of colours. They, therefore, often err in their judgments. The third class comprises the vast majority of women, in which the sexual appetite is as moderate as all other appetites.

It is a false notion, and contrary to nature, that this passion in a woman is a derogation to her sex. The science of physiology indicates most clearly its propriety and dignity. There are wives who plume themselves on their repugnance or their distaste for their conjugal obligations. They speak of their coldness and of the calmness of their senses, as if these were not defects. Excepting those afflicted with vices of conformation or with disorders of sensibility—which amount to the same thing—all wives are called upon to receive and pay the imposts of love, and those who can withdraw themselves from the operation of this mysterious law without suffering and with satisfaction, show themselves by that fact to be incomplete in their organization, and deficient in the special function of their being. There should be no passion for one which is not shared by both. Generation is a duty. The feeling which excites to the preservation of the species is as proper as that which induces the preservation of the individual. Passionate, exclusive, and durable love for a particular individual of the opposite sex is characteristic of the human race, and is a mark of distinction from other animals. The instinct of reproduction in mankind is thus joined to an affectionate sentiment, which adds to its sweetness and prolongs infinitely its duration.

Many physiologists have assigned to the feelings an important rôle in conception, the possibility of which has even been doubted if there be no passion on the side of the woman. Although this extreme view is not tenable in the light of modern research, yet all recent authorities agree that conception is more assured when the two individuals who co-operate in it participate at the same time in the transports of which it is the fruit. It is also, without doubt, true that the disposition of the woman at that time has much power in the formation of the fœtus, both in modifying its physical constitution and in determining the character and temperament of its mind. The influence long ago attributed by Shakspeare to "a dull, stale, tired bed" in creating a "tribe of fops" is not a mere poet's fancy.

In this manner, also, may be explained the results of prolonged continence upon the offspring, for desires are usually vivid in proportion to the previous period of rest. The father of Montaigne returning after an absence of thirty-two years, during which he was engaged in the wars of Italy, begot his son, so justly celebrated in French literature. The father of J. J. Rousseau, after a considerable absence in Constantinople, brought to his wife the reward of a long fidelity.

Sexual passion exerts, therefore, a marked influence upon the future being, before conception, by the impression made upon the elements which come together to form it. The question now occurs, what effect does its presence and gratification produce upon the parents? We answer, it is a natural and healthful impulse. Its influence is salutary. A marked improvement in the physical condition of delicate women often follows a happy marriage. This sometimes occurs even in those cases where, from the nature of the disorder, the reverse might be expected. The utility of the passions well directed has become a maxim in medicine as in morality. And what passion is more important and fervent than that of which we write!

The fathers in medecine, and their modern followers, agree in ascribing to the pleasures of love, indulged in with moderation, activity and lightness of the body, vigour and vivacity of the mind.

Music, apart from its immense influence on the nervous system in general, seems sometimes to exercise a special action on the sexual instinct. Science possesses at the present day some facts beyond dispute which prove the great power of music in this respect.

ON THE INDULGENCE AND THE RESTRAINT OF SEXUAL DESIRE.

The act of generation is a voluntary one. But, nature has so placed it under the empire of pleasure, that the voice of discretion is no longer heard, and the will is often led captive. Hence it is well, for hygienic reasons, to consider its laws.

The too frequent repetition of the reproductive act is known to be followed by consequences injurious to the general health. Too rigid continence is not unattended, in many constitutions, with danger, for the victory over passion may be dearly bought. Science recommends the adoption of a wise mean between two extremes equally destructive. By following her counsel, woman may escape from the hysterical and other disorders which often wait as well upon excess as upon too great denial of that passion, which claims satisfaction as a natural right.

As men have made laws upon all subjects, we need not be surprised to learn that they have legislated upon this History informs us that the legislators of ancient times have not failed to occupy themselves with this grave question of conjugal economy. The ordinances of Solon required that the married should acquit themselves of their duties at least three times a month; those of Zoroaster prescribed once a week. Mahomet ordained that any wife neglected by her husband longer than a week could demand and obtain a divorce. It is not, however, in these and other enactments which might be quoted, that guidance is to be sought. The principles derived from nature and experience are more valuable than human laws, however venerable, for these too often serve only to reflect the profound ignorance of their makers.

Moderation should here prevail. Health is thus preserved and strengthened, and the gratification doubled. The art of seasoning pleasures in general consists in being avaricious with them. To abstain from enjoyment is the philosophy of the sage, the epicurism of reason.

Proper self-denial in the gratification of the wants of physical love is a source of good, not only to the individual practising it, but to the community, as we shall show hereafter. It may be practised for one's own advantage only, or for the benefit of another. The latter is in the end more conducive to self-interest than the former. A double profit grows therefrom: gratitude and sympathy returned, and increase of appetite and power of future enjoyment. The love which first united any pair soon becomes extinguished through excess of indulgence, and sometimes terminates in the pain of a surfeit. Earnest love, satisfying itself with small gratifications, is a more copious source of pleasure than that frequently quenched by full gratification.

What then, is this moderation which both Hygeia and Venus command? Here, again, invariable rules are not possible. Science rarely lays down laws as inflexible as those of the Medes and Persians. She designates limits. The passage between Scylla and Charybdis is often a wide one. The folly of the ancient statutes which have been referred to, consists mainly in their failure to recognise the divers influence of age, temperament, seasons, etc.

It almost appears as if there were but one season for generation, that in which the sun re-warms and vivifies the earth, trees dress in verdure, and animals respire the soft breath of spring. Then every living thing reanimates itself. The impulse of reproduction is excited. Now, also, its gratification is most beneficial to the individual and to the species. Children conceived in the spring time have greater vitality, are less apt to die during infancy, than those conceived at any other time of the year. The statistics of many thousand cases recently carefully collected in England prove this beyond peradventure. It is well known that a late calf, or one born at the end of the summer, is not likely to become a well-developed and healthy animal. This has been attributed to the chilling influence of the approaching winter; but it is capable of another, and perhaps a truer explanation. Nature's impulses, therefore, in the spring of the year, are for the good of the race, and may then be more frequently indulged without prejudice to the individual. Summer is the season which agrees the least with the exercise of the generative organs. The autumn months are the most unfruitful. Then, also, derangements of the economy are readily excited by marital intemperance.

The temperaments exert over reproduction, as over all the other functions of the body, a powerful influence. Love is said to be the ruling passion in the sanguine temperament, as ambition is in the bilious. There is also in some cases a peculiar condition of the nervous system which impels to, or diverts from, sexual indulgence. In some women, even in moderation, it acts as a poison, being followed by headache and prostration, lasting for days.

With advancing years, the fading of sexual desire calls attention to the general law, that animals and plants when they become old are dead to reproduction. What in early life is followed by temporary languor, in matured years is succeeded by a train of symptoms much graver and more durable.

Those who are in feeble health, and particularly those

who have delicate chests, ought to be sober in the gratification of love. Sexual intercourse has proved mortal after severe hemorrhages.

All organized beings are powerfully affected by propagation. Animals become depressed and dejected after it. The flower which shines so brightly at the moment of its amours, after the consummation of that act withers and falls. It is wise, therefore, in imparting life, to have a care not to shorten one's own existence. Nothing is more certain than that animals and plants lessen the duration of their lives by multiplied sexual enjoyments. The abuse of these pleasures produces lassitude and weakness, Beauty of figure and grace of movement are sacrificed. When the excess is long continued, it occasions spasmodic and convulsive affections, enfeeblement of the senses, particularly that of sight, deprivation of the mental functions, loss of memory, pulmonary consumption, and death. One of the most eminent of living physiologists has asserted that "development of the individual and the reproduction of the species stand in a reverse ratio to each other," and that " the highest degree of bodily vigour is inconsistent with more than a very moderate indulgence in sexual intercourse."

The general principles we have just enunciated are of great importance in the regulation of the health. They are more suggestive and useful than the precise rules which have from time to time been laid down on this subject.

TIMES WHEN MARITAL RELATIONS SHOULD BE SUSPENDED.

There are times at which marital relations are eminently improper. We are told, 1 Corinth. vii. 3, 4, that the husband and wife are equally bound to fulfil the conjugal obligation when the debt is demanded. But there are certain legitimate causes for denial by the wife.

A condition of intoxication in the husband is a proper ground for refusal. Fecundation taking place while either parent has been in this state has produced idiots and epileptics. This has happened again and again. The cases on record are so numerous and well authenticated, as to admit of no doubt in regard to the fatal effect upon the mind of the offspring of conception under such circumstances.

Physical degeneracy is also often a consequence of procreation during the alcoholic intoxication of one or both parents. A peculiar arrest of growth and development of body and mind takes place, and in some instances, the unfortunate children, although living to years of manhood remain permanent infants, just able to stand by the side of a chair, to utter a few simple sounds, and to be amused with childish toys.

During convalescence from a severe sickness, or when there is any local or constitutional disease which would be aggravated by sexual intercourse, it should be abstained from. There is reason for believing that a being procreated at a period of ill-humour, bodily indisposition, or nervous debility, may carry with it, during its whole existence, some small particles of these evils. When there exists any contagious disease, refusals are of course valid, and often a duty to the unborn. Poverty, or the wish to have no more children, cannot lawfully be urged against the rendering of conjugal rights.

The opinion that sexual relations practised during the time of the menses engender children liable to scrofulous disease is a mere popular prejudice. But there are other and better founded reasons for continence during these periods.

The question of intercourse during pregnancy and suckling will come up for consideration when speaking of these conditions hereafter.

CONDITIONS WHEN MARITAL RELATIONS ARE PAINFUL.

Nature has not designed that a function of great moment to the human race—one involving its very existence

—should be attended with pain. The presence of pleasure is indicative of health; its absence, of disease. But to a woman who has systematically displaced her womb by years of imprudence in conduct or dress, this act, which should be a physiological one, and free from any hurtful tendencies, becomes a source of distress, and even of illness. The diseases of the womb which sometimes follow matrimony are not to be traced to excessive indulgence in many cases, but to indulgence *to any extent* by those who have altered the natural relation of the parts before marriage. A prominent physician, Professor T. Gaillard Thomas, of New York, has said that "upon a woman who has enfeebled her system by habits of indulgence and luxury, pressed her uterus entirely out of its normal place, and who, perhaps, comes to the nuptial bed with some marked uterine disorder, the result of imprudence at menstrual epochs, sexual intercourse has a *poisonous* influence. The taking of food into the stomach exerts no hurtful induence on the digestive system; but the taking of food by a dyspeptic, who has abused and injured that organ, does so."

When excessive pain exists, and every attempt occasions nervous trepidation and apprehension, it is absolutely certain that there is some diseased condition present, for which proper advice should be secured at once. Delay in doing so will not remove the necessity for medical interference in the end, while it will assuredly aggravate the trouble.

STERILITY.

Wives who never become mothers are said to be sterile or barren. This condition is frequently a cause of much unhappiness. Fortune may favour the married couple in every other respect, yet if she refuse to accord the boon of even a single heir to heart and home, her smiles will bear the aspect of frowns. It is, then, of some interest to inquire into the causes of this condition, and how to prevent or remedy their operation.

Dr. Duncan, of Edinburgh, has shown by elaborate research that, in those wives who are destined to have children. there intervenes, on the average, about seventeen months between the marriage ceremony and the birth of the first child, and that the question whether a woman will be sterile is decided in the first three years of married life. If she have no children in that time, the chances are thirteen to one against her having any. In those cases, therefore, in which the first three years of married life are fruitless, it is highly desirable for those wishing a family to ascertain whether or not the barrenness is dependent upon any defective condition capable of relief.

The age of a wife at the time of marriage has much to do with the expectation of children. As the age increases over twenty-five years, the interval between the marriage and the birth of the first child is lengthened. For it has been ascertained that not only are women most fecund from twenty to twenty-four, but that they begin their career of child-bearing sooner after marriage than their younger or elder sister. Early marriages (those before the age of twenty) are sometimes more fruitful than late ones (those after twenty-four). The interesting result has further been arrived at in England, that about one in fourteen of all marriages of women between fifteen and nineteen are without offspring; that wives married at ages from twenty to twenty-four inclusive are almost all fertile; and that after that age the chances of having no children gradually increase with the greater age at the time of marriage.

There are two kinds of sterility which are physiological, natural to all women—that of young girls before puberty, and that of women who are past the epoch of the cessation of the menses. In some very rare cases conception takes place after cessation. In one published case it occurred nine months afterwards, and in another eighteen months. In some very rare cases, also, conception has taken place before the first menstruation.

The older a woman is at the time of her marriage, the longer deferred is the age at which she naturally becomes sterile. She bears children later in life, in order to compensate, as it were, for her late commencement. But, although she continues to have children until a more advanced age than the earlier married, yet her actual childbearing period is shorter. Nature does not entirely make up at the end of life for the time lost from the duties of maternity in early womanhood. For the younger married have really a longer era of fertility than the older, though it terminates at an earlier age.

A wife who, having had children, has ceased for three years to conceive, will probably bear no more, and the probability increases as time elapses. After the first births take place with an average interval, in those who continue to be fertile, of about twenty months.

Nursing women are generally sterile, above all during the first months which follow accouchement, because the vital forces are then concentrated on the secretion of the milk. In a majority of instances, when suckling is prolonged to even nineteen and twenty months, pregnancy does not take place at all until after weaning.

Climate has also an influence upon the fertility of marriages. In southern regions more children are born, fewer in northern. The number of children is in inverse proportion to the amount of food in a country and in a season. In Belgium, the higher the price of bread, the greater the number of children, and the greater the number of infant deaths.

The seasons exert a power over the increase of population. The spring of the year, as has already been stated, is the most favourable to fecundity. It is not known whether day and night have any effect upon conception.

The worldly condition seems to have much to do with the size of a family. Rich and fashionable women have fewer children than their poor and hard-working neighbours. Wealth and pleasure seem to be often gladly exchanged for the title of mother.

But it is our more particular object now to inquire into the causes of absolute sterility in individual cases, rather than to discuss the operation of general laws upon the fertility of the community at large, however inviting such a discussion may be. When marriages are fruitless, the wife is almost always blamed. It is not to be supposed that she is always in fault. Many husbands are absolutely sterile: for it is a mistake to consider that every man must be prolific who is vigorous and enjoys good health. Neither does it follow because a woman has never given birth to a living child, that she has not conceived. About one marriage in eight is unproductive of living children, and therefore fails to add to the population. The seeds of life have, however, been more extensively sown among women than these figures would seem to indicate. If the life of an infant for a long time after birth is a frail one, before birth its existence is precarious in the extreme. It often perishes soon after conception. A sickness, unusually long and profuse, occurring in a young married woman, a few days beyond the regular time, is often the only evidence she will ever have that a life she has communicated has been ended almost as soon as begun. A tendency to miscarriage may, therefore, be all that stands in the way of a family. This is generally remediable.

It is a well-known fact that frigidity is a frequent cause of barrenness, as well as a barrier to matrimonial happiness. Its removal, so desirable, is in many cases possible by detecting and doing away with the cause. The causes are so various that their enumeration here would be tedious and unprofitable, for most of them can only be discovered and remedied by a practical physician who has studied the particular case under consideration. So, also, in regard to the various displacements and diseases of the womb preventing conception. Proper medical treatment is usually followed by the best results.

While the fact that pleasure is found in the marital re-

...tion is a favourable augury for impregnation, it has been long noticed that Messalinas are sterile. It was observed in Paris that, out of one thousand, only six bore children in the course of a year, whereas the ordinary proportion in that city, for that time, is three and a half births for every one hundred of the population.

In some women nothing seems amiss but too intense passion. Such cases are much more rare than instances of the opposite extreme producing the same effect.

A condition of debility, or the presence of certain special poisons in the blood, may prevent conception, or, what is to all intents the same thing, cause miscarriage. Many apparently feeble women have large families. But in numerous instances a tonic and sometimes an alterative constitutional treatment is required before pregnancy will take place. On the contrary, there are well-authenticated cases of women, who are stout and barren in opulence, becoming thin and prolific in poverty.

The stimulus of novelty to matrimonial intercourse imparted by a short separation of husband and wife is often salutary in its influence upon fertility.

To show upon what slight constitutional differences infertility often depends, it is merely necessary to allude to the fact, known to every one, that women who have not had children with one husband often have them with another. This condition of physiological incompatibility is evidently not altogether one of the emotional nature, for it is observed in animals, among whom it is by no means rare to find certain males and females who will not breed together, although both are known to be perfectly fruitful with other females and males. The ancients, believing that sterility was more common with couples of the same temperament and condition, advised, with Hippocrates, that blonde women should unite with dark men, thin women with stout men, and *vice versa.*

Barren women should not despair. They sometimes become fecund after a long lapse of years. In other words, they are sterile only during a certain period of their lives, and then, a change occurring in their temperament with age, they become fruitful. History affords a striking example of this eccentricity of generation in the birth of Louis XIV., whom Anne of Austria, Queen of France, brought into the world after a sterility of twenty-two years. Catherine de Medicis, wife of Henry II., became the mother of ten children after a sterility of ten years. Dr. Tilt, of London, mentions the case of a woman who was married at eighteen, but, although both herself and her husband enjoyed habitual good health, conception did not take place until she was forty-eight, when she bore a child. Another case is reported where a well-formed female married at nineteen, and did not bear a child until she had reached her fiftieth year.

Families often suffer from the effects of sterility. Civilized nations never do. It has been found by observation, in countries where loss of life by war is inconsiderable, and where the pressure of the population, through excess of propagation, against the bounds of subsistence, is not very severe, that annual births equal in number to the annual deaths of the total population, are obtained by means of one-half only of the women exerting their full procreating power. Nature, therefore, has made ample provision for preventing a decrease of population through failure of reproduction.

She has also instituted laws to prevent its undue increase. It would seem as if the extension of material, mental, and social comfort and culture has a tendency to render marriage less prolific, and population stationary, or nearly so. So evident is this tendency, that it has been laid down as a maxim in sociology, by Sismondi, that "where the number of marriages is proportionately the greatest, where the greatest number of persons participate in the duties and virtues and the happiness of marriage, the smaller number of children does each marriage produce." Thus, to a certain extent, does nature endorse the opinions of those political economists who assert that increase of population beyond certain limits is an evil, happily averted by wars, famines, and pestilence, which hence become national blessings in disguise. She, however, points to the extension of moral and mental education and refinement as gentler and surer means of reducing plethoric population than those suggested by Malthus and Mill.

Many causes of sterility, it will therefore be seen, are beyond the power of man to control. They operate on a large scale for the good of the whole. With these we have little concern. But there are others which may be influenced by intelligent endeavour. Some have been already alluded to, and the remedy suggested; but we will proceed to give more specific

ADVICE TO WIVES WHO DESIRE TO HAVE CHILDREN.

It has long been known that menstruation presents a group of phenomena closely allied to fecundity. The first eruption of the menses is an unequivocal sign of the awakening of the faculty of reproduction. The cessation of the menstrual epochs is a sign equally certain of the loss of the faculty of reproduction. When conception has taken place, the periodical flow is interrupted. Labour occurs at about the time in which the menses would have appeared. In short, it is a fact now completely established, that the time immediately before and particularly that immediately after the monthly sickness is the period the most favourable to fecundation. It is said that by following the counsel to this effect given him by the celebrated Fernel, Henry II., the King of France, secured to himself offspring after the long sterility of his wife referred to. Professor Bedford, of New York, says that he can point to more than one instance in which, by this advice, he has succeeded in adding to the happiness of parties who for years had been vainly hoping for the accomplishment of their wishes

Repose of the woman, and, above all, sojourn on the bed after the act of generation, also facilitates conception. Hippocrates, the great father of medicine, was aware of this, and laid stress upon it in his advice to sterile wives.

The womb and the breasts are bound together by very strong sympathies; that which excites the one will stimulate the other. Dr. Charles Loudon mentions that four out of seven patients by acting on this hint became mothers. A similar idea occurred to the illustrious Marshall Hall, who advised the application of a strong infant to the breast. Fomentations of warm milk to the breasts and the corresponding portion of the spinal column, and the use of the breast-pump two or three times a day, just before the menstrual period, have also been recommended by good medical authorities. Horseback exercise carried to fatigue seems occasionally to have conduced to pregnancy.

The greatest hope of success against sterility is to change the dominant state of the constitution. But this can only be affected under suitable medical advice. The treatment of sterility—thanks to the recent researches of Dr. Marion Sims—is much more certain than formerly, and the intelligent physician is now able to ascertain the cause, and point out the remedy, where before all was conjecture and experiment.

ON THE LIMITATION OF OFFSPRING.

No part of our subject is more delicate than this. Very few people are willing to listen to a dispassionate discussion of the propriety or impropriety of limiting within certain bounds the number of children in a family. On the one side are many worthy physicians and pious clergymen, who, without listening to any arguments, condemn every effort to avoid large families; on the other are numberless wives and husbands who turn a deaf ear to the warnings of doctors and the thunders of divines, and, eager to escape a responsibility they have assumed, hesitate not to resort to the most dangerous and immoral means to accomplish this end.

We ask both parties to lay aside prejudices and prepossession, and examine with us this most important social question in all its bearings.

Let us first inquire whether there is such a thing as *over-production*—having *too many* children. Unquestionably there is. Its disastrous effects on both mother and children are known to every intelligent physician. Two-thirds of all cases of womb disease, says Dr Tilt, are traceable to child-bearing in feeble women. Hardly a day passes that a physician in large practice does not see instances of debility and disease resulting from over-much child-bearing. Even the lower animals illustrate this. Every farmer is aware of the necessity of limiting the offspring of his mares and cows. How much more severe are the injuries inflicted on the delicate organization of women. "A very great mortality," says Dr. Duncan, of Edinburgh, "attends upon confinements when they become too frequent."

The evils of a too rapid succession of pregnancies are likewise conspicuous in the children. "There is no more frequent cause," says Dr. Hillier, whose authority in such matters none will dispute, "of rickets than this." Puny, sickly, short-lived offspring, follows over-production. Worse than this, the carefully-compiled statistics of Scotland show that such children are peculiarly liable to idiocy. Adding to an already excessive number, they come to overburden a mother already overwhelmed with progeny. They cannot receive at her hands the attention they require. Weakly herself, she brings forth weakly infants. "Thus," concludes Dr. Duncan, "are the accumulated evils of an excessive family manifest."

Apart from these considerations, there are certain social relations which have been thought by some to advise small families. When either parent suffers from a disease

IMAGE EVALUATION
TEST TARGET (MT-3)

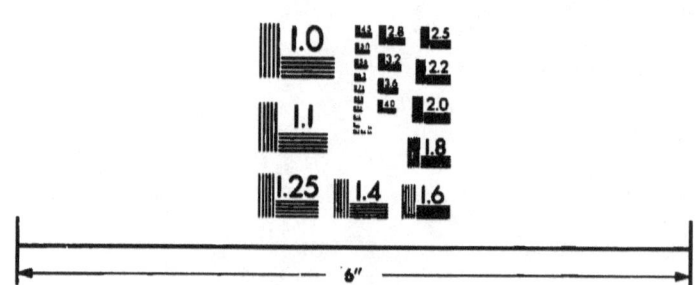

Photographic
Sciences
Corporation

23 WEST MAIN STREET
WEBSTER, N.Y. 14580
(716) 872-4503

which is transmissible, and wishes to avoid inflicting mi
sery on an unborn generation, it has been urged that they
should avoid children. Such diseases not unfrequently
manifest themselves after marriage, which is answer
enough to the objection that if they did not wish children they should not marry. There are also women to
whom pregnancy is a nine months' torture, and others to
whom it is nearly certain to prove fatal. Such condition
cannot be discovered before marriage, and therefore cannot be provided against by a single life. Can such women
be asked to immolate themselves?

It is strange, says that distinguished writer, John Stuart
Mill, that intemperance in drink, or in any other appetite,
should be condemned so readily, but that incontinence in
this respect should always meet not only with indulgence
but praise. "Little improvement," he adds, "can be expected in morality until the producing too large families
is regarded with the same feeling as drunkenness, or any
other physical excess." A well-known medical writer of
London, Dr. Drysdale, in commenting on these words
adds, "In this error, if error it be, I also humbly share."

"When dangerous prejudices," says Sismondi, the learned historian of South Europe, "have not become accre
dited, when our true duties towards those to whom we
gave life are not obscured in the name of a sacred authority, no married man will have more children than he car
bring up properly."

Such is the language of physicians and statesmen. But
a stronger appeal has been made for the sake of morality
itself. The detestable crime of *abortion* is appallingly rife
in our day; it is abroad in our land to an extent which
would have shocked the dissolute women of pagan Rome.
Testimony from all quarters, especially from New England,
has accumulated within the past few years to sap our
faith in the morality and religion of American women.
This wholesale fashionable murder, how are we stop it?
Hundreds of vile men and women in our large cities wh-

aist by this slaughter of the innocents, and flaunt their ill-gotten gains—the price of blood—in our public thoroughfares. Their advertisements are seen in the newspapers; their soul and body destroying means are hawked in every town. With such temptations strewn in her path, what will the woman threatened with an excessive family do? Will she not yield to evil, and sear her conscience with the repetition of her wickedness? Alas! daily experience in the heart of a great city discloses to us only too frequently the fatal ease of such a course.

In view of the injuries of excessive child-bearing on the one hand, and of this prevalent crime on the other, a man of genius and sympathy, Dr. Raciborski, of Paris, took the position that the avoidance of offspring to a certain extent is not only legitimate, but should be recommended as a measure of public good, "We know how bitterly we shall be attacked," he says, "for promulgating this doctrine; if our ideas only render to society the services we expect of them, we shall have effaced from the list of crimes the one most atrocious without exception—that of child-murder, before or after birth, and we shall have poured a little happiness into the bosoms of despairing families, where poverty is allied to the knowledge that offspring can be born only to prostitution or mendicity. The realization of such hopes will console us under the attacks upon our doctrines.

It has been eagerly repeated by some, that the wish to limit offspring arises most frequently from an inordinate desire of indulgence. We reply to such that they do not know the human heart, and that they do it discredit. More frequently the wish springs from a love of children. The parents seek to avoid having more than they can properly nourish and educate. They do not wish to leave their sons and daughters in want. "This," says a writer in *The Nation*, (of New York), in an article on this interesting subject—"this is not the noblest motive of action, of course, but there is something finely human about it,"

"Very much, indeed, is it to be wished," says Dr. Edward Reich,—after reviewing the multitudinous evils which result to individuals and society from a too rapid increase in families,—"that the function of reproduction be placed under the dominion of the will."

Men are very ready to find an excuse for self-indulgence, and if they cannot get one anywhere else, they seek it in religion. They tell the woman it is her duty to bear all the children she can. They refer her to the sturdy strong-limbed women of the early colonies, to the peasant women in Europe, who emigrate to our shores, and ask and expect the American wife to rival them in fecundity. They do not reflect that she has been brought up to light indoor employment, that her organization is more nervous and frail, that she absolutely has not the stamina required for many confinements.

Moreover they presume too much in asking her to bear them. "If a woman has a right to decide on any question," said a genial physician in the Massachussetts Medical Society a few years since, "it certainly is as to how many children she shall bear." "Certainly," say the editors of a prominent medical journal of our country "wives have a right to demand of their husbands at least the same consideration which a breeder extends to his stock." "Whenever it becomes unwise that the family should be increased," says Sismondi again, "*justice* and *humanity* require that the husband should impose on himself the same restraint which is submitted to by the unmarried."

An eminent English writer on English statistics, Dr. Henry MacCormack, says: "The brute yields to the generative impulse when it is experienced. He is troubled by no compunction about the matter. Now, a man ought not to act like a brute. He has reason to guide and control his appetites. Too many, however, forget and act like brutes instead of men. It would, in effect, prove very greatly conducive to man's interests were the generative impulses placed absolutely under the sway of right reason, chastity, forecast and justice.

There is no lack of authorities, medical and non-medical, on this point. Few who weigh them well will deny that there is such a thing as too large a family, that there does not come a time when a mother can rightly demand rest from her labours in the interest of herself, her children and society. When is this time? Here again the impossibility meets us, of stating a definite number of children, and saying: This many and no more. As in every other department of medicine, averages are of no avail in guiding individuals. There are women who require no limitation whatever. They can bear healthy children with rapidity, and suffer no ill results; there are others—and they are the majority—who should use temperance in this as in every other function; and there are a few who should bear no children at all. It is absurd for physicians or theologians to insist that it is either the physical or moral duty of the female to have as many children as she possibly can have. It is time that such an injurious prejudice was discarded, and the truth recognised that, while marriage looks to offspring as its natural sequence, there should be inculcated such a thing as marital continence, and that excess here as elsewhere is repugnant to morality, and is visited by the laws of physiology with certain and severe punishment on parent and child.

Continence, self-control, a willingness to deny himself, —that is what is required from the husband. But a thousand voices reach us from suffering women in all parts of our land, that this will not suffice; that men refuse thus to restrain themselves; that it leads to a loss of domestic happiness and to illegal amours, or that it is injurious physically and mentally—that in short, such advice is useless because impracticable.

To such sufferers we reply that nature herself has provided to some extent against over-production, and that it is well to avail ourselves of her provisions. It is well known that women when nursing rarely become pregnant, and for this reason, if for no other, women should nurse their own children, and continue the period until the child is at least a year old. Be it remembered, however, that nursing continued too long weakens both mother and child, and, moreover, ceases to accomplish the end for which we now recommend it.

Another provision of nature is, that for a certain period between her monthly illnesses every woman is sterile. The vesicle which matures in her ovaries, and is discharged from them by menstruation, remains some days in the womb before it is passed forth and lost. How long its stay is, we do not definitely know, and probably it differs in individuals. From ten to twelve days at most are supposed to elapse after the *cessation* of the flow before the final ejection of the vesicle. For some days after this, the female is incapable of reproduction, but for some days *before* her monthly illness she is liable to conception, as for that length of time the male element can survive. This period, therefore, becomes a variable and an undetermined one, and even when known, its observation demands a large amount of self-control.

What, then, is left to her whom an inconsiderate husband does not spare, and in whom the condition of nursing does not offer—as sometimes it does not—any immunity from pregnancy?

It is amiss to hope that science will find resources, simple and certain, which will enable a woman to let reason and sound judgment, not blind passion, control the increase of her family.

Such resources are not patents, or secrets hawked about by charlatans or advertised by quacks. Were they familiar to intelligent physicians, yet with a wise discrimination, and a conscientious regard for morality, they could not reveal them except where they were convinced that they will not be abused. Therefore, they, as a rule, have refrained from discussing the subject.

Let women be warned in the most emphatic manner against the employment of the secret methods which quacks in the newspapers are constantly offering. Such means are the almost certain cause of painful uterine diseases, and of shortened life. They are productive of more misery by far than over-production itself. "The workings of nature in this as in all other physiological processes," says Dr. Gaillard Thomas, "are too perfect, too accurately and delicately adjusted, to be interfered with materially by clumsy and inappropriate measures adopted to frustrate her laws."

None of these clumsy expedients is more frequent than the use of injections. None is more hurtful. It is almost certain to bring on inflammation and ulceration. "We are prepared to assert," says the editor of an ably-conducted journal in the west, "that fully *three-fourths* of the cases we have met of the various forms and effects of inflammation of the uterus and appendages in married women are directly traceable to this method of preventing pregnancy."

Equally injurious to the husband is the habit of uncompleted intercourse. Nervous prostration, paralysis, premature debility and decay are its frequent consequences.

On the contrary, when that due moderation which medical skill inculcates is employed to attain the same end, the danger seems less. "Long observation proves to us," says the editor of a prominent medical journal of this country, "that such women are the healthiest women in the world."*

There is one method widely in use in this country for the limitation of offspring, which deserves only the most unqualified condemnation, which is certain to bring upon the perpetrators swift and terrible retribution, and which is opposed to every sentiment of nature and morality We mean

---

* Dr. N. K. Bowling, Nashville Journal of Medicine and Surgery, October, 1868.

THE CRIME OF ABORTION.

From the moment of conception a new life commences; a new individual exists; another child is added to the family. The mother who deliberately sets about to destroy this life, either by want of care, or by taking drugs, or using instruments, commits as great a crime, is just as guilty as if she strangled her new-born infant, or as if she snatched from her own breast her six months' darling and dashed out its brains against the wall. Its blood is upon her head, and as sure as there is a God and a judgment that blood will be required of her. The crime she commits is *murder, child murder*—the slaughter of a speechless, helpless being, whom it is her duty, beyond all things else, to cherish and preserve.

This crime is common. It is fearfully prevalent. Hundreds of persons in every one of our largest cities are devoted to its perpetration. It is their trade. In nearly every village its ministers stretch out their bloody hands to lead the weak women to suffering, remorse, and death. Those who submit to their treatment are not generally unmarried women who have lost their virtue, but the mothers of families, respectable *Christian* matrons, members of churches, and walking in the better class of society.

We appeal to all such with earnest and with threatening words. If they have no feeling for the fruit of their womb, if maternal sentiment is so callous in their breasts let them know that such produced abortions are the constant cause of violent and dangerous womb diseases, and frequently of early death; that they bring on mental weakness, and often insanity; that they are the most certain means to destroy domestic happiness which can be adopted. Better, far better, to bear a child every year for twenty years than to resort to such a wicked and injurious step; better to die, if needs be, in the pangs of child-birth, than to live with such a weight of sin on the conscience.

There is no need of either. By the moderation we have mentioned, it is in the power of any woman to avoid the evils of an excessive family, without injury and without criminality.

We feel obliged to speak in plain language of this hidden sin, because so many are ignorant that it is a sin. Only within a few years have those who take in charge the public morals spoken of it in such terms that this excuse of ignorance is no longer admissible.

Bishop Coxe, of New York, in a pastoral letter; Archbishop Spaulding, Catholic Primate of the United States, in an address at the close of the last Provincial Council at Baltimore; the Old and New School Presbyterian Churches, at a recent meeting in Philadelphia, have all pronounced the severest judgments against those guilty of ante-natal infanticide. Appeals through the press have been made by physicians of high standing, and by eminent divines, which should be in the hands of every one.

The chiefest difficulty, hitherto, has been, that while women were warned against the evils of abortion, they were offered no escape from the exhaustion and dangers of excessive child-bearing. This difficulty we have fully recognised and fairly met, and, we believe, in such a manner that neither the accuracy of our statements nor the purity of our motives can be doubted. Should our position be attacked, however, the medical man must know that, in opposing our views, he opposes those of the most distinguished physicans in this country and in Europe; and the theologian should be warned that when a neglect of physical laws leads to moral evil, the only way to correct this evil is to remedy the neglect. In this case the neglect is in over-production—the evil is abortion.

NATURE OF CONCEPTION.

The theories which have been advanced to explain the manner in which the human species is continued and reproduced are very numerous. Including the hypotheses of the ancient philosophers, some two hundred and fifty have been promulgated by the greatest thinkers of all times. The older ones do not deserve mention, as they are replete with absurdities. Such, for instance, as that of Pythagoras, which supposed that a vapour descended from the brain and formed the embryo. The Scythians therefore took blood from the veins behind the ears to produce impotence and sterility. Modern science has shown the total error of this and many other views formerly entertained on this subject. Has galvanism or electricity any share in the mysterious function? Some among the modern physiologists have supposed that there is an electrical or magnetic influence which effects generation. Even within a few months, Dr. Harvey L. Byrd, Professor of Obstetrics in the Medical Department of Washington University of Baltimore, Md., has asserted that he has "every reason for believing that fecundation or impregnation is always an electrical phenomenon; . . . it results from the completion of an electric circle—the union of positive and negative electricities." This, however, is not accepted by all as the dictum of modern science. Physiology has clearly established that the new being is the result of contact between the male element, an independent, living animal, on the one part, and the female element, a matured egg, on the other, involving the union of the contents of two peculiar cells. Without such contact fecundation cannot take place.

The only matter of practical moment in connection with this most interesting function which we have to announce, is the influence of the mind on the offspring at the time of generation. This influence has long been remarked in regard to animals as well as men. Jacob was aware of it when he made his shrewd bargain with Laban for "all the speckled and spotted cattle" as his hire. For we are told that then "Jacob took him rods of green poplar, and of the hazel and chestnut tree ; and pilled white strakes in them, and made the white appear which was in the rods. And he set the rods which he had pilled before the flocks in the gutters in the watering troughs when the flocks came to drink, that they should conceive when they came to drink. And the flock conceived before the rods, and brought forth cattle ringstraked, speckled and spotted. And Jacob did separate the lambs and set the faces of the flocks towards the ringstraked and all the brown in the flock of Laban; and he put his own flock by themselves, and put them not unto Laban's cattle. And it came to pass whensoever the stronger cattle did conceive, that Jacob laid the rods before the eyes of the cattle in the gutters, that they might conceive among the rods. But when the cattle were feeble, he put them not in; so the feebler were Laban's and the stronger Jacob's.'

The impressions conveyed to the brain through the sense of sight are here asserted by the writer of Genesis to have influenced the system of the ewes so that they brought forth young in the same manner as the rods placed before their eyes. It is not said that there was any miraculous interposition; but the whole account is given as if it were an everyday, natural, and well-known occurrence.

The Greeks, a people renowned for their physical beauty, seemed to be aware of the value of mental impressions; for in their apartments they were lavish of statues and paintings representing the gods and goddesses, delineated in accordance with the best models of art.

Dionysius, tyrant of Syracuse, caused the portraits of the beautiful Jason to be suspended before the nuptial bed, in order to obtain a handsome child.

The following is related of the celebrated Galen. A Roman magistrate, little, ugly, and hunchbacked, had by his wife a child exactly resembling the statue of Æsop. Frightened at the sight of this little monster, and fearful of becoming the father of a posterity so deformed, he went to consult Galen, the most distinguished physician of his time, who counselled him to place three statues of love around the conjugal bed, one at the foot, the others, one on each side, in order that the eyes of his young spouse might be constantly feasted on those charming figures. The magistrate followed strictly the advice of the physician, and it is recorded that his wife bore him a child surpassing in beauty all his hopes.

The fact that the attributes of the child are determined to an important extent by the bodily and mental condition of the parents at the time of conception, explains the marked difference almost constantly observed between children born to the same parents, however strong the family likeness may be among them. The changes constantly going on in the physical, intellectual and emotional states of the parents produces a corresponding alteration in offspring conceived at successive intervals. Twins generally resemble each other very closely in every respect.

Inasmuch, therefore, as the moment of generation is of much more importance than is commonly believed, in its effect upon the moral and physical life of the future being, it is to be wished that parents would pay some attention to this subject. It is the moment of creation, that in which the first vital power is communicated to the new creature. Not without reason has nature associated with it the highest sensual exaltation of our existence. Dr. Hufeland, the author of the "Art of Prolonging Life," has said, "In my opinion it is of the utmost importance that this moment should be confined to a period when the sensation of collected powers, ardent passion, and a mind cheerful and free from care, invite to it on both sides."

SIGNS OF FRUITFUL CONCEPTION.

There are some women in whom the act of conception is attended with certain sympathetic affections, such as faintness, vertigo, etc., by which they know that it has taken place.

Swelling of the neck was regarded in ancient times as a sign of conception. Its truthfulness has been reaffirmed by modern authorities.

It has also been asserted that impregnation generally excites a universal tremor in all parts of the body, and that it is associated with more than an ordinary degree of pleasure.

It must not be supposed, however, that enjoyment and impregnation bear necessarily to each other the relation of cause and effect, although this is the popular opinion. From too implicit a reliance upon this current belief, wives are often incredulous as to their true condition.

It is a fact that in some cases sickness at the stomach manifests itself almost simultaneously with the act of fecundation. Authentic instances are on record of wives reckoning their confinement nine months from the first feeling of nausea, without ever making a mistake.

In conclusion, it may be said that peculiar sensations are often experienced frequently of a character difficult to explain, and many modern authors attach to them a marked value. In this manner it is possible for a woman to be satisfied at the moment as to the change which has taken place; yet the evidence is often deceptive, and sometimes nothing peculiar is noticed.

From the period of conception the mother has no direct knowledge of the process that is going on within, excepting by the effects of the increasing pressure upon other parts, until "quickening" takes place, which belongs to another part of our subject.

HOW TO RETAIN THE AFFECTIONS OF A HUSBAND.

Ah! this is a secret indeed!—worth the wand of the magician, the lamp of Alladin, or the wishing cap of the fairy. What could any of these give in exchange for the love of a husband? Yet this pearl of great price, how often it is treated as lightly and carelessly as if it was any bauble of Brummagem?

"My husband!" we have heard young wives say, "why it is his duty to love me. Why did he marry me if he is not going to love me, love me fondly, love me for ever?"

"Love the gift, is love the debt."

But in this world of ours it is often hard to get one's own, and when got, our care must never cease, lest it be wrested from us. The plant you bought at the greenhouse, that now blossoms on your window-sill, became yours by purchase, but it has required your daily care to keep it alive and persuade it to unfold its blossoms. Infinitely more delicate is this plant of love. It, too, you purchased. You gave in exchange for it your own heart. It, too, you must daily tend with constant solicitude, lest it wither and die.

In this country some women think that anything is good enough to wear at home. They go about in slatternly morning dresses, unkempt hair, and slippers down at heel. "Nobody will see me," say they, "but my husband." Let them learn a lesson from the wives of the Orient.

In those countries a wife never goes abroad except in long sombre robes and thick veil. An English lady visiting the wife of one of the wealthy merchants, found her always in full dress, with toilet as carefully arranged as if she were going to a ball.

"Why," exclaimed the visitor at length, "is it possible that you take all this trouble to dress for nobody but your husband?"

"Do then," asked the lady in reply, "the wives of Englishmen dress for the sake of pleasing other men?"

The visitor was mute.

Not that we would wish American ladies to be forever in full costume at home. That would be alarming. But she who neglects neatness in attire, and above all, cleanliness of person, runs a great danger of creating a sentiment of disgust in those around her. Nothing is more repugnant to the senses than bad odours, and for reasons which every woman knows, women who neglect cleanliness are peculiarly liable to them. When simple means do not remove them, recourse should be promptly had to a physician.

So it is with bad breath. This sometimes arises from the neglect of the teeth, sometimes from diseases of the stomach, lungs, etc. A man of delicate olfactories is almost forced to hold at arm's length a wife with a fetid breath.

There are some women—we have treated several—who are plagued with a most disagreeable perspiration, especially about the feet, the arms, etc. Such should not marry until this is cured. It is a rule among army surgeons to be chary about giving men their discharge from military service on a surgeon's certificate. But fetid feet are at times so horribly offensive, that they are considered an allowable cause for discharge. No doubt in some of our States they would be received as a valid ground for divorce!—certainly with as much reason as many of the grounds usually alleged.

In short, the judicious employment of all the harmless arts of the toilet, and of those numerous and effective means which modern science offers, to acquire, preserve, and to embellish beauty, is a duty which women, whether married or single, should never forget. With very little trouble, the good looks and freshness of youth can be guarded to almost old age, and even when hopelessly gone, simple and harmless means are at hand to repair the injuries of years, or at least to conceal them. But this is an art which would require a whole volume to treat of, and which we cannot here touch upon.

INHERITANCE.

We now come to the consideration of a very wonderful subject, that of inheritance. It is one of absorbing interest, both because of the curious facts it presents and of the great practical bearing it has upon the welfare of every individual.

In order to the better understanding of this matter, it is necessary at the outset to make a distinction between four kinds or varieties of inheritance. The most generally recognised is direct inheritance, that in which the children partake of the qualities of the father and mother. But a child may not resemble either parent, while it bears a striking likeness to an uncle or aunt. This constitutes indirect inheritance. Again, a child may be more like one of its grand-parents than either its father or mother. Or, what is still more astonishing, it may display some of the characteristics possessed only by a remote ancestor. This form of inheritance is known by the scientific term *atavism*, derived from the Latin word *atavus*, meaning an ancestor. It is curious to note in this connection that a son resembles more closely his maternal than his paternal grandsire in some male attribute, as a peculiarity of beard or certain diseases confined to the male sex. Though the mother cannot possess or exhibit such male qualities, she has transmitted them through her blood, from her father to her son.

The fourth variety of inheritance is that in which the child resembles neither parents, but the first husband of its mother. A woman contracting a second marriage transmits to the offspring of that marriage the peculiarities she has received through the first union. Breeders of stock know this tendency, and prevent their brood mares, cows, or sheep, from running with males of an inferior stock. Thus the diseases of a man may be transmitted to children which are not his own. Even though dead, he continues to exert an influence over the future offspring of his wife by means of the ineffaceable impress he had made in the conjugal relation upon her whole system, as we have previously mentioned. The mother finds in the children of her second marriage

"* * * the touch of a vanished hand,
And the sound of a voice that is still."

A child may, therefore, suffer, through the operation of this mysterious and inexorable law, for sins committed, not by its own father, but by the first husband of its mother. What a serious matter, then, is that relation between the sexes called marriage! How far-reaching are its responsibilities!

A distinction must here be drawn between hereditary transmission and the possession of qualities of birth which have not been the result of any impression received from the system of father or mother, but due to mental influences or accidents operating through the mother. A child may be born idiotic or deformed, not because either parent or one of its ancestors was thus affected, but from the influence of some severe mental shock received by the mother during her pregnancy. This subject of maternal impressions will come up for separate consideration in the discussion of pregnancy. Again, a child may be epileptic, although there is no epilepsy in the family, simply because of the intoxication of the father or mother at the time of the intercourse, resulting in conception. Such cases are not due to hereditary transmission, for that cannot be hereditary which has been possessed by neither the parents nor any other relatives.

In considering the effects of inheritance, we will first pass in review those connected with the physical constitution. These are exceedingly common and universally known. Fortunately, not merely are evil qualities inherited, but also beauty, health, vigour, and longevity.

BEAUTY.

Good looks are characteristic of certain families. Alcibiades, the handsomest among the Grecians of his time descended from ancestors remarkable for their beauty. So well and long has the desirable influence of inheritance in this respect been recognised, that there existed in Crete an ancient law which ordained that each year the most beautiful among the young men and women should be chosen and forced to marry in order to perpetuate the type of their beauty. Irregularities of feature are transmitted from parent to child through many generations The aquiline nose has existed some centuries, and is yet hereditary in the Bourbon family, The hereditary under lip of the House of Hapsburg is another example. When the poet Savage speaks of

"The tenth transmitter of a foolish face,"

he scarcely exaggerates what is often seen in families where some strongly-marked feature or expression is long predominant, or re-appears in successive generations.

NECK AND LIMBS.

The form and length of the neck and limbs are frequently hereditary, as is also the height of the body. The union of two tall persons engenders tall children. The father of Frederick the Great secured for himself a regiment of men of gigantic stature by permitting the marriage of his guards only with women of similar height. A tendency to obesity often appears in generation after generation of a family. Yet such cases are within the reach of medical art.

COMPLEXION.

Even the complexion is not exempt from this influence. Blondes ordinarily procreate blondes, and dark parents have dark-skinned children. An union in marriage of fair and dark complexions results in an intermediate shade in the offspring. Not always, however, for it has been asserted that the complexion chiefly follows that of the father. The offspring of a black father and a white mother is much darker than the progeny of a white father and a dark mother. In explanation of this fact, it has been said that the mother is not impressed by her own colour, because she does not look upon herself, while the father's complexion attracts her attention, and thus gives a darker tinge to the offspring. Black hens frequently lay dark eggs; but the reverse is more generally found to be the case.

PHYSICAL QUALITIES TRANSMITTED BY EACH PARENT.

In general, it may be said there exists a tendency on the part of the father to transmit the external appearance, the configuration of the head and limbs, the peculiarities of the senses, and of the skin and muscular condition, while the size of the body, and the general temperament or constitution of the child, is derived from the mother. Among animals, the mule, which is the produce of the male ass and the mare, is essentially a modified ass, having the general configuration of its sire but the rounded trunk and larger size of its dam. On the other hand, the hinny, which is the offspring of the stallion and the she ass, is essentially a modified horse, having the general configuration of the horse, but being a much smaller animal than its sire, and therefore approaching the dam in size as well as in the comparative narrowness of its trunk. The operation of this principle, though general, is not universal. Exceptions may easily be cited. In almost every large family it will be observed that the likeness to the father predominates in some children, while others most resemble the mother. It is rare to meet with instances in which some distinctive traits of both parents may not be traced in the offspring.

HAIR.

Peculiarities in the colour and structure of the hair are transmitted. Darwin mentions an English family in which, for many generations, some of the members had a single lock differently coloured from the rest of the hair.

TEMPERAMENT.

The law of inheritance rules in regard to the production of the temperament. The crossing of one temperament with another in marriage produces a modification in the offspring generally advantageous.

FERTILITY.

A peculiar aptitude for procreation is sometimes hereditary. The children of prolific parents are themselves prolific. It is related that a French peasant woman was confined ten times in fifteen years. Her pregnancies, always multiple, produced twenty-eight children. At her last confinement she had three daughters, who all lived, married, and gave birth to children; the first to twenty-six, the second to thirty-one, and the third to twenty-seven. On the contrary, sometimes a tendency to sterility is found fixed upon certain families, from which they can only escape by the most assiduous care.

LONGEVITY.

In the vegetable kingdom, the oak inherits the power to live many years, while the peach tree must die in a short time. In the animal kingdom, the robin becomes gray and toothless at ten years of age; the rook caws lustily until a hundred. The ass is much longer lived than the horse. The mule illustrates in a striking manner the hereditary tendency of longevity. It has the size of the horse, the long life of the ass. The weaker the ass, the larger, the stronger, and the shorter-lived and more horse-like the mule. It is also a curious and instructive fact, that this animal is the toughest after it has passed the age of the horse; the inherited influence of the horse having been expended, the vitality and hardness of the ass remains.

It is universally conceded that longevity is the privileged possession of some lineages. The famous instance of old age, Thomas Parr, the best authenticated on record, may be mentioned in illustration. It is vouched for by Harvey, the distinguished discoverer of the circulation of the blood. Parr died in the reign of Charles the First, at the age of 152, after having lived under nine sovereigns of England. He left a daughter aged 127. His father had attained to a great age, and his great-grandson died at Cork at the age of 103.

DEFORMITIES.

Deformities are undoubtedly sometimes transmitted to the progeny. It is by no means rare to find that the immediate ancestors of those afflicted with superfluous fingers and toes, club feet, or hare lips, were also the subject of these malformations. There are one or two families in Germany, whose members pride themselves upon the possession of an extra thumb; and there is an Arab chieftain whose ancestors have from time immemorial been distinguished by a double thumb upon the right hand. Darwin gives many similar instances. A case of curious displacement of the knee-pans is recorded, in which the father, sister, son, and the son of the half brother by the same father, had all the same malformation.

PERSONAL PECULIARITIES.

Gait, gestures, voice, general bearing, are all inherited. Peculiar manners, passing into tricks, are often transmitted, as in the case, often quoted, of the father who generally slept on his back with his right leg crossed over the left, and whose daughter, whilst an infant, in the cradle, followed exactly the same habit, though an attempt was made to cure her. Left-handedness is not unfrequently hereditary. It would be very easy to go on multitiplying instances, but we forbear.

HOW TO HAVE BEAUTIFUL CHILDREN.

A practical question now naturally suggests itself. How can the vices of conformation be avoided and beauty secured? The art of having handsome children, known under the name of *callipædia*, has received much attention, more, perhaps, in years gone by, than of late. The noted Abbot Quillet wrote a book in Latin on the subject. Many other works, in which astrology plays a prominent part, were written on this art in the sixteenth and seventeenth centuries.

We have already stated that well-informed parents will transmit these qualities to their children, with scarcely an exception. Like begets like. Unfortunately all parents are not beautiful. Yet all desire beautiful offspring. The body of the child can be influenced by the mind of the parent, particularly of the mother. A mind habitually filled with pleasant fancies and charming images is not without its effect upon the offspring.

The statues of Apollo, Castor and Pollox, Venus, Hebe, and other gods and goddesses which were so numerous in the gardens and public places of Greece, reproduced themselves in the sons and daughters of the passers by. We know also that marriages contracted at an age too early or too late are apt to give imperfectly developed children. The crossing of temperaments and of nationalities beautifies the offspring. The custom which has prevailed in many countries among the nobility of purchasing the handsomest girls they could find for their wives, has laid the foundation of a higher type of features among the ruling classes. To obtain this desired end, conception should take place only when both parents are in the best physical condition, at the proper season of the year, and with mutual passion. (We have already hinted how this can be regulated.) During pregnancy the mother should often have some painting or engraving representing cheerful and beautiful figures before her eyes or often contemplate some graceful statue. She should avoid looking at or thinking of ugly people, or those marked with disfiguring diseases. She should take every precaution to escape injury, fright and disease of any kind, especially chicken-pox, erysipelas, or such disorders as leave marks on the person. She should keep herself well nourished, as want of food nearly always injures the child. She should avoid ungraceful positions and awkward attitudes, as by some mysterious sympathy these are impressed on the child she carries. Let her cultivate grace and beauty in herself at such a time, and she will endow her child with them; as anger and irritability leave imprints on the features, she should maintain serenity and calmness.

INHERITANCE OF TALENT AND GENIUS.

The effects of inheritance are perhaps more marked upon the mind than upon the body. This need not surprise us. If the peculiar form of the brain can be transmitted, the mental attributes, the result of its organization, must necessarily also be transmitted.

It is a matter of daily observation that parents gifted with bright minds, cultivated by education, generally engender intelligent children; while the offspring of those steeped in ignorance are stupid from birth. It may be objected that men, the most remarkable in ancient or modern times. as Socrates, Plato, Aristotle, Shakespeare, Milton, Buffon, Cuvier, etc., have not transmitted their vast intellectual powers to their progeny. In explanation it has been stated that what is known as genius is not transmissible. The creation of a man of genius seems to require a special effort of nature, after which as if fatigued, she reposes a long time before again making a similar effort. But it may well be doubted whether even those complex mental attributes on which genius and talent depend are not inheritable, particularly when both parents are thus endowed. That distinguished men do not more frequently have distinguished sons may readily be accounted for, when it is recollected that the inherited character is due to the combined influence of both parents. The desirable qualities of the father may therefore be neutralized in the offspring by the opposite or defective qualities of the mother. That contrasts in the disposition of parents are rather the rule than the exception, we have already shown. Every one tends to unite himself in friendship or love with a different character from his own, seeking thereby to supplement the qualities in which he feels his own nature to be deficient. The mother, therefore, may weaken and perhaps obliterate the qualities transmitted by the father. Again, the influence of some remote ancestors may make itself felt upon the offspring, through the operation of the law of atavism, before alluded to, and thus prevent the children from equalling their parents in their natural endowments. Notwithstanding the working of these opposing forces, and others which might be mentioned, we find abundant illustration of the hereditary nature of talent and character.

Of six hundred and five names occurring in the "Biographical Dictionary" devoted to men distinguished as great founders and originators, between the years 1453 and 1853, there were no less than one hundred and two relationships, or one in six. Walford's "Men of the Time" contains an account of the distinguished men in England, the Continent, and America, then living. Under the letter A there are eighty-five names, and no less than twenty-five of these, or one in three and a half, have relatives also in the list; twelve of them are brothers, and eleven fathers and sons. In Bryan's "Dictionary of Painters," the letter A contains three hundred and ninety-one names of men, of whom sixty-five are near relatives, or one in six; thirty-three of them are fathers and sons, and thirty are brothers. In Feti's "Biographie Universelle des Musiciens," the letter A contains five hundred and fifteen names, of which fifty are near relatives, or one in ten. Confining ourselves to literature alone, it has been found that it is one to six and a half that a very distinguished literary man has a very distinguished literary relative. And it is one in twenty-eight that the relation is father and son or brother and brother respectively. Out of the thirty-nine Chancellors of England, sixteen had kinsmen of eminence; thirteen of them had kinsmen of great eminence. These thirteen out of thirty-nine, or one in three, are certainly remarkable instances of the influence of inheritance. A similar examination has been instituted in regard to the judges of the Supreme Court of Massachusetts, and other States, with like results. The Greek poet, Æschylus, counted eight poets and four musicians among his ancestors. The greater part of the celebrated sculptors of ancient Greece descended from a family of sculptors. The same is true of the great painters. The sister of Mozart shared the musical talent of her brother. As there are reasons, to be detailed hereafter, for believing that the influence of the mother is even greater than that of the father, how vastly would the offspring be improved if distinguished men united themselves in marriage to distinguished women for generation after generation!

INFUENCE OF FATHERS OVER DAUGHTERS; OF MOTHERS OVER SONS.

We have already called attention to the parts of the physical organization transmitted by the father and by the mother. It would seem, moreover, that each parent exercises a special influence over the child according to its sex. The father transmits to the daughters the form of the head, the framework of the chest and of the superior extremities, while the conformation of the lower portion of the body and the inferior extremities are transmitted by the mother. With the sons this is reversed. They derive from the mother the shape of the head and of the superior extremities, and resemble the father in the trunk and inferior extremities. From this it therefore results, that boys procreated by intelligent women will be intelligent, and that girls procreated by fathers of talent will inherit their mental capacity. The mothers of a nation, though unseen and acknowledged in the halls of legislation, determine in this subtle manner the character of the laws.

History informs us that the greater part of the women who have been celebrated for their intelligence, reflected the genius of their fathers. Arete, the most celebrated woman of her time, on account of the extent of her knowledge, was the daughter of the distinguished philosopher Aristippus, disciple of Socrates. Cornelia, the mother of the Gracchi, was a daughter of Scipio. The daughter of the Roman emperor Caligula was as cruel as her father, Marcus Aurelius inherited the virtues of his mother, and Commodus the vices of his. Charlemagne shut his eyes upon the faults of his daughters, because they recalled his own. Gengis-Khan, the renowned Asiatic conqueror, had for his mother a warlike woman. Tamerlane, the greatest warrior of the fourteenth century, was descended from Gengis-Khan by the female side. Catherine de Medicis was as crafty and deceitful as her father, and more superstitious and cruel. She had two sons worthy of herself, Charles IX., who shot the Protestants, and Henry III., who assassinated the Guises. Her daughter, Margaret of Valois, recalled her father by her gentle manners. Henry VIII., who put two of his wives to death on the scaffold, had two sons distinguished for the meekness of their characters, and two daughters as cruel as himself. Arete, Hypatia, Madame de Stael, and George Sand, all four had philosophers for their fathers. The mother of Bernardo Tasso had the gift of poetry. Buffon often speaks of the rich imagination of his mother. The poet Burns, "Rare Ben Jonson," Goethe, Walter Scott, Byron, and Lamartine—all were born by women remarkable for their vivacity and brilliancy of language. Byron, in his journal, attributes his hypochondria to an hereditary taint derived from his mother, who was its victim in its furious forms; and her father "was strongly suspected of suicide." He was said to have resembled more his maternal grandfather than any of his father's family. The daughter of Molière was like her father in her wit and humour. Beethoven had for a maternal grandmother an excellent musician. The mother of Mozart gave the first lessons to her son. A crowd of composers have descended from John Sebastian Bach, who long stood unrivalled as a performer on the organ, and composer for that instrument. It may be remarked here that it is almost invariably true that the ability or inability to acquire a knowledge of music is derived from the ancestry. Parents who cannot turn a tune, or tell one note from another, bring forth children equally unmoved "with concord of sweet sounds." Examples could easily be adduced at still greater length illustrating the direct influence of the father over the daughter, and of the mother over the son. Those given will suffice.

INFLUENCE OF EDUCATION OVER INHERITED QUALITIES.

In correcting the evil effects of inheritance on the mind, education plays a very important part. A child born with a tendency to some vice or intellectual trait, may have this tendency entirely overcome, or at least modified, by training. So, also, virtues implanted by nature may be lost during the plastic days of youth, in consequence of bad associations and habits.

Education can therefore do much to alter inherited mental and moral qualities. Can it be invoked to prevent the transmission of undesirable traits, and secure the good? Everything that we have at birth is an heritage from our ancestors. Can virtuous habits be transmitted? Can we secure virtues in our children by possessing them ourselves? Science sadly says, through her latest votaries, that we are scarcely more than passive transmitters of a nature we have received, and which we have no power to modify. It is only after exposure during several generations to changed conditions or habits that any modification in the offspring ensues. The son of an old soldier learns his drill more quickly than the son of an artisan. We must, therefore, come to the conclusion that, to a great extent, our own embryos have sprung immediately from the embryos whence our parents were developed, and these from the embryos of their parents, and so on forever. Hence, we are still barbarians in our nature. We show it in a thousand ways. Children, who love to dig and play in the dirt, have inherited that instinct from untold generations of ancestors. Our remote forefathers were barbarians, who dug with their nails to get at the roots on which they lived. The delicately-reared child reverts to primeval habits. In like manner, the silk-haired parlour-nurtured spaniel springs from the caressing arms of its mistress to revel in the filth of the road-side. It is the breaking out of inherited instinct.

TRANSMISSION OF DISEASE.

Perhaps the most important part of the subject of inheritance is that which remains for us to consider, in relation to the transmission of, or the predisposition to, disease.

Consumption, that dread foe of American life, is the most frequently encountered of all affections as the result of inherited predisposition. Indeed, some of the most eminent physicians have believed it is never produced in any other way. Heart disease, disease of the throat, excessive obesity, affections of the skin, asthma, disorders of the brain and nervous system, gout, rheumatism, and cancer are all hereditary. A tendency to bleed frequently, profusely, and uncontrollably, from trifling wounds, is often met with as a family affection.

The inheritance of diseased conditions is also *influenced by the sex.* A parent may transmit disease exclusively to children of the same sex, or exclusively to those of the opposite sex. Thus a horn-like projection on the skin, peculiar to the Lambert family, was transmitted from the father to his sons and grandsons alone. So mothers have through several generations, transmitted to their daughters alone, supernumerary fingers, colour-blindness, and other deformities and diseases. As a general rule, any disease acquired during the life of either parent strongly tends to be inherited by the offspring of the same sex rather than the opposite. We have spoken of the apparently reverse tendency in regard to the transmission of genius and talent.

ARE MUTILATIONS INHERITABLE?

How, it may be inquired, is it in regard to the inheritance of parts mutilated and altered by injuries and disease during the life of either parent? In some cases mutilations have been practised for many generations without any inherited result. Different races of men have knocked out their upper teeth, cut off the joints of their fingers, made immense holes through their ears and nostrils, and deep gashes in various parts of their bodies, and yet there is no reason for supposing that those mutilations have been inherited. The *Comprachicos*, a hidden and strange association of men and women, existed in the seventeenth century, whose business it was to buy children, and make of them monsters. Victor Hugo, in his last work, has graphically told how they took a face and made of it a snout, how they bent down growth, kneaded the physiognomy, distorted the eyes, and in other ways disfigured "the human form divine," in order to make fantastic playthings for the amusement of the noble born. But history does not state that these deformities were inherited certainly no race of monsters has resulted. The pits from small-pox are not inherited, though many successive generations must have been thus pitted by that disease before the beneficent discovery of the immortal Jenner. Children born with the scars left by pustules have had small-pox in the womb, acquired through the system of the mother. On the other hand, the lower animals, cats, dogs, and horses, which have had their tails and legs artificially altered or injured, have produced offspring with the same condition of parts. A man who had his little finger on the right hand almost cut off, and which in consequence grew crooked, had sons with the same finger on the same hand similarly crooked. The eminent physiologist, Dr. Brown-Séquard, mentions that many young guinea-pigs inherited an epileptic tendency from parents which had been subjected to an operation at his hands, resulting in the artificial production of fits; while a large number of guinea-pigs bred from animals which had not been operated on, were not thus affected. At any rate, it cannot but be admitted that injuries and mutilations which cause disease, are occasionally inherited. But many cases of deformities existing at birth, as harelip, are not due to inheritance, although present in the father. They arise from a change effected in the child while in the womb through an impression made upon the mind of the mother as will be shewn hereafter.

LATE MANIFESTATIONS OF THE EFFECTS OF INHERITANCE.

Not only are diseases inherited which make their appearance at birth, but those which defer their exhibition until a certain period of life corresponding with that at which they showed themselves in the parents. Thus in the Lambert Family, before referred to, the porcupine excrescence on the skin began to grow in the father and sons at the same age, namely, about nine weeks after birth. In an extraordinary hairy family, which has been described, children were produced during three generations with hairy ears; in the father, the hair began to grow over his body at six years old; in his daughte somewhat earlier, namely, at one year; and in both generations the milk teeth appeared late in life, the permanent teeth being deficient. Grayness of hair at an unusually early age has been transmitted in some families. So also, is the premature appearance of baldness.

HOW TO AVOID THE TENDENCY OF INHERITANCE.

These facts suggest the practical consideration that in those diseases the predisposition to which alone is inherited, and which break out only after a lapse of time, it is often altogether possible to prevent the predisposition being developed into positive disease. Thus, for instance, the inherited tendency to *consumption* remains asleep in the system until about the age of puberty or later. Therefore, by the use of a diet in which animal food forms a large portion, properly regulated, and systematic exercise in the open air, the practice of the long inhalations before recommended, warm, comfortable clothing, together with a residence, if practicable, during the changeable and inclement seasons of the year, in an equable climate, we can often entirely arrest the development of the disease. Prevention here is not only better than cure, but often all that is possible. Those in whom the disease has become active must too often, like those who entered Dante's infernal regions, "abandon hope." Let our words of caution therefore be heeded.

When there is reason to believe that an individual possesses an inherent tendency to any disease, it is the duty of the medical adviser to study the constitution of the patient thoroughly, and after such study to recommend those measures of prevention best suited to avert the threatened disorder. Above all, let the physician look closely to the child at the period of life when any grave constitutional inheritable disease attacked the parent. This supervision should be carried into adult years, for there are instances on record of inherited diseases coming on at an advanced age, as in that of a grandfather, father, and son, who all became insane and committed suicide near their fiftieth year. Gout, apoplexy, insanity, chronic disease of the heart, epilepsy, consumption, asthma, and other diseases, are all more or less under the control of preventive measures. Some hereditary diseases, such as idiocy and cancer, we are impotent to prevent in the present state of our knowledge.

A singular fact in connection with the transmission of disease, is the readiness with which a whole generation is passed over, the affection appearing in the next. A father or mother with consumption may, in some instances, have healthy children, but the grand-children will die of the disease. Nature kindly favours one generation, but only at the expense of the next.

Some diseases require, in addition to the general means of prevention to be found in a strict observance of the laws of health, some special measures in order to effectually ward off their appearance. But the extent of this work will not admit of their discussion. Already, indeed, have we unduly, perhaps, extended our remarks upon inheritance. The interest and importance of the facts must be our justification.

WHY ARE WOMEN REDUNDANT.

It cannot be without interest to look into the relative proportion of men and women now living. It will interest us still more to inquire into the reason why one sex preponderate over the other in numbers? This done, we will answer the question, is the production of the sex at all under the influence of the human will?

The female sex is the more numerous in all parts of the world, where we have reliable statistics. In Austria, England and Wales, there are nearly one hundred and five women for every one hundred men. In Sweden they are as one hundred and nine to one hundred. In all cities the disproportion is greater than in the country. In London there are one hundred and thirteen women to every one hundred men; and in the large towns of Sweden, they stand as one hundred and sixteen to one hundred.

This is not true, however, of newly-populated regions The relative difference is reversed in recent and thinly-settled localities. In our Western States, for instance, the number of the men exceeds that of the women. In California they are as three to one; in Nevada, as eight to one; in Colorado, twenty to one. In the State of Illinois there were, according to the last United States' census, ninety-three thousand more men than women. In Massachusetts, on the contrary, there are between fifty and sixty thousand more women than men.

The disproportion of men to women in new countries is due to the disinclination of women to emigrate. They are also unfitted for the hardships of pioneer life.

How is this general preponderance in the number of women produced? Is it because there are more girls born than boys? Not at all. The statistics of over fifty-eight millions of persons show that there are one hundred and six living boys born, to every one hundred girls. In the State of Rhode Island, for instance, the proportion for three years, from 1853 to 1855, was one thousand and sixty-four boys born to one thousand girls. But now we meet with the wonderful arrangement of nature that a larger proportional number of male infants die during the first year of their lives than of females. In the second year, the mortality, though less excessive, still remains far greater on the male side. It subsequently decreases, and at the age of four or five years is nearly equal for both sexes. In after life, from the age of fifteen to forty, the mortality is something greater among women, but not sufficiently to make the number of the two sexes equal. The greater tendency of male offspring to die early is seen even before birth, for more male children are still-born than female, namely, as three to two. For this reason, the term, "the stronger sex," applied to men, has been regarded by some authors as a misnomer. They are physically weaker in early life, and succumb more readily to noxious influences.

Having thus pointed out that there are more women actually living in the world than men, although a larger number of boys are born than girls, we will consider for a moment some of the laws of nature which determine the number of the sexes. Without giving the figures—which would make dry reading—we will state in brief the conclusions derived from many observations, extending over many years and many nationalities. The relative age of the parents has an especial influence upon the sex of the children. Seniority on the father's side gives excess of male offspring. This tallies with the fact that in all civilized countries, as has been stated, the proportion of male births is greater than that of females; for in accordance with the customs of society, the husband is generally older than the wife. A curious instance in confirmation of this law has recently come under our own observation. A patient married for the second time, is ten years older than her husband. She has two children by him, both girls. Singular to relate, her former husband was ten years older than herself, and by him she had four children, of whom three were boys, and the fourth, a girl, had a twin brother.

Still the relative age is not the sole cause which fixes the sex of the child. Its operation is sometimes overruled by conflicting agencies. In some districts of Norway, for instance, there has been a constant deficiency in boys, while in others the reverse has been the case. The circumstance is well known that after great wars, and sometimes epidemics, in which a disproportionate number of men have died, more boys are born than usual. Men who pass a sedentary life, and especially scholars who exhaust their nervous force to a great extent beget more girl than boys. So also a very advanced age on the man's side diminishes the number of males among the offspring. The quantity and quality of the food; the elevation of the abode; the conditions of temperature; the parents' mode of life, rank, religious belief, frequency of sexual intercourse, have all been shown to be causes contributing to the disproportion of the sexes, besides the relative ages of the parents.

Some writers have stated that a southerly or warm and humid constitution of the year is most favourable to the birth of female infants; while in cold and dry years most males are produced. This statement has not been supported by reliable statistics in regard to the human race, but among domestic animals the agriculturists of France have long observed that the season has much to do with the sex. When the weather is dry and cold and the wind northerly, mares, ewes, and heifers produce more males than when the opposite meteorological condition prevails.

The saying among nurses that "This is the year for sons or daughters," is based upon the erroneous supposition that mothers bring forth more male infants in one year than in another.

That, however, which concerns us the most in this connection is the question,

CAN THE SEXES BE PRODUCED AT WILL

This question was asked many centuries ago. It was a hard one, and remained without a satisfactory answer until quite recently. Science has at last replied to it with authority. M. Thury, Professor in the Academy of Geneva, has shown how males and females may be produced in accordance with our wishes.

Some families are most anxious for male offspring, others ardently desire daughters. And would it not often be a matter of national concern to control the percentage of sexes in the population? Is it not a "consummation most devoutly to be wished" to bring about that Utopian condition when there would be no sighing maids at home nor want of warriors in the field? The discussion of this subject is therefore important and allowable.

It has been observed that queen bees lay female eggs first and male eggs afterwards. So with hens; the first laid eggs give female, the last, male products. Mares shown the stallion late in their periods, drop horse-colts rather than fillies.

Professor Thury, from the consideration of these and other like facts, formed this law for stock-raisers: "If you wish to produce females, give the male at the first signs of heat; if you wish males, give him at the end of the heat." But it is easy to form a theory. How was this law sustained in practice? We have now in our possession the certificate of a Swiss stock-grower, son of the President of the Swiss Agricultural Society, Canton de Vaud, under date of February, 1867, which says:

"In the first place, on twenty-two successive occasions I desired to have heifers. My cows were of Schurtz breed, and my bull a pure Durham. I succeeded in these cases. Having bought a pure Durham cow, it was very important for me to have a new bull, to supersede the one I had bought at great expense, without leaving to chance the production of a male. So I followed accordingly the prescription of Professor Thury, and the success has proved once more the truth of the law. I have obtained from my Durham bull six more bulls (Schurtz-Durham cross) for field work; and having chosen cows of the same colour and height, I obtained perfect matches of oxen. My herd amounted to forty cows of every age.

"In short, I have made in all twenty-nine experiments after the new method, and in every one I succeeded in the production of what I was looking for—male and female. I had not one single failure. All the experiments have been made by myself, without any other person's

intervention; consequently, I do declare that I consider
as real, and certainly perfect, the method of Professor
Thury."

A perfectly trustworthy observer of this city communicates to the *Medical and Surgical Reporter* of this city for May 2nd, 1868, the results of similar experiments on animals with like conclusions.

The plan of M. Thury had also been tried on the farms of the Emperor of the French, with, it is asserted, the most unvarying success.

What is the result of the application of this law to the human race? Dr. F. J. W. Packman, of Wimborne, England, has stated in the *London Lancet* that "in the human female, conception in the first half of the time between menstrual periods produces female offspring, and male in the latter. When a female has gone beyond the time she calculated upon, it will generally turn out to be a boy."

In the *Philadelphia Medical and Surgical Reporter* for February 8th, 1868, a respectable physician writes that in numerous instances that have come under his observation, Professor Thury's theory has proved correct. "Whenever intercourse has taken place in from two to six days after the cessation of the menses, girls have been produced; and whenever intercourse has taken place in from nine to twelve days after the cessation of the menses boys have been produced. In every case I have ascertained not only the date at which the mother placed conception, but also the time when the menses ceased, the date of the first and subsequent intercourse for a month or more after the cessation of the menses," etc.

Again, a physician writes to the same journal for June 20th, 1868, recording the result of his own experience.

A farmer in Louisiana states, in the "Turf, Field, and Farm," in support of this law, that "I have already been able in many cases to guess with certainty the sex of a future infant. More than thirty times among my friends I have predicted the sex of a child before its birth, and the event proved nearly every time that I was right."

The wife, therefore, who would wish as Macbeth desired of his, to,

"Bring forth men-children only,"

should avoid exposing herself to conception during the first half of the time between her menstrual periods.

The prediction of the sex of the child before birth can now be with some accuracy made by the intelligent and skilful physician. The method of doing so will be mentioned in treating of pregnancy.

TWIN-BEARING.

As a rule, a woman has one child at a time. Twins when they occur are looked upon with disfavour by most people. There is a popular notion that they are apt to be wanting in physical strength and mental vigour. This opinion is not without foundation. A careful scientific examination of the subject has shown that of imbeciles and idiots a much larger proportion is actually found among the twins born than in the general community. In families where twinning is frequent, bodily deformities likewise occur with frequency. Among the relatives of imbeciles and idiots twin-bearing is common. In fact the whole history of twin-births is of an exceptional character, indicating imperfect development and feeble organization in the product, and leading us to regard twins in the human species as a departure from the physiological rule, and therefore injurious to all concerned. Monsters born without brains have rarely occurred except among twins.

The birth of twins occurs once in about eighty deliveries. A woman is more apt to have no children than to have more than one child at a time. In view of the increased danger to both mother and child, this rarity of a plural birth is fortunate.

WHY ARE TWINS BORN?

What are the causes or favouring circumstances bringing about this abnormal child-bearing? For it is brought about by the operation of laws. It is not an accident. There are no accidents in nature. By some it is supposed to be due to the mother, by some to the father. There are facts in favour of both opinions. Certain women married successively to several men have always had twins, while their husbands with other wives have determined single births. Certain men have presented the phenomenon. We can scarcely cite an example more astonishing than that of a countryman who was presented to the Empress of Russia, in 1755. He had had two wives. The first had fifty-seven children in twenty-one confinements. The second thirty-three in thirteen. All the confinements had been quadruple, triple, or double. A case has come under our observation in which the bearing of twins has seemed to be due to a constitutional cause. The wife has nine children. The first was a single birth, a girl. The others were all twin-births and boys.

It has been asserted that compound pregnancies are more frequent in certain years than in others. But what seems to exert the greatest actual influence over the production of twins is the age of the mother. Very extensive statistics have demonstrated that from the earliest child-bearing period until the age of forty is reached, the fertility of mothers in twins gradually increases.

Between the ages of twenty and thirty, fewest wives have twins. The average age of the twin-bearers is older than the general run of bearers. It is well known that by far the greater number of twins are born of elderly women. While three-fifths of all births occur among women under thirty-years of age, three-fifths of all the twins are born to those over thirty years of age. Newly-married women are more likely to have twins at the first labour, the older they are. The chance that a young wife from fifteen to nineteen shall bear twins is only as one to one hundred and eighty-nine; from thirty-five to thirty-nine the chance is one to forty-five; that is, the wives married youngest have fewest twins, and there is an increase as age advances, until forty is reached.

Race seems to have some influence over plural births. They occur relatively oftener among the Irish than the English.

INFLUENCE OF TWIN-BEARING ON SIZE OF FAMILIES.

Do women bearing twins have in the end larger families than those having but one at a time? Popular belief would answer this question in the affirmative. Such a reply would also seem to receive support from the fact, well established, that twins are more frequent additions to an already considerable family than they are either the first of a family or additional to a small family. But statistics have not answered this question as yet positively. They seem, however, in favour of the supposition that twin-bearing women have larger families than their neighbours.

Women are more apt to have twins in their *first pregnancy* than any other, but after the second confinement the bearing of twins increases in frequency with the number of the pregnancy. It becomes, therefore, an indication of an excessive family, and is to be deplored.

MORE THAN TWO CHILDREN AT A BIRTH.

Cases of the birth of more than two children at a time are still less frequently met with than twins. They are scarcely ever encountered, excepting in women who have passed their thirtieth year.

THREE AT A BIRTH.

The births of triplets are not exclusively confined to women above thirty years, but in those younger they are

EXTRAORDINARY BIRTHS.

so rare as to be great curiosities. Neither are they apt to occur in the first pregnancy. In this respect they differ from twins, who, as has just been said, are peculiarly prone to make their appearance at the first child-birth. Only four cases of treble births occurred among the thirty-six thousand accouchements which have taken place in the Hospice de Maternité of Paris in a determined time. Out of forty-eight thousand cases of labour in the Royal Maternity Charity of London, only three triplets occurred. History informs us that the three Roman brothers, the Horatii, were triplets. They fought and conquered the Curiatii of Alba (667 B.C.) who were likewise triplets.

As an interesting fact in connection with this subject we may mention, that in the St. Petersburg Midwives Institute, between 1845-59, there were three women admitted, who, in their fifteenth pregnancies, had triplets, and each had triplets three times in succession. Happily, the fifteenth pregnancy is not reached by most women.

FOUR AT A BIRTH.

Instances of quadruplets are fewer than triplets. But four vigorous infants have been born at one birth.

FIVE AT A BIRTH.

The birth of *five* living children at a time is very exceptional, and is usually fatal to the offspring. A remarkable case of this kind is reported in a late English medical journal. A woman, aged thirty, the wife of a labourer, and the mother of six children, was taken in labour about the seventh month of her pregnancy. Five children, and all alive, were given birth to—three boys and two girls. Four of the children survived an hour, and died within a few moments of each other. The fifth, a female, and the last born, lived six hours, and was so vigorous that, notwithstanding its diminutive size, hopes were entertained of its surviving.

Another case is reported in a recent French medical journal. The woman was forty years old. She had had twins once, and five times single children. On her seventh pregnancy, when five months gone, she was as large as women usually are at the end of their full term. At the close of the month she was delivered of five children. They were all born alive, and lived from four to seven minutes. All five children were males, well built and as well developed as fœtuses of five and one-half months usually are in a single birth. The woman made a good recovery. Other cases of five at a birth might be quoted. They are known to medical science as very singular and noteworthy occurrences.

INCREDIBLE NUMBERS.

Some books speak of seven, eight, nine, ten, and more children at a birth. But these statements are so marvellous, so incredible, and unsupported by proper testimony, that they do not merit any degree of confidence. The climax of such extraordinary assertions is reached, and a good illustration of the credulity of the seventeenth century furnished by a writer named Goftr. This traveller, in 1630, saw a tablet in a church at Leusdown (Lausdunum), about five miles from the Hague, with an inscription stating that a certain illustrious countess, whose name and family he records, brought forth, at one birth, in the fortieth year of her age, in the year 1276, three hundred and sixty-five infants. They were all baptised by Guido the Suffragan. The males were called John, and the females Elizabeth. They all, with their mother, died on the same day, and were buried in the above-mentioned church. This monstrous birth was said to have been caused by the sin of the countess in insulting a poor woman with twins in her arms, who prayed that her insulter might have at one birth the same number of children as there were days in the year. Of course, notwithstanding the story is attested by a tablet in a church, it must be placed among the many other instances of superstition afforded by an ignorant and credulous era.

We may remark, in closing this subject, that fewer plural births come to maturity than pregnancies with single children. Miscarriages are comparatively more frequent in such pregnancies than in ordinary ones.

PREGNANCY.

We have been considering woman hitherto as maiden and wife. She now approaches the sacred threshold of maternity. She is with child. In no period of her life is she the subject of an interest so profound and general. The young virgin and the new wife have pleased by their grace, spirit, and beauty. The pregnant wife is an object of active benevolence and religious respect. It is interesting to note how, in all times, and in all countries, she has been considered with considerate kindness and great deference. She has been made the subject of public veneration, and sometimes even of religious worship. At Athens and at Carthage the murderer escaped from the sword of justice, if he sought refuge in the house of a pregnant woman. The Jews allowed her to eat forbidden meats. The laws of Moses pronounced the penalty of death against all those who by bad treatment, or any act of violence, caused a woman to abort. Lycurgus compared women who died in pregnancy to the brave dead on the field of honour, and accorded to them sepuchral inscriptions. In ancient Rome, where all citizens were obliged to rise and stand during the passage of a magistrate, wives were excused from rendering this mark of respect, for the reason that the exertion and hurry of the movement might be injurious to them in the state in which they were supposed to be. In the kingdom of Pannonia, all enceinte women were in such veneration that a man meeting one on the road was obliged, under penalty of a fine, to turn back and accompany and protect her to her place of destination. The Catholic Church has at all times exempted pregnant wives from fasts. The Egyptians decreed, and in most Christian countries the law at the present time obtains, that if a woman shall be convicted of an offence the punishment of which is death, the sentence shall not be executed if it be proved that she is pregnant.

"HOW CAN I TELL WHETHER I AM PREGNANT?"

The first sign which is calculated to give rise to the suspicion is the *ceasing to be unwell*. This, taken alone, is not conclusive. There are many other conditions of the system which produce it besides pregnancy. We have already referred to several.

It should be borne in mind that young married women sometimes have a slight show for two or three periods after their first impregnation. Ignorance of this fact has very frequently led to a miscalculation of the time of confinement. On the other hand, the menses will sometimes become arrested soon after marriage, and continue so for one or two months, without there existing any pregnancy The temporary disappearance of the monthly sickness in such cases is due to the profound impression made upon the system by the new relations of the individual.

It not unfrequently happens that menstruation continues with regularity during the whole period of pregnancy. Exceptional cases are given by distinguished writers on midwifery, of women menstruating during their pregnancy and at no other time.

As a general rule, when a healthy wife misses her monthly sickness, she is pregnant. But this symptom though a strong one, must be supported by others before it can be regarded as establishing anything.

2. *Morning sickness* is a very common, a very early, and, in the opinion of most mothers, a very conclusive symptom of pregnancy. We have already had occasion

to remark that it sometimes makes its appearance almost simultaneously with conception. It usually comes on in the first few weeks, and continues until the third or fourth month, or until quickening. This symptom is apt to be a troublesome one. Often the vomiting is slight, and immmediately followed by relief. But it may produce violent and ineffectual straining for some time. It is however, not to be called a disease. Unless it proceeds to an exhausting degree, it must be looked upon as favourable and salutary. There is an old and true proverb, that "a sick pregnancy is a safe one." The absence of nausea and vomiting is a source of danger to the mother and child. Women who habitually fail to experience them are exceedingly apt to miscarry. In such cases medical skill should be invoked to bring about the return of these symptoms, of such importance to healthful pregnancy.

Morning sickness is therefore a very general, almost constant, accompaniment of the pregnant condition, and great reliance may be placed upon it as a sign.

3. *Changes in the breasts* are valuable as symptoms. They become larger and firmer, and the seat of a pricking or stinging sensation. The nipples are swollen prominent, and sometimes sore or painful. The veins beneath the skin appear more conspicuous and of a deeper blue than ordinary. The peculiar circles of rose-coloured skin which surround the nipples increase in extent, change to a darker colour, and become covered with a number of little elevations. Subsequently, numerous mottled patches, or round spots of a whitish hue, scatter themselves over the outer part of this circle.

The time at which these changes make their appearance is variable. They may begin to develop themselves in two or three weeks, oftener not until the second or third month, and, in women of a delicate build, sometimes not until the latter end of pregnancy. Occasionally no alteration whatever occurs in the breasts until after confinement, in which cases the secretion of milk is delayed for several days after the birth of the child. In some rare instances, the breasts never assume maternal proportions, and the mother is debarred from the pleasure and duty of nursing her own child.

4. *Quickening* is the next symptom we will consider. By this term is meant the arrival of that time when the mother first becomes conscious by the movements of the child of its presence. The ancients thought that then life was imparted to the new being. Modern physiology emphatically condemns this absurdity. The embryo is as much alive in the very earliest moments of pregnancy as at any future stage of its existence. Let every woman therefore remember that she who produces ABORTION is EQUALLY GUILTY in the eyes of science and of Heaven, whether the act be committed before or after the period of quickening.

How is quickening produced? Undoubtedly by the movements of the child. So soon as its nervous and muscular systems become sufficiently developed to enable it to move its limbs, the mother, if the movements be sufficiently active, is rendered sensible of her situation. But the muscular contractions may not be strong enough to impart any sensation to the mother. In many cases in which they are too feeble to be noticed by herself, the skilled accoucheur is capable of recognising them. And the movements of the fœtus may be excited in various ways known to physicians.

Time of Quickening.—This symptom usually occurs about the middle of pregnancy, near the eighteenth week.

Some women feel the movements of the fœtus as early as the third month of pregnancy; others not till the sixth month. Cases occur in which no movement whatever is felt until the eighth or ninth month, or even not at all. It has been suggested that a fœtus which does not indicate its presence in this way is a kind of "Lazy Lawrence," too indolent to move. Certainly many of both sexes ex-habit, after birth, such indomitable love of repose, that it can readily be supposed they were equally passive in foetal life.

The non-occurrence of this sign may, however, be due to debility of the young child, or to a want of sensibility in the walls of the womb itself.

A woman may be deceived, and suppose she has quickened, when her sensations are to be traced to flatulence of the bowels, or, perhaps, a dropsical effusion. Many ludicrous instances of self-deception are on record. The historian Hume states that Queen Mary of England, in her extreme desire to have issue, so confidently asserted that she felt the movements of the child, that public proclamation was made of the interesting event. Despatches were sent to foreign courts; national rejoicings were had; the sex of the child was settled, for everybody was certain it was going to be a male, and Bonner, Bishop of London, made public prayers, praying that Heaven would pledge to make him beautiful, vigorous and witty. But all those high hopes and eager expectations were destined never to be realized. The future disclosed that the supposed quickening was merely a consequence of disordered health and commencing dropsy.

Some women possess the power of imitating the movement of a foetus by a voluntary contraction of the abdominal muscles. A well-known coloured woman of Charleston, "Aunt Betty," had a great reputation as having "been pregnant for fifteen years." She made a good deal of money by exhibiting to those who were curious, the pretended movements of her unborn child. She was repeatedly exhibited to the medical classes in the city. No pregnancy existed, as was revealed by a post-mortem examination. She imposed upon the credulous by the habit she had acquired of jerking her muscles at pleasure, and thus closely simulating the movements of an embryo.

5. *Changes in the abdomen.*—In the first two months of pregnancy the abdomen is *less* prominent than usual

it recedes and presents a flat appearance. The navel is also drawn in and depressed. About the third month a swelling frequently shows itself in the lower part of the abdomen, and then diminishes, thus leading the wife to suppose that she was mistaken in her condition, for she finds herself at the fourth month smaller than at the third. After this, however, there is a gradual increase in the size and hardness of the abdomen. What is of more value is the peculiar form of the swelling. It is pear-shaped, and is thus distinguished from the swelling of dropsy and other affections. The navel begins to come forward, and finally protrudes. The pouting appearance it then presents is very characteristic.

In this connection it may be remarked that towards the change of life, childless married women often think they perceive that "hope deferred" is about to be gratified An enlargment of the abdomen takes place at this time, from a deposit of fatty matter. The nervous perturbations and the cessation of menses, which are natural to this period, are looked upon as confirmations of the opinion that pregnancy exists. But the day of generation with them has passed. These symptoms herald the approach of the winter of life, which brings with it death to the reproductive system.

6. *Changes in the skin.*—The alterations occurring in the skin are worth observing. Those women who have a delicate complexion and are naturally pale, take a high colour, and *vice versa*. In some cases a considerable quantity of hair appears on those parts of the face occupied by the beard in men; it disappears after labour, and returns on every subsequent pregnancy. Oftentimes the skin becomes loose and wrinkled, giving a haggard, aged air to the face, and spoiling good looks. Women who ordinarily perspire freely have now a dry, rough skin, whereas those whose skin is not naturally moist have copious perspiration, which may be of a peculiar strong odour. Copper-coloured or yellow blotches sometimes appear upon the skin,

mole spots become darker and larger, and a dark ring develops itself beneath the eyes. The whole appearance is thus in many cases altered. On the other hand, obstinate, long existing skin affections sometimes take their departure during pregnancy, perhaps never to return. These alterations do not occur in all women, nor in all pregnancies of the same woman.

7. We may now group together a number of less important and less constant signs, such as *depraved appetite, longings for unnatural food, excessive formation of saliva in the mouth, heartburn, loss of appetite* in the first two or three months, succeeded by a voracious desire for food, which sometimes compels the woman to rise at night in order to eat, *toothache, sleepiness, diarrhœa, palpitation of the heart, pain in the right side,* etc. These when they occur singly are of little value as evidence.

Among these that of *depraved appetite* is by far the most important, and may be regarded as quite significant. A married woman in her ordinary health, suddenly feeling this morbid taste for chalk, charcoal, slate pencil, etc., may look upon it as strong presumptive evidence of impregnation.

When any or all of this group of symptoms accompany the ceasing to be "regular," the morning sickness, the changes in the breasts and the other signs which have been enumerated, the wife may be quite sure that she is pregnant.

8. *Changes in the mind.*—The most wonderful of all the changes which attend pregnaucy are those in the nervous system. The woman is rendered more susceptible, more impressionable. Her character is transformed. She is no longer pleasant, confiding, gentle, and gay. She becomes hasty, passionate, jealous, and bitter. But in those who are naturally fretful and bad-tempered a change for the better is sometimes observed, so that the members of the household learn from experience to hail with delight the mother's pregnancy as a period when clouds and storms

give place to sunshine and quietness. In some rare cases, also, pregnancy confers increased force and elevation to the ideas, and augmented power to the intellect.

As this book is written for women only, we do not mention any of the signs or symptoms of pregnancy which the physician alone can recognise. We will merely state that there are many other signs beside those referred to, of great value to the doctor. One, the sound of the heart of the child, which the practised ear can detect at about the fifth month, is positive and conclusive.

MISCARRIAGE.

Miscarriage is a fruitful source of disease and often of danger to wives. It is also a frightful waste of human life. Unborn thousands annually die in this manner.

Frequency.—Miscarriage is by no means a rare occurrence. Statistics show that thirty-seven out of one hundred mothers miscarry before they attain the age of thirty years. But this accident is much more apt to occur during the latter than the first half of the child-bearing period, and therefore it is estimated that ninety out of one hundred of all women who continue in matrimony until the change of life, miscarry.

Influence of age of mother.—A woman who marries at forty is very much disposed to miscarry, whereas had she married at thirty, she might have borne children when older than forty. As a mother approaches the end of her child-bearing period, it is likely that she will terminate her career of fertility with a premature birth. The last pregnancies are not only most commonly unsuccessful, but there is also reason to believe that the occurrence of idiocy in a child may be associated with the circumstance of its being the last born of its mother. It has been asserted, in this connection, that men of genius are frequently the first-born. First pregnancies are also fraught with the danger of miscarriage, which occurs more often in them than in others, excepting the latest. A woman is particularly apt to miscarry with her first child, if she be either exceedingly nervous or full-blooded.

Influence of period of pregnancy.—Miscarriage is most frequent in the earlier months of pregnancy—from the first to the third. It is also very prone to happen about the sixth month. Habit makes itself felt here: for women who have many times experienced this sad accident, encounter it nearly always at the same epoch of their pregnancy.

How long can the child live ?—The infant is incapable, as a rule, of an independent existence if brought into the world before the end of the sixth month. The law of France regards a child born one hundred and eighty days after wedlock as not only capable of living, but as legitimate and worthy of all legal and civil rights. There are many cases mentioned by the older medical writers, of children born previous to this period living. One of the most curious is that recorded by Van Swieten. The boy, Fortunio Liceti, was brought into the world before the sixth month, in consequence of a fright his mother had at sea. When born, it is said, he was the size of a hand, and his father placed him in an oven, for the purpose, probably, it has been suggested, of making him *rise*. Although born prematurely, he died late, for we are told he attained his seventy-ninth year. Professor Gunning S. Bedford, of New York, records the case of a woman, in her fourth confinement, who was delivered before she had completed her sixth month, of a female infant weighing two pounds nine ounces. The surface of the body was of a scarlet hue. It breathed, and in a short time after birth cried freely. After being wrapped in soft cotton, well lubricated with warm sweet-oil, it was fed with the mother's milk, by having a few drops at a time put into its mouth. At first it had great difficulty in swallowing, but gradually it succeeded in taking sufficient nourishment, and is now a vigorous, healthy young woman.

Danger to mothers.—Wives are too much in the habit of making light of miscarriages. They are much more frequently followed by disease of the womb than are confinements at full terms. There is a greater amount of injury done to the parts than in natural labour. While after confinement ample time is afforded by a long period of repose for the bruised and lacerated parts to heal, after a miscarriage no such rest is obtained. Menstruation soon returns; conception may quickly follow. Unhappily there is no custom requiring husband and wife to sleep apart for a month after a miscarriage, as there is after a confinement. Hence, especially if there be any pre-existing uterine disease or a predisposition thereto, miscarriage is a serious thing.

Causes.—The irritation of hemorrhoids or straining at stool will sometimes provoke an early expulsion of a child. Excessive intercourse by the newly married is a very frequent cause. Bathing in the ocean has been known to produce it. Nursing is exceedingly apt to do so. It has been shown by a distinguished medical writer that in a given number of instances miscarriage occurred in seventeen per cent. of cases in which the woman conceived while nursing, and in only ten per cent. where conception occurred at some other time. A wife, therefore, who suspects herself to be pregnant should wean her child. The extraction of a tooth, over-exertion and over-excitement, a fall, a blow, any violent emotion, such as anger, sudden and excessive joy, or fright, running, dancing, horseback exercise or riding in a badly-built carriage over a rough road, great fatigue, lifting heavy weights, the abuse of purgative medicines, disease or displacement of the womb, small-pox, or a general condition of ill-health, are all fruitful and well-known exciting causes of this unfortunate mishap, in addition to those which have been before mentioned.

Prevention.—Dr. Tilt, the eminent practitioner of London, says:—" The way to prevent miscarriage is to lead a quiet life, particularly during those days of each successive month when, under other circumstances, the woman would menstruate; and to abstain during those days not only from long walks and parties, but also from sexual intercourse."

It is especially desirable to avoid a miscarriage in the first pregnancy, for fear that the habit of miscarriage shall then be set up, which will be very difficult to eradicate. Therefore, newly-married women should carefully avoid all causes which are known to induce the premature expulsion of the child. If it should take place in spite of all precautions, extraordinary care should be exercised in the subsequent pregnancy to prevent its recurrence. Professor Bedford, of New York, has said he has found that an excellent expedient in such cases is, as soon as pregnancy is known it exist, " to interdict sexual intercourse until after the fifth month, for if the pregnancy pass beyond this period, the chances of miscarriage will be much diminished."

If the *symptoms of miscarriage* which may be expressed in the two words, *pain* and *flooding*, should make their appearance, the physician ought at once to be sent for, the wife awaiting his arrival in a recumbent position. He may even then be able to avert the impending danger. At any rate, his services are as necessary, and often even more so, as in a labour at full term.

MOTHERS' MARKS.

It is a popular belief that the imagination of the mother affects the child in the womb. It is asserted that infants are often born with various marks and deformities corresponding in character with objects which had made a vivid impression on the maternal mind during pregnancy. This is a subject of great practical interest. We shall, therefore, give it the careful attention which it deserves.

We have already discussed the operation of the laws of

inheritance. It was then stated that the whole story of maternal influence had not been told: that the mother could communicate qualities she never possessed. The potency of imagination at the time of conception over the child has been mentioned. It is now our design to consider its effects, during the period of pregnancy, upon the physical structure and the mental attributes of the offspring. We shall have occasion hereafter, in speaking of nursing, to illustrate the manner in which the child may be affected by maternal impressions acting through the mother's milk. What can be more wonderful than this intimate union between the mother and her child? It is only equalled by that mysterious influence of the husband over the wife, by which he so impresses her system that she often comes in time to resemble him both in mental and physical characteristics, and even transmits his peculiarities to her children by her second marriage. Father, mother and child are one.

We wish here to premise that our remarks will be based upon the conclusions of skilled and scientific observers only, whose position and experience no physician will question. All the instances to be related are given upon unimpeachable authority. They are not the narrations of ignorant, credulous people; they are all fully vouched for. We record here, as elsewhere, only the sober utterances of science. The great importance and utility of an acquaintance with them will be patent to every intelligent man and woman.

The effect of the mind upon the body is well known. Strong, long-continued mental emotion may induce or cure disease. Heart-disease may be produced by a morbid direction of the thoughts to that organ. Warts disappear under the operation of a strong belief in the efficacy of some nonsensical application. In olden times scrofula, or the "king's evil," was cured by the touch of the king. The mind of the patient of course accomplished the cure. Under the influence of profound mental emotion, the hair of the beautiful Marie Antoinette became white in a short time. During the solitary voyage of Madame Condamine down the wild and lonely Amazon, a similar change took place. Many other instances might be adduced, but those given are sufficient to show that strong and persistent mental impressions will exert a mysterious transforming power over the body. These facts will pave the way to the consideration of corresponding effects, through the mother's mind, upon the development of the unborn child, forming a part of herself *in utero*.

Influence of mind of mother on form and colour of infant.—There are numerous facts on record which prove that *habitual*, long continued mental conditions of the mother at an early period of pregnancy induce deformity or other abnormal development of the infant.

Professor William A. Hammond, of New York, relates the following striking case, which occurred in his own experience, and which scarcely admits of a doubt as to the influence of the maternal mind over the physical structure of the fœtus.

A lady in the third month of her pregnancy was very much horrified by her husband being brought home one evening with a severe wound on the face, from which the blood was streaming. The shock to her was so great that she fainted, and subsequently had an hysterical attack, during which she was under Dr. Hammond's care. Soon after her recovery she told him that she was afraid her child would be affected in some way, and that even then she could not get rid of the impression the sight of her husband's bloody face had made upon her. In due time the child, a girl, was born. She had a dark red mark upon the face, corresponding in situation and extent with that which had been upon her father's face. She also proved to be idiotic.

Professor Dalton, of New York, states that the wife of the janitor of the College of Physicians and Surgeons of that city, during her pregnancy dreamed that she saw a

man who had lost part of the ear. The drea[m made a]
great impression upon her mind, and she ment[ioned it to]
her husband. When her child was born, a port[ion of the]
ear was deficient, and the organ was exactly li[ke the de-]
fective ear she had seen in her dream. When [Professor]
Dalton was lecturing upon the development of [the foetus]
as affected by the mind of the mother, the jan[itor called]
his attention to the foregoing instance. The ea[r looked ex-]
actly as if a portion had been cut off with a sh[arp knife.]

Professor J. Lewis Smith, of Bellevue Hosp[ital Medi-]
cal College, New York, has met with the follow[ing case:]
An Irish woman, of strong emotions and su[perstitious,]
was passing along a street, in the first mon[th of her]
pregnancy, when she was accosted by a be[ggar, who]
raised her hand, destitute of thumb and finge[rs, and in]
" God's name " asked for alms. The woman pas[sed on, but]
reflecting in whose name the money was aske[d, thought]
she had committed a great sin in refusing [the alms.]
She returned to the place where she had met [the beggar]
and on different days, but never afterwards [found her.]
Harrassed by the thought of her imaginary s[in for]
for weeks, according to her statement, she was [troubled]
by it, she approached her confinement. A fe[male child]
as born, otherwise perfect but lacking the [fingers and]
thumb on one hand. The deformed limb was o[n the same]
side, and it seemed to the mother to resembl[e exactly]
that of the beggar. In another case which [Professor]
Smith met, a very similar malformation was [traced]
by the mother of the child to an accident occu[rr-]
ing the time of her pregnancy to a near relat[ive, which]
necessitated amputation. He examined bot[h of these]
children with defective limbs, and has no do[ubt of the]
truthfulness of the parents. In May, 1868, he [removed a]
supernumerary thumb from an infant, whose [mother, a]
baker's wife, gave the following history :—No [one in the]
family, and no ancestor, to her knowledge, pre[sented this]
deformity. In the early months of her preg[nancy]

sold bread from the counter, and nearly every day a child with a double thumb came in for a penny roll, presenting the penny between the thumb and the finger. After the third month she left the bakery, but the malformation was so impressed upon her mind that she was not surprised to see it reproduced in her infant.

In all those cases the impression was reproduced in the early months of pregnancy; but many have been recorded in which malformations in the infant appeared distinctly traceable to strong mental emotions of the mother only a few months previous to confinement, these impressions having been persistent during the remaining period of the pregnancy, and giving rise to a full expectation on the part of the mother that the child would be affected in the particular manner which actually occurred. Professor Carpenter, the distinguished physiologist of London, is personally cognizant of a very striking case of the kind, which occurred in the family of a near connection of his own.

All the above instances have been those of the effects of persistent mental emotion. But it is also true that *violent and sudden emotion* in the mother leaves sometimes its impress upon the unborn infant, although it may be quickly forgotten.

It is related on good authority that a lady, who, during her pregnancy, was struck with the unpleasant view of leeches applied to a relative's foot, gave birth to a child with the mark of a leech coiled up in the act of suction on the intended spot.

Dr. Delacoux, of Paris, says that in the month of January, 1825, he was called to attend a woman in the village of Batignoles, near Paris, who, the evening before, had been delivered of a six months' fœtus, horribly deformed. The upper lip was in a confused mass with the jaw and the gums, and the right leg was amputated at the middle, the stump having the form of a cone. The mother of this being, who was a cook, on entering one morning, about

the third month of her pregnancy, the house
was employed, was seized with horror at the
porter with a hare-lip and an amputated leg.

At a meeting of the Society of Physicians, at
August, 1868, Herr Dupré stated that a wom:
the first weeks of her third pregnancy, a boy v
lip, and not only was the child she then carried
a frightful hare lip, but also three children sul
Another one, a woman in the fifth week of]
saw a sheep wounded and with its bowels]
She was greatly shocked, and did not recov
sure for several days. She was delivered at
child in other respects well developed, but l:
walls of the abdomen.

Many remarkable instances have been collec
power of *imagination* over the unborn offsprin

Ambrose Paré, the illustrious French surge
sixteenth century, in one of his treatises. devot
ter to the subject of "monsters which take t
and shape from imagination," and was evidentl
believer in this influence.

A black child is generally believed to have
to Marie Thérèse, the wife of Louis XIV., in co
of a little negro page in her service having sta
a hiding-plac· and stumbled over her dress ea
pregnancy. The child was educated at the (
Moret, near Fontainebleau, where she took th
where, till the shock of the Revolution, her po
shown.

Examples are given by authors of the force
in causing deformities in infants, and the forma
them of fruits, such as apples, pears, grapes, a;
which the mother may have longed for.

The following is related upon excellent medi
rity :—A woman gave birth to a child with a la:
of globular tumours growing from the tongue,
venting the closure of the mouth, in colour, shap

exactly resembling our common grapes; and with a red excrescence from the chest, as exactly resembling in figure and appearance a turkey's wattles. On being questioned before the child was shown to her, she answered that while pregnant she had seen some grapes, longed intensely for them, and constantly thought of them; and that she was also once attacked and much alarmed by a turkey-cock.

Dr. DeMangeon, of Paris, quotes, in his work on the Imagination, the "Journal de Verdun," as mentioning the case of a child, born at Blois, in the eyes of which the face of a watch was distinctly seen. The image was situated around the pupil, and the figures representing the hours were plainly perceived. The mother had expressed a strong desire to see a watch whilst she was pregnant with this child.

Professor Dalton says, in his "Human Physiology," that "there is now little room for doubt that various deformities and deficiencies of the fœtus, conformably to the popular belief, do really originate in certain cases, from nervous impressions, such as disgust, fear, or anger, experienced by the mother." We will now consider the

Influence of the mind of the mother on the mind of the infant, which subject we have not yet touched upon, having confined ourselves to the influence of the maternal mind over the form and colour of the unborn child. It will not be necessary to illustrate at length this branch of our topic. Instances are sufficiently common and well known. Dr. Seguin, of New York, in his work on Idiocy, gives several cases in which there was reason to believe that fright, anxiety, or other emotions in the mother, had produced idiocy in the offspring. As he remarks: "Impressions will sometimes reach the fœtus in its recess, cut off its legs or arms, or inflict large flesh wounds before birth—inexplicable as well as indisputable facts, from which we surmise that idiocy holds unknown, though certain relations to maternal impressions."

We have given many strong cases and mos[t]
authority for the doctrine that the purely me[ntal influ]-
ence of the mother may produce bodily a[nd mental]
changes in the unborn infant. But the child [is af]-
fected by *physical impressions made upon the* [mother.]

Dr. Russegger reports that a woman, who h[ad]
borne four healthy children, was, in the sevent[h month of]
her pregnancy, bitten in the right calf by a [dog. The]
author saw the wound made by the animal's t[eeth. The]
wound consisted of three small triangular depr[essions,]
two of which the skin was only slightly ruffle[d. No]
appearance of blood was perceptible in the t[hird. The]
woman was at the moment of the accident [much]
alarmed, but neither then nor afterwards ha[d any fear]
that her fœtus would be affected by the occurr[ence. Six]
weeks after she was bitten, the woman bore [a healthy]
child, which, however, to the surprise of every [one, had]
three marks corresponding in size and appearan[ce to those]
caused by the dog's teeth in the mother's le[g, con]-
sisting, like those, of one large and two smaller i[mpressions.]
The two latter, which were pale, disappeared in [time, and]
the larger one had also become less, and was n[ot so highly]
coloured as it was at birth. At the time of w[riting the]
child was four months old.

Dr. S. P. Crawford, of Greenville, Tennessee, [reports in]
a recent number of the *Nashville Journal o*[f Medicine]
the following sad case:—A lady, in the last sta[ge of preg]-
nancy, was burned by the explosion of a keros[ene lamp.]
She lived twelve hours after the accident. T[he legs,]
arms and abdomen were badly burned. The [motions]
of the child were felt three or four hours aft[er the acci]-
dent. A short time before the death of the [mother she]
gave birth to the child at full maturity, bu[t dead.]
It bore the mark of the fire, corresponding to [that of the]
mother. Its legs, arms, and abdomen were [all much]
blistered, having all the appearance of a recen[t burn.]

These instances of a decided influence exert[ed]

body and mind of the child in the womb, by physical and mental impression, made upon the mother, might be doubled or trebled. They are as numerous as they are wonderful. Physiologists of the present day do not hesitate to admit the existence of the influence we have been discussing. Reason also comes to the support of facts, to demonstrate and establish its reality. For if a sudden and powerful emotion of the mind can so disturb the stomach and heart as to cause vomiting and fainting, is it not probable that it can affect the womb and the impressible being within it? Pregnancy is a function of the woman as much as digestion or pulsation of the heart, and if the latter are controlled by moral and mental impressions, why should not the former be also?

In what manner does this influence of the maternal mind act?—Through the blood of the mother. Only a very delicate membrane separates the vital fluid of the mother from that of the infant in her womb. There is a constant interchange of the blood in its body, with that in hers, through this exceedingly thin membrane, and thus all nervous impressions which have produced an alteration of either a temporary or permanent character in the circulating fluid of the mother are communicated to the child. Since the mother, as has been shown, can transmit through her blood certain characteristics of mind and body not her own—for instance, a disease peculiar to a male from her father to her son, or the physical and mental traits of her first husband to the children by her second—it does not seem at all strange that she should, through this same medium, her blood, impart other peculiarities which have made a strong impression upon her mind. Anatomy and physiology therefore fully explain and account for this seemingly mysterious influence.

The view here stated, and endorsed by modern science, is one which ought to have great weight with the mother, her relatives and friends. The *practical conclusion* which it suggests is, that as during pregnancy there is unusual

THE WIFE DURING PREGNANCY.

susceptibility to mental impressions, and as these
sions may operate on the fragile structure of the
being, this tendency should be well considered a
stantly remembered, not only by the woman hers
by all those who associate or are thrown in conta
her. Upon the care displayed in the managemen
corporeal and mental health of the mother dur
whole period of pregnancy, the ultimate constitu
the offspring greatly depends. All the surroundi
employments of the pregnant woman should be
conduce to cheerfulness and equanimity. Above
should avoid the presence of disagreeable and u
objects. Vivid and unpleasant impressions sho
removed as soon as possible by quiet diversion
mind. All causes of excitement should be c
guarded against.

In leaving the subject of maternal impressions,
call attention to the manifest difference in extent
gree between the influence of the father and tha
mother over the offspring. That of the father
with impregnation. That of the mother continues
the whole term of pregnancy, and, as we shall sho
even during that of nursing.

EDUCATION OF THE CHILD IN THE WOMB.

The outlines drawn by the artist Flaxman are e
the most perfect and graceful in existence. From
childhood he manifested a delight in drawing. I
ther, a woman of refined and artistic tastes, used t
that, for months previous to his birth, she spen
daily in studying engravings, and fixing in her
the most beautiful proportions of the human fig
trayed by masters. She was convinced that th
of her son was the fruit of her own self-culture.
charming idea is this! What an incentive to tho
to become mothers, to cultivate refinement, high t

pure emotions, elevated sentiments! Thus they endow their children with what no after education can give them.

The plastic brain of the foetus is prompt to receive all impressions. It retains them, and they become the characteristics of the child and the man. Low spirits, violent passions, irritability, frivolity, in the pregnant woman, leave indelible marks on the unborn child. So do their contraries, and thus it becomes of the utmost moment that during this period all that is cheerful, inspiring, and elevating should surround the woman. Such emotions educate the child, they form its disposition, they shape its faculties, they create its mental and intellectual traits. Of all education, this is the most momentous.

CAN A WOMAN BECOME AGAIN PREGNANT DURING PREGNANCY?

Can a woman during pregnancy conceive, and add a second and a younger child to that already in the womb?

It is not uncommon in the canine race for a mother to give birth at the same time to dogs of different species, showing conclusively the possibility, in these animals, of one conception closely following another. So a mare has been known to produce within a quarter of an hour, first a horse, and then a mule. And in the human race cases are on record in which women have had twins of which the one was white and the other coloured, in consequence of intercourse on the same day with men of those two races. Dr. Henry relates that in Brazil a Creole woman, a native, brought into the world at one birth three children of three different colours, white, brown, and black, each child exhibiting the features peculiar to the respective races.

In all such instances the two conceptions followed each other very rapidly, the offspring arriving at maturity to-

...ther, and being born at the same accouchen
...e curious and wonderful examples of socon
...urrent pregnancies have been published tha...
for instance, those in which a child, bearing al...
butes of a fœtus at full term, is born two, three
even five months after the first, which appea...
have been born at full term. Marie Anne Bi...
thirty-seven, gave birth, April 30, 1748, t...
boy at full term, and on the ensuing Septeml...
living girl, which was recognised, by the size
developed condition of its body and limbs, to
also carried until full term. This fact was o...
Professor Eiseman, and by Leriche, surgeon m...
military hospital of Strasbourg. It will be n...
there was an interval of four and a half mont...
the two accouchements. The first child lived
half months, and the second a year. In th...
there was not a double womb, as might perh...
posed, for after the mother's death an examina...
that the uterus was single.

Another case of this kind is the following
Franquet, of Lyons, brought into the world
January 20, 1780, and five months and six days
a second girl, also apparently at term and well
Two years later these two children were pres...
their certificates of baptism, to two notaries
MM. Calliot and Desurgey, in order that the
be placed on record and vouched for, because
in legal medicine.

The number of the entirely authenticated
birth of fully developed children within from
months of each other now known, can leave no
the possibility of such an occurrence. The on...
which remains is in regard to the periods of
Are the two children in such cases twins, c...
the same time, but the growth of the last born
that it did not arrive at maturity until a...

months after its fellow? or has a second conception taken place at an interval of several months after the first? If this latter view be true, then in the instance of Marie Anne Bigaud, above related, the second must have been conceived after the first had quickened. Then, also, two children of different ages, the offspring of different fathers, may exist in the womb at the same time. The weight of scientific observation and authority has now established the fact that, in very rare instances, a second conception may take place during pregnancy. It must not be understood, as necessarily following from this statement, that when two children are born at the same time, one fully developed and the other small and apparently prematurely born, the two were conceived at different times. The smaller may have been blighted and its growth hindered by the same causes which bring about such effects in cases of single births of incompletely developed children. A similar supposition may account for the birth of a second child within a month or two after the first, for the first may have been prematurely born, and the second carried to full term. But no such supposition can explain the cases referred to, and others which might be mentioned, in which the interval has been five or six months, each child presenting every indication of perfect maturity. The only explanation possible in such instances, which, as has been said, are well authenticated, although few in number, is that a second pregnancy has occurred during the first.

The above facts would seem sufficiently wonderful. There are others, however, of the same nature, still more so. In some instances the product of the second conception, instead of developing independently of the first, has become attached to it, and the phenomenon has been presented of the growth of a child within a child—a fœtus within a fœtus. Such a singular occurrence has been lately recorded in a German journal. A correspondent of the *Duntzic Gazette* states that on Sunday, Feb-

ruary 1, 1869, at Schliewen, near Dirschau, " a
blooming shepherd's wife was delivered of a
wise sound, but having on the lower part of
between the hips, a swelling as big as two
fists, through the walls of which a well-devel
may be felt. Its limbs indicate a growth of f
six months, and its movements are very li
father called in the health commissioner, Dr. P
Dirschau, and begged him to remove the sv
gether with the fœtus. The doctor, however, a
ful examination, declared that there was a po
this extraordinary case of the child within t
coming to fruition. Its existence and acti
were palpable to all present. No physicia
justified in destroying this marvellous being
rather to be protected and cherished. The
girl, notwithstanding her strange burden, is
strength and beauty, and takes the breas
fully."

We find something further in regard to t
birth in the *Weser Zeitung* of February 20
quotes from the *Dantzic Gazette* some rem
health commissioner, Dr. Preuss, of Dirscha
the doctor declares the facts contained in the r
above to be correct. He was summoned on
February to the child, and saw the vigorous
and felt the members of a fœtus within the
described. It was evidently a double creation
thus far, though rare, is not unique. "But wh
and hitherto perfectly unnoticed in medical l
the fact that not only the girl which has beer
full term is alive to-day, but the fœtus withi
ing has also, the eleven days after birth,
veloped and palpably increased in size. The
now four and a half inches long, three and a
wide, and high and pear-shaped ; the head
neath on the left. the body towards the right.'

Further particulars, and the latest intelligence we have concerning the progress of this case are to the effect that the child was brought by special request before the Natural History Society of Dantzic, and thence the mother went to Berlin for medical advice.

MORAL ASPECTS OF THE QUESTION.

Upon proper judgment and discrimination in the application of the facts we have just been dwelling upon, may depend a wife's honour and the happiness of the dearest social relations. We will suppose an example. A husband, immediately after the impregnation of his wife, is obliged to quit her, and remains absent a year. In the meanwhile she gives birth to two children at an interval of a number of weeks. The question will then come up whether, under such circumstances, it is possible for her to do so consistently with conjugal purity.

It will be recollected that in speaking of twins we remarked that it was not very uncommon for an interval of days and weeks to elapse between the births, and it has just been stated that impregnation during pregnancy is extremely rare. The presumption, therefore, in the case supposed, is as very many to one, that the two births were the result of a twin pregnancy. In the absence of any other evidence against the wife's chastity, it should not even be called in question. The decision receives the support of the maxim in law, that a reasonable doubt is the property of the accused, and of the Christian principle, that it is better that ninety-nine guilty should escape than that one innocent should be condemned. Hence, the teachings of science and of human and divine law all coincide to protect the sacred rights and the precious interests at stake against an unjust suspicion, which even the doctrine of chance would render untenable.

CAN A CHILD CRY IN THE WOMB?

There are some cases recorded, on undoubted
in which the child has been heard to cry w
womb. These are very exceptional. Unde
circumstances it is impossible for the child
breathe or cry, because of the absence of air,
when the bag of membranes has been torn, and
of the child is applied at or near the neck of
that this can take place. The infant is not u
heard to cry just before birth, after labour has
but before the extrusion of the head from th
consequence of the penetration of air into
cavity.

IS IT A SON OR DAUGHTER?

It is a common saying among nurses that
difference in the size and form of the pregn
according to the sex she carries. This m
doubted. Neither is it true that one sex is
in its "movements" than the other. It is qu
however, for the wife to know the sex of t
she can tell about what time in her month
took place. If it occurred directly after a m
ness, the child is a girl; if directly before,
When a woman is "out" in her reckoning, a
yond the period of her expected confinement,
narily turn out to be a boy. The skilful ph
in the latter months of pregnancy, settle the
sex in some cases. The beats of the fœtal hea
frequent in females than in males. The averag
of pulsations of twenty eight female fœtuse
found to be one hundred and forty-four in
the lowest figure being one hundred and thirt
twenty-two male fœtuses, one hundred and
lowest figure being one hundred and twelve.
when the pulsations of the heart of the child i

DURATION OF PREGNANCY.

are counted—as can easily be done by a practised medical ear, during the last month of pregnancy—and are found to be over one hundred and thirty in a minute, it is a daughter, if under one hundred and thirty, a son. In this manner the sex of an unborn child can be predicted with tolerable accuracy, excepting only when illness of the fœtus has deranged the action of its heart.

ARE THERE TWINS PRESENT?

Certain signs lead to the suspicion of twins, such as being unusually large, and the fact that the increase in size has been more than ordinarily rapid. Sometimes also the abdomen is divided into two distinct portions by a perpendicular fissure. In other cases the movements of a child can be felt on each side at the same time. And in twin pregnancies the morning sickness is apt to be more distressing, and all the other discomforts incident to this condition increased. But these signs and symptoms, when present in any given case, are not conclusive, for they may be noticed where there is only one child. The doctor has one characteristic and infallible sign by which he can ascertain whether the woman be pregnant with twins. It is furnished to him, again, by the art of listening, or auscultation, as it is technically called, the same that, as we have already seen, enables him to determine the sex of the child. When the beatings of two fœtal hearts are heard on opposite portions of the abdomen, the nature of the pregnancy is apparent.

LENGTH OF PREGNANCY.

What is the ordinary duration of pregnancy? Almost every woman considers herself competent to make the answer—nine months. She may be surprised to learn, however, that such an answer is wanting in scientific precision. It is too indefinite, and is erroneous. There is a great difference between the calendar and the lunar months. Each lunar month having twenty-eight days the period of nine lunar months is two hundred and fifty two days. Nine calendar months, including February, represent, on the contrary, two hundred and seventy-three days. Now the average duration of pregnancy is two hundred and eighty days, that is forty weeks, or ten lunar months.

Whilst most extended observations have shown that, as a general rule, forty weeks, or two hundred and eighty days, is the true period of pregnancy, are we justified in the conclusion that this is its invariable duration? This important question, upon the answer to which so often depends the honour of families, the rights of individuals and sometimes the interests of nationalities, has been in all times the subject of careful research by physicians, philosophers, and legislators. On the one side have been those who contend that the laws of nature are invariable, and that the term of pregnancy is fixed and immutable. On the other side have been those who assert that the epoch of accouchement can be greatly advanced or retarded by various causes, some of which are known and others not yet appreciated. Abundant and satisfactory testimony has proved that the prolongation of pregnancy beyond the ordinary period of two hundred and eighty days, or forty weeks, is possible. Nor is this contrary to what is observed in regard to other functions of the human body. There is no process depending on the laws of life which is absolutely invariable either as to the period of its appearance or its duration. It is known, as we have already pointed out, that puberty may be advanced or retarded the time at which the change of life occurs in woman, as we shall have occasion hereafter to show, is also subject to variation; and it is a matter of common observation with mothers that the period of teething is sometimes strangely hurried or delayed. A certain degree of variability, therefore, being frequently observed, and entirely compatible with health in the various other natural processes, why should that of pregnancy form an exception, and be invariably fixed in its duration? And observation upon the lower animals affords most convincing evidence that nature is not controlled by any uniform law in reference to the length of pregnancy. In the cow, the usual period of whose pregnancy is the same as in the human female, instances of calving six weeks beyond the ordinary term are not at all uncommon.

As an illustration of the great interest sometimes attaching to the inquiry under discussion, we may cite the celebrated Gardner peerage case, tried by the House of Lords in 1825. Allen Legge Gardner petitioned to have his name inscribed as a peer on the Parliament roll. He was the son of Lord Gardner by his second wife. There was another claimant for the peerage, however—Henry Fenton Iadis—on the ground, as alleged, that he was the son of Lord Gardner by his first and subsequently divorced wife. Medical and moral evidence was adduced to establish that the latter was illegitimate. Lady Gardner, the mother of the alleged illegitimate child, parted from her husband on the 30th of January, 1802, he going to the West Indies, and not again seeing his wife until the 11th of July following. The child, whose legitimacy was called in question, was born on the 8th of December of that year. The plain medical query therefore arose whether this child, born either three hundred and eleven days after intercourse (from January 30th to December 8th) or one hundred and fifty days (from July 11th to December 8th), could be the son of Lord Gardner. As there was no pretence that there was a premature birth, the child having been well developed when born, the conception must have been dated from January 30th. The medical question was therefore narrowed down to this: Was the alleged protracted pregnancy (three hundred and eleven days) consistent with experience? Sixteen of the principal obstetric practitioners of Great Britain were examined on this point.

Eleven concurred in the opinion that natural
might be protracted to a period which would
birth of the alleged illegitimate child. Becaus
of the moral evidence alone, which proved the
intercourse of Lady Gardner with a Mr. Iadis,
decided that the title should descend to the sor
cond Lady Gardner.

There is on record one fact well observed, w
lishes beyond cavil the possibility of the pro
pregnancy beyond two hundred and eighty da
weeks. The case is reported by the learned
meaux, of Paris, and occurred under his own ne
Hôpital de Maternité of that city. A woman,
of three children, became insane. Her physici
that a new pregnancy might re-establish her
faculties. Her husband consented to enter or
ter of the hospital each visit he was allowed to
which took place only every three months.
evidence of pregnancy showed itself, the visits w
tinued. The woman was confined two hundred
days after conception.

The late distinguished Professor Charles I
Philadelphia, published a case, which he deer
trustworthy, of the prolongation of pregnan
hundred and twenty days, or sixty weeks.
reports two cases, which nearly equalled thre
and fifty-six days each. Professor Simpsor
burgh, records, as having occurred in his ow
cases in which the period reached three hu
thirty-six, three hundred and thirty-two, thr
and twenty-four, and three hundred and ninete
the "Dublin Quarterly Journal of Medical Scie
of protracted pregnancy is related by Dr. J
evidence is positive that the minimum dur
have been three hundred and seventeen day
six weeks more than the average. Dr. Elsa
in one hundred and sixty cases of pregnancy

tracted to periods varying from three hundred to three hundred and eighteen days.

In treating of the subject of miscarriage, we mentioned instances recorded by physicians of skill and probity, proving beyond a shade of doubt that a woman may give birth to a living child long before the expiration of forty weeks. The Presbytery of Edinburgh, Scotland, some time since decided in favour of the legitimacy of an infant born alive within twenty-five weeks after marriage, to the Rev. Fergus Jardine.

One of the most enlightened countries in Europe has, in view of the facts in reference to the extreme limits of pregnancy, enacted, in the Code Napoleon, that a child born within three hundred days after the departure or death of the husband, or one hundred and eighty days after marriage, shall be considered legitimate. The law further states that a child born after more than three hundred days shall not be necessarily declared a bastard, but its legitimacy may be contested. The Scotch legislation on this subject is very similar to the French.

CAUSES OF PROTRACTED PREGNANCY.

It has been asserted by some that an infant is born at ten or eleven months because that at nine months it has not acquired the growth which is necessary in order to induce the womb to dislodge it. The popular notion is that a child carried beyond the usual time must necessarily be a large one. Rabelais has reflected this common opinion in his celebrated romance entitled "Gargantua," in which he represents the royal giant of that name as having been carried by his mother, Gargamelle, eleven months. When born, the child was so vigorous that he sucked the milk from ten nurses. He lived for several centuries, and at last begat a son, Pantagruel, as wonderful as himself. Such reasoning cannot, however, be seriously maintained, as many children carried longer than nine months have not been more fully developed than some born a few weeks prematurely, and the size of the child has nothing to do with the bringing on of labour, as we shall show hereafter. Protracted pregnancies are caused by a defect in the energy of the womb, induced by moral as well as physical influences. As a rule, a woman who leads a regular life and observes the physiological laws of her being, which laws it has been our aim to point out, will be confined at the term that nature usually marks out, that is, at the expiration of two hundred and eighty days, or forty weeks, from conception.

This brings us to the consideration of the question,

HOW TO CALCULATE THE TIME OF EXPECTED LABOUR.

Many rules for this purpose have been laid down. We shall merely give one, the most satisfactory and the most easily applied. It was suggested by the celebrated Professor Naegelé of Heidelberg, and is now generally recommended and employed by physicians. The point of departure in making the calculation is *the day of the disappearance of the last monthly sickness;* three months are subtracted and seven days added. The result corresponds to the day on which labour will commence, and will be found to be two hundred and eighty days from the time of conception, if that event has occurred, as ordinarily, immediately after the last menstrual period. Suppose, for instance, the cessation of the last monthly sickness happened on the 14th day of January. Subtract three months, and we have October 14th; then add seven days, and we obtain the 21st day of the ensuing October (two hundred and eighty days from January 14th) as the time of the expected confinement. This method of making the "count" may be relied upon with confidence, and only fails, by a few days in those exceptional cases in which conception takes place just before the monthly period, or during the menstrual flow.

CARE OF HEALTH DURING PREGNANCY.

This subject, the proper management of the health from conception to childbirth, is worthy of careful consideration. The condition of pregnancy, though not one of disease, calls for peculiar solicitude, lest it should lead to some affection in the mother or in the child. For it ought to be remembered that the welfare of a new being is now in the balance. The woman has no longer an independent existence. She has entered upon the circle of her maternal duties. She became a mother when she conceived. The child, though unborn, lives within her; its life is a part of her own, and so frail that any indiscretion on her part may destroy it. The danger to the child is not imaginary, as the large number of miscarriages and still-births proves.

All mothers desire to have healthy, well-formed, intelligent children. How few conduct themselves in such a manner as to secure a happy development of their offspring! Puny, deformed, and feeble-minded infants are daily ushered into the world because of a want of knowledge, or a sinful neglect of those special measures imperatively demanded in the ordering of the daily life, by the changed state of system consequent upon pregnancy. We shall therefore point out those laws which cannot be infringed with impunity, and indicate the diet, exercise, dress, and, in general, the conduct most favourable to the mother and child during this critical period, in which the wife occupies, as it were, an intermediate state between health and sickness.

FOOD.

The nourishment taken should be abundant, but not, in the early months, larger in quantity than usual. Excess in eating or drinking ought to be most carefully avoided. The food is to be taken at shorter intervals than is common, and it should be plain, simple, and nutri-

tious. Fatty articles, the coarser vegetables, hi[gh]
and sweet food, if found to disagree, as is ofte[n]
should be abstained from. The flesh of youn[g]
as lamb, veal, chicken, and fresh fish, are whol[ly]
generaly agree with the stomach. Ripe fruit[s]
ficial. The diet should be varied as much as po[ssible]
day to day. The craving which some women [feel at]
night or early morning may be relieved by
a little milk, or a cup of coffee. When taken a[t night]
before rising, this will generally be retained,
very grateful, even though the morning s[ickness is]
troublesome. Any food or medicine that will
derange the bowels is to be forbidden. The ta[ste is a]
rule, a safe guide, and may be reasonably
But inordinate, capricious desires for improp[er]
articles should, of course, be opposed. Suc[h desires,]
however, are not often experienced by thos[e well]
brought up. It is a curious fact that the mod[e of]
the digestive system during pregnancy is so[metimes so]
great that substances ordinarily the most indi[gestible are]
eaten without any inconvenience, and even w[hile]
while the most healthful articles become hurt[ful]
like poison.

As pregnancy advances, particularly abou[t the]
month, a larger amount of food, and that of [a sub-]
stantial character, will be required. The numb[er of meals]
in a day should then be increased, rather tha[n the quan-]
tity taken at each meal.

CLOTHING.

The dress should be loose and comfortabl[e, not]
pressing tightly or unequally. The word [by]
which a pregnant woman is designated, mean[s a woman]
without a cincture,—that is, unbound. The [Roman ma-]
trons so soon as they conceived were oblige[d to loosen]
their girdles. Lycurgus caused the enactm[ent]

Spartan law that pregnant women should wear large dresses, so as not to prejudice the free development of the precious charges of which nature had rendered them the momentary depositaries. Stays or corsets may be used, in a proper manner, during the first five or six months of pregnancy, but after that they should either be laid aside or worn very loosely. Any attempt at concealing pregnancy, by tight lacing and the application of a stronger busk, cannot be too severely condemned. By this false delicacy the mother is subjected to great suffering and the child placed in jeopardy. The shape of the stays should be moulded to that of the changing figure, and great care should be taken that they do not depress the nipple or irritate the enlarging breasts.

The amount of clothing should be suited to the season, but rather increased than diminished, owing to the great susceptibility of the system to the vicissitudes of the weather. It is especially important that flannel drawers should be worn during advanced pregnancy, as the loose dress favours the admission of cold air to the unprotected parts of the body. A neglect of this precaution sometimes leads to the establishment of the painful disease known as rheumatism of the womb.

Pressure upon the lower limbs, in the neighbourhood of the knee or the ankle joint, should be avoided, more particularly towards the last months. It is apt to produce enlargement and knotting of the veins, swelling and ulcers of the legs, by which many women are crippled during their pregnancies and sometimes through life. Therefore the garters should not be tightly drawn, and the gaiters should not be too closely fitted, while yet they should firmly support the ankle.

EXERCISE.

Moderate exercise in the open air is proper and conducive to health during the whole period of pregnancy. It should never be so active or so prolonged as to induce fatigue. Walking is the best form of exercise. Riding in a badly constructed carriage, or over a rough road, or upon horseback, as well as running, dancing, and the carrying of heavy weights, should be scrupulously avoided, as liable to cause rupture, severe flooding and miscarriage. During the early months in particular, extraordinary long walks and dancing ought not to be indulged in. Journeys are not to be taken while in the pregnant state. Railway travelling is decidedly objectionable. The vibratory motion of the cars is apt to produce headache, sickness at the stomach, faintness and premature labour. All these precautions are especially to be observed in the first pregnancy.

We must not be understood as condemning exercise and fresh air. They are of the greatest importance to mother and child. But the amount of exercise should be regulated by the dictates of common sense and the woman's own sensations. If she can only walk a short distance each day with comfort, let that suffice. She should not force herself to go to a certain place or to promenade during a certain time in the twenty-four hours. So soon as fatigue is felt, the walk should cease. Let the walks be frequent and short rather than few and long. They should also be made as pleasant as possible by companionship and surroundings that will occupy the feelings and imagination in an agreeable manner with new and cheerful impressions. A tendency to indolence is to be combated. A gently active life is best calculated to preserve the health of the mother and her unborn child. But with even the most robust a moderation of the ordinary pursuits and avocations is called for. The nervous and delicate cannot make with safety their customary daily exertions in the performance of their household or social duties and pleasures.

Towards the end of pregnancy the wife should economise her forces. She should not remain long standing or kneeling, nor sing in either of these postures.

BATHING.

Those who have not been accustomed to bathing should not begin the practice during pregnancy, and in any case great care should be exercised during the latter months of pregnancy. It is better to preserve cleanliness by sponging with tepid water than by entire baths. Foot-baths are always dangerous. Sea-bathing sometimes causes miscarriage, but sea air and the sponging of the body with salt water are beneficial. The shower bath is, of course, too great a shock to the system, and a very warm bath is too relaxing. In some women of a nervous temperament, a lukewarm bath taken occasionally at night during pregnancy has a calming influence. This is especially the case in the first and last month. But women of a lymphatic temperament and of a relaxed habit of body are always injured by the bath.

VENTILATION.

We have spoken of the benefits of out-door air. Attention should also be directed to keeping the atmosphere in the sitting and sleeping rooms of the house fresh. This can only be accomplished by constantly changing it. The doors and windows of every room, while unoccupied, should be kept thrown open in the summer time, and opened sufficiently often in the winter to wash out the apartments several times a day with fresh air. The extremes of heat and cold are to be, with equal care, avoided. The house should be kept light. Young plants will not grow well in the dark; neither will the young child nor its mother flourish without sunlight. The ancients were so well aware of this that they constructed on the top of each house a solarium, or solar air-bath, where they basked daily, in thin attire, in the sunlight.

SLEEP.

During pregnancy a large amount of sleep i[s]
It has a sedative influence upon the disturbe[d]
system of the mother. It favours, by the calm[ing]
the functions which attend it, the growth of
Neither the pursuit of pleasure in the evenin[g]
observance of any trite maxims in regard to e[arly rising]
in the morning, should be allowed to curtail the
voted to slumber. Pregnant women have an
desire to lie abed late, which, like the other pro[mptings of]
nature during this period, should not be disrega[rded. At]
least eight hours out of the twenty-four can be
spent in bed. No night-watching ought ever t[o be]
taken during pregnancy.

Feather beds should be avoided. The heat
maintain about the body is inconvenient and
predisposing to flooding and exhausting per[spirations.]
The hair or sponge mattress is to be preferred.
clothing should not be too heavy. Blankets ar[e em-]
ployed rather than coverlids, as they are lighter
permeable to perspiration. The mattress and co[verings should]
be well aired during the day. The sleeping-ro[om should]
be capacious and well-ventilated, and no cur[tains per-]
mitted about the bed.

Occasional rest is also necessary in the daytim[e. A nap]
of an hour or two upon a sofa or lounge will
very refreshing. In the earlier months of pr[egnancy it]
will tend to prevent miscarriage, and in latt[er months,]
to relieve the distress consequent upon the inc[reased size]
of the womb. It is not unusual, as the close of
approaches, for a feeling of suffocation to ensue
woman attempts to lie down. This may be ov[ercome by]
supporting the back and shoulders with cushion[s or pil-]
lows. Or, a bed chair may be employed. Th[is, properly]
constructed and covered, will often be found ver[y useful]
at night, in the last few weeks of pregnancy.

THE MIND.

A tranquil mind is of the first importance. Gloomy forebodings should not be encouraged. Pregnancy and labour are not, we repeat, diseased conditions. They are healthful processes, and should be looked upon as such by every woman. Bad labours are very unfrequent. It is as foolish to dread them as it is for the railway traveller to give way to misgivings in regard to his safety. Instead of desponding, science bids the woman to look forward with cheerfulness and hope to the joys of maternity.

The bad effects of fear upon the mother's mind are illustrated by Plutarch, who, in his life of Publicola, mentions that "at a time when a superstitious fear overran the City of Rome, all the women then pregnant brought forth imperfect children, and were prematurely delivered." But we have already spoken, in treating of mothers' marks, of the influence of mental emotions over the unborn child, and the necessity of avoiding their exciting causes.

Because of their deleterious tendency, severe study, as well as arduous and protracted manual labour, ought to be avoided. The nervous systems of many women are also injuriously affected during pregnancy by perfumes, which at other times are agreeable and innocuous. It is, therefore, prudent not only to exclude all offensive scents, but also to abstain from the strong odours of various colognes and of flowers. Large bouquets often cause feelings of faintness and sometimes temporary loss of consciousness. The extreme liability of the nervous system of the pregnant woman to be affected injuriously to herself and child by scenes of suffering or distress, and by disgusting or frightful objects, cannot be too strongly impressed upon every one. She should be protected from all that will disturb her, and should be constantly treated with soothing and encouraging kindness. Her manifestations of irritability, her caprices, her melancholy anticipations, are not

to be scoffed at, but combated with a mixture of reas[oning]
ing and patient forbearance. On her part she should [en]
deavour to co-operate with those around her in sedulou[sly]
shunning all injurious influences, and in banishing [as]
quickly as possible all improper longings. She should [re]
member that, although she herself may escape misch[ief]
from them, her child may suffer. She is the custodia[n of]
interests dearer to her than her own.

RELATION OF HUSBAND AND WIFE.

During that time when the wife, if she were not pr[eg]
nant, would have been "unwell," marital intercourse sho[uld]
be abstained from. It is then injurious to the mother, [and]
dangerous to the life of the child, as it is liable to ex[cite]
miscarriage. If this habitual epoch of the mont[hly]
sickness be avoided, there is no reason why passion sho[uld]
not be gratified in moderation and with caution dur[ing]
the whole period of pregnancy. There is one except[ion]
to be made to this general course of conduct. In th[ose]
cases in which a miscarriage has occurred in the first pr[eg]
nancy, every precaution should be employed—for reas[ons]
which have been dwelt upon in a previous article—to prev[ent]
its happening again after the second conception. Unders[uch]
exceptional circumstances, therefore, the husband [and]
wife should sleep apart during the first five months [of]
pregnancy. After that period their ordinary relations m[ay]
be resumed. When a miscarriage has taken place, int[er]
course should not be permitted within a month of the [ac]
cident. The observance of this direction is of the utm[ost]
importance. Its neglect is the frequent cause of sev[ere]
and intractable diseases of the womb.

EFFECT OF PREGNANCY ON HEALTH.

We have had occasion to remark that pregnancy is [not]
a condition of disease. It is not only an evidence

health, but during its continuance it confers increased physical vigour. As a rule, a woman enjoys *better health* during her pregnancy than at any other time; she is less liable to contagious and other maladies; she is less apt to die than at any other period of her life; and her general constitution seems also then to receive a favourable impress, for wives and mothers live longer than celibates. It is wisely decreed that when woman is engaged in this, to her, anxious stage of reproduction, she shall not be exposed to the pains and dangers of disease, and that those great covenants of nature, marriage and child-bearing, shall be rewarded by added strength and length of days.

There are certain disorders incident, in exceptional cases, to pregnancy, of which we shall shortly speak. In general, however, we repeat that this condition is one of extraordinary health. More than this, in numerous instances it exerts an ameliorating influence upon pre-existing diseases, suspending their march, or bringing about a decidedly curative effect. Thus, various obstinate chronic affections of the skin, of the womb and ovaries, and of the brain and nervous system, frequently get well during pregnancy; and it is well known to every physician that, by the judicious management of this state, and of the lying-in period, troublesome displacements of the womb may be arrested.

It should nevertheless ever be recollected that the condition of pregnancy is one of excitement and enhanced susceptibility to impressions of all kinds. For this reason a change in the habits of life is necessary, and the importance of the directions just laid down for the care of the health during this period cannot be too strongly insisted upon.

DISEASES OF PREGNANCY.

Notwithstanding the general immunity from disease, and the improvement in the health upon which we have

been dwelling, as ordinary attendants upon p
there are certain inconveniences or discomfort
to this state which demand a little attention.

Morning sickness.—This affection when cont
usually the case, to the morning and early pa:
day, rarely requires much medical care. Its
which, as we have said, is a frequent cause of mi
is more to be regretted than its presence, especi
is apt to be replaced by more serious troubles.

Relief will be afforded by washing the face
in cold water, and taking a cup of milk or a li(
and a biscuit or sandwich, *before raising the h
the pillow* in the morning, remaining in bed abo
ter of an hour after this early meal; then
quickly, and immediately going out for a l
walk. Rest in a half recumbent posture durin(
particularly after meals, is beneficial. The a:
mostly a nervous one, and is best combated 1
The food should be plain and unirritating, but
and should be taken frequently, in small quan
time,

When the nausea and vomiting are excessive
tinue during the day, there is generally some
condition of the digestive apparatus.

This may be corrected by taking at night a t(
of the *confection* of senna, a pleasant preparati
ordinary disagreeable medicine, and by drink
times a day, before each meal, a wineglassful
made with columbo. Half an ounce of pow(
umbo should be added for this purpose, to a pi
ing water.

Dr. John H. Griscom, of New York, recomt
bromide of potassium, which is a harmless me
domestic practice, as affording the most useful
arresting the nausea attendant on pregnancy.

The following prescription may be compound
druggist, and will often be found very effective

Take of Bromide of Potassium, two drachms.
" Cinnamon water, three ounces.

Of this a dessertspoonful may be taken two or three times a day. It may be used with confidence as an entirely safe and harmless remedy in this troublesome affection.

A prescription frequently ordered for the nausea of pregnancy by the late distinguished Dr. Meigs, of this city, consisted of equal parts of sweet tincture of rhubarb and compound tincture of gentian: a dessertspoonful to be taken after meals.

Often when the bowels require to be regulated, the use of bran bread, wheaten grits, oatmeal gruel, and other laxative articles of food, will be found very beneficial.

Constipation should be attended to, if it exist to such an extent as to cause inconvenience. Often when the mother suffers from headache, perversion of sight, dimness of vision, etc., they may all be happily relieved by small doses of citrate of magnesia, a Seidlitz powder taken before breakfast, or the use of the Saratoga and Bedford waters.

Pain in the abdomen, caused by the distention of its walls, may be relieved by the application of equal parts of sweet-oil and laudanum.

PREPARATIONS FOR CONFINEMENT.

Certain foolish preparations are sometimes made by wives with the best intentions. Perhaps one of the most common and absurd of these is the local use of sweet-oil, in order to facilitate the dilatation of the parts, for which purpose it is perfectly inert. There are, however, some wise and even necessary precautions which every wife should know and employ, to guard against unpleasant and dangerous complications in childbirth.

In particular, *the condition of the breasts* towards the close of pregnancy demands attention. Scarcely any pain

in the lying-in chamber is greater and more difficult
bear than that which the young mother suffers from
coriated nipples. This troublesome and very often
tractable affection is nearly always the consequence
the want of care previous to confinement. During
latter part of pregnancy the nipples sometimes beco
sunken or flat, being retracted as the breasts increase
size, because of the want of elasticity on the part of
milk-tubes. In order to remedy this fault, we have kno
a breast-pump or puppy to be applied. Such treatm
is dangerous, as it may excite premature contractio
the womb and miscarriage. Nipple-shields, with br
bases and openings, should always be obtained. They
safe, and effectually secure the prominence of the nipp
when worn constantly, day and night, during the
month or so of pregnancy. Wives who have never
children ought to take special care to ascertain be
labour whether this depressed condition of the ni
exists, and to correct it in the manner indicated.

In the first pregnancy it is also important to *har
the nipple*. This may be done by occasionally ge
rubbing them between the thumb and finger, and
bathing them twice a day during the last six weeks
tincture of myrrh, or with a mixture of equal part
brandy and water, to which a little alum has been ad
This procedure will render the surfaces less sensitiv
the friction of the child's mouth, and thus avert the
tress so often occasioned in the first confinement by
derness of the nipples.

If the nipples be rough or nodulated in appearance,
a strawberry or raspberry, they are more apt to bec
excoriated or fissured, than if they present a smooth
face. Under such circumstances, make a solution o
sulphate of zinc, of the strength of one grain to the o
of rose water, in a wide-mouthed bottle, then tilt
bottle upon the nipple, and allow it to remain there f
few minutes, several times a day. Simple tendernes

CARE OF NIPPLES.

the nipples and slight fissures may be averted by the application either of a lotion of borax (two scruples of borax in three ounces of water, and an ounce of glycerine), of the honey of borax, or of the tincture of catechu, and by protecting the parts from the pressure of the stays and the friction of the flannel vest.

It is of the greatest moment to the comfort of the mother that all affections of the nipples should be prevented or remedied before labour, for the treatment of sore nipples, when the child is at the breast, is often unsatisfactory, while the suffering they occasion is very great, even sometimes giving rise to mammary abscess.

There are certain *articles of clothing* and *dressing for the bed* which should be cared for in advance, in order that they may be ready when required.

The mother should be provided with short gowns, to be worn over the chemise instead of the ordinary nightgowns. It is of consequence to procure a proper *bandage*. It should be made of heavy muslin, neither too coarse nor too fine; an ordinary good quality of unbleached muslin is best. The material is to be cut bias, about one and a quarter yards in length, and from twelve to eighteen inches in breadth, varying, of course, with the size of the person. It should be just large enough to encircle the body after confinement, with a margin of a couple of inches, and to extend down below the fulness of the hips. The measurement should be taken and the bandage made to fit when four and a half months advanced. It should be narrow above, wider below, and gored in such a manner, that it will be a little narrower at the lower extremity than a few inches above, so as to prevent it, when adjusted, from sliding upwards. A bandage constructed in this manner will be very comfortable, and is not apt to become displaced after application, as is invariably the case when a towel or a piece of straight muslin is used. The way in which it is to be applied will be detailed hereafter.

The *child's clothing* should consist first of a piece of

flannel or some woollen material for a binder. This
be from four to six inches in width, and from tw
sixteen inches in length; that is to say, wide en
extend from the arm pits to the lower part of th
men, and long enough to go once and a half time
the child, having the double fold to come over th
men. There should be no embroidery about this.
which it is desirable should be woollen, is to be p
to place over the binder. It should be made to c
tolerably high in the neck and to extend down t
Neither it nor any portion of the child's clothing
be starched. The petticoat, which may be ope
whole length behind, is to be put over the shirt; t
be used, a short one and a long one. Next co
child's ordinary frock or slip, and above this, an a
protect the dress from the frequent discharges f
stomach. Then a shawl, of flannel, or any othe
material, is to be provided to throw over the shou
the weather be cold. Socks and pieces of old soft
free from stiffening, for napkins or diapers, comp
child's outfit.

For the *permanent and temporary dressing of*
there should be provided a piece of imperviou
(oiled silk is the neatest) about a yard square, a
ordinary table oil-cloth or rubber cloth, a numbe
sheets and comfortables, and a piece of thick carpe
manner in which these are to be used will be ex
shortly.

A pair of small rounded scissors, a package o
pins, one and a half inches in length, for the ban
the mother, and smaller ones for that of the child
good linen bobbin for the doctor to tie the navel
good toilet-soap and fine surgical sponge for wash
child; a piece of soft linen or muslin for dress
navel; a box of unirritating powder; and a
towels, should all be had and laid aside many we
fore they are wanted. These, together with the n

SYMPTOMS OF LABOUR.

r dressing the bed, the child's clothing, and the mother's
ndage, ought to be placed together in a basket got for
e purpose, in order that they may all be easily and
rtainly found at a time when perhaps the hurry and ex-
ement of the moment would render it difficult other-
ise to collect them all immediately.

SIGNS OF APPROACHING LABOUR.

One of the earliest of the preliminary signs of the
ming on of confinement occurs about two weeks before
at event. It is a dropping or subsidence of the womb.
ie summit of that organ then descends, in most cases,
om above to below the umbilicus, and the abdomen
comes smaller. The stomach and lungs are relieved
om pressure, the woman breathes more freely, the sense
 oppression which troubled her previously is lost, and
e says she feels "very comfortable." This sensation of
ghtness and buoyancy increases, and a few days before
e setting in of labour she feels so much better that she
inks she will take an extra amount of exercise. The
other of a number of children is acquainted with this
gn, but the wife with her first child may exert herself
duly in the house or out-doors, and induce labour when
 the street or away from home. Hence the importance
a knowledge of this premonitory symptom.

A second precursory sign of labour is found in the
reased fulness of the external parts and an augmented
cous secretion, which may amount even to a discharge
embling whites, and requiring the wearing of a napkin.
is symptom is a good one, indicating a disposition to
xation, and promising an easy time.

he third preliminary sign which we shall mention is
 change in the mental state of the pregnant woman.
 has a feeling of anxiety and of fidgetiness, sometimes
mpanied with depression of spirits. This condition
motional distress, modified in particular cases by rea-

son, self-control, and religion, may continue 1
days, perhaps, when

THE SYMPTOMS OF ACTUAL LABOUR

make their appearance. The first of these is ge
"show." It is the discharge of the plug of m
has occupied the neck of the womb up to this t
ordinarily accompanied by a little blood. Perl
this, or perhaps not for some hours after, the "
develop themselves. These recur periodically a
of an hour or half an hour at the outset, and a
ing" in character. *True* labour pains are dis
from false by the fact that they are felt in
passing on to the thighs, while *false* pains are
the abdomen; by their intermittent char
spurious pains being more or less continuous—
steady increase in their frequency and severity
of doubt as to their exact nature, the physician
summoned, who will be able to determine
whether labo... has begun.

The other symptoms which point to the a
mencement of labour are a frequent desire to
bowels and bladder, nausea and vomiting, wh
early part of confinement, is a good sign; shiv
attended with any sensation of cold; and 1
rupture and discharge of the contents of th
water."

Before passing on to the consideration of th
ment of the confinement into which the wife
entered, a few words may be appropriately sai

CAUSE OF LABOUR.

Neither the size nor the vigour of the child 1
fluence in bringing about delivery at full t
ancient theory—which received the support

…guished naturalist, Buffon—that the infant was the …tive agent in causing its own expulsion, is an exploded …e. It was asserted by some that hunger excited the …tus to struggle to free itself from the womb; others …re disposed to attribute its efforts to accomplish its en…nce into the world to the need of respiration which it …perienced. But all these ingenious theories, which pre…pposed the embryo to be actuated by the same feelings …ich would influence a grown person if shut up in such a …nfined abode, are unsatisfactory and not tenable. It is …ll known that the child may die in the womb without …tarding or interfering in any way with the coming on of …e process of labour. This fact alone shows that the …tus is, or at any rate may be, absolutely passive either …regard to the induction or advancement of delivery. …e determining cause of labour is seated in the womb …elf. The contractions of this organ occasion the " pains" …d expel the child, assisted by the muscles of the abdomen …d the diaphragm. That the assistance of the latt r …rces is not necessary is conclusively proved by the …urrence of childbirth after the decease of the mother. …r instance, a case is on record in which labour commenced …d twins were born after the mother had been dead for …ree days.

THE CONFINEMENT.

We will suppose labour to have commenced. The *preparation of the bed* for the occupancy of the mother is …w to be attended to. As she is to lie on the *left side* …the bed, this is the side, and the only one, which is to …dressed for the occasion. In order to do so, remove …outer bed-clothes one at a time, folding them neatly …the right side of the bed so that they can easily be …wn over when desired. The *permanent dressing* is …be placed beneath the lower sheet and upon the mat-…. A soft impervious cloth—which, in speaking of the …paration for confinement we directed to be procured—

is placed next to the surface of the bed. The
should be nearly as high as the margin of
and it should extend down to a distance at
below the level of the hips, so as to certainly
bed from the discharges. Upon the top of thi
or sheet is laid, and the whole fastened by
lower sheet of the bed, which had been turn
the right side to permit the application of th
is now to be replaced. Over the position of
nent dressing, on the top of the bed sheet, a ne
sheet, with the folded edge down, is adjusted
in its place. It is upon this sheet that the p
be drawn up after her confinement, which will
upon the *temporary dressing* of the bed, no
ranged. It consists of an oil-cloth, which sho
up beyond the lower edge of the permanent dre
lapping the folded sheet which has been place
and should fall over the side and bottom of t
comfortable, or any soft absorbent material, is
this impervious cloth and covered with a fo
completing the temporary dressing. The bed-c
now be adjusted, concealing the dressings fro
til they are wanted. The valances at the foot
should be raised and a piece of carpet placed o
The bed should have no foot-board, or a very

The dress of the mother.—Either a folded s
be adjusted around the waist as the only skir
to interfere with walking, or a second chemis
put on, with the arms outside the sleeves, to e
the waist to the feet. Then the chemise nex
should be drawn up and folded high up a
breast. It should be plaited neatly along the
brought forward and fastened by pins. This
thoroughly done, so that the linen may not
wet nor soiled when it is drawn down after co
A wrapper or dressing-gown may be worn
first stage of labour, before it is necessary to

When, however, that time comes, the wife will take her place on her left side on the temporary dressing, with a sheet thrown over her, her head on a pillow so situated that her body will be bent well forward, and her feet against the bed-post. A sheet should be twisted into a cord and fastened to the foot of the bed, for her to seize with her hands during the accession of the "bearing down pains." Care should be taken to have a number of napkins, a pot of fresh lard, and the basket containing the scissors, ligature, bandages, etc.—which have been previously enumerated in the article on preparations for confinement—at hand, for the use of the doctor.

We have now noted all that it is useful for the wife to know in regard to the preparation for the management of confinement, when a physician is in attendance, as for obvious reasons he should always be. In some instances, however, the absence of the doctor is unavoidable, or the labour is complete before his arrival. As a guide to the performance of the necessary duties of the lying-in room under such circumstances, we give some

HINTS TO ATTENDANTS

The room should be kept quiet. Too many persons must not be allowed in it, as they contaminate the air, and are apt, by their conversation, to disturb the patient, either exciting or depressing her. So soon as the head is born, it should be immediately ascertained whether the neck is encircled by the cord; if so, it should be removed or loosened. The neglect of this precaution may result fatally to the infant, as happened a short time since in our own practice, the infant, born a few minutes before our arrival, being found strangled with the cord about its neck. It is also of importance at once to allow of the entrance of air to the face, to put the finger in the mouth to remove any obstruction which may interfere with respiration, and to lay the babe on its right side, with the

head removed from the discharges. The cord
be tied until the infant is heard to cry. The
to be applied in the following manner. A pie
bin is thrown around the navel string, and t:
double knot at the distance of three finger
from the umbilicus; a second piece is tied a:
yond the first, and the cord divided, with tl
between the two—care being taken not to cli
ger or otherwise injure the unsuspecting little
has occurred in careless hands more than once.
child is separated from the mother, a warm bl
piece of flannel should be ready to receive it.
hold of the little stranger it may slip out of
and be injured. To guard against this accider
very apt to occur with awkward or inexperi
sons, always seize the back portion of the n
space bounded by the thumb and first finger o
and grasp the thighs with the other. In this
bo safely carried. It should be transferred h
in its blanket, to some *secure* place, and ne
an arm chair, where it may be crushed by son
does not observe that the chair is already occu
head of the child should not be so covered as t
danger of suffocation.

ATTENTION TO THE MOTHER.

When the after-birth has come away, t
should be drawn up a short distance—six or e
—in bed, and the sheet which has been pinned
together with the temporary dressing, removed,
folded sheet introduced under the hips. The p
be gently washed with warm water and a t
or cloth, after which an application of equal pa
wine and water will prove pleasant and bene
have also found the anointing of the external
nal parts with goose grease, which has been

washed in several hot waters, to be very soothing and efficient in speedily allaying all irritation. This ought all to be done under cover, to guard against the taking of cold. The chemise pinned up around the breast should now be loosened, and the woman is ready for the application of the bandage, which is to be put on next the skin. If properly and nicely adjusted, it will prove very grateful. The directions for making it have already been given. In order to apply it, one-half of its length should be folded up into plaits, and the mother should lie on her left side. Lay the plaited end of the bandage underneath the left side of the patient, carrying it as far under as possible, and draw the loose end over the abdomen. Then let the mother roll over on her back and draw out the plaited end. If the abdominal muscles are much relaxed and the hip bones prominent, a compress of two or three towels will be wanted. The bandage should be first tightened in the middle by a pin applied laterally, for strings should never be employed. The pins should be placed at intervals of about an inch. The lower portion of the bandage should be made quite tight, to prevent it slipping up. The mother is now ready to be drawn up in bed upon the permanent dressing; this should be done without any exertion on her part. A napkin should be laid smoothly *under* the hips (never folded up) to receive the discharges. If she prefer to lie on her left side, place a pillow behind her back.

ATTENTION TO THE CHILD.

The baby may be now washed and dressed. Before beginning, everything that is wanted should be close at hand, namely, a basin of warm water, a large quantity of lard or some other unctuous material, soap, fine sponge, and a basket containing the binder, shirt, and other articles of clothing. First rub the child's body thoroughly with lard. The covering can only be removed in this way;

IMAGE EVALUATION
TEST TARGET (MT-3)

Photographic
Sciences
Corporation

23 WEST MAIN STREET
WEBSTER, N.Y. 14580
(716) 872-4503

the use of soap alone will have no effect unless the
so great as to take off also the skin. The nurse s
a handful of lard and rub it in with the palm o:
particularly in the flexures of the joints. In
one part, the others should be covered, to p
child from taking cold. If the child is thus mad
clean, do not use any soap and water, because 1
left in a more healthful condition by the lard, a
risk of the child taking cold from the eva]
the water. But the face may be washed wit]
water, great care being taken not to let the soa
the child's eyes, which is one of the most frequ
of sore eyes in infants. The navel-string is
dressed. This is done by wrapping it up in
piece of muslin, well oiled, with a hole in its ce
bandage is next to be applied. The object of i
protect the child's abdomen against cold and t
dressing of the cord in its position. The nature,
size of the binder have been described. It sho
ned in front; three pins being generally suffic:
rest of the clothing before enumerated is then

The child is now to be *applied to the brea*
This is done for three reasons. First, it very.
vents flooding, which is apt otherwise to occur.
it tends to prevent milk fever, by averting t]
rush of the milk on the third day, and the cons
gorgement of the breast, and constitutional di
The third reason is, that there is always a se
the breast from the first, which it is desirab
child to have, for it acts as a cathartic, stimu
liver and cleansing the bowels from the secreti
fill them at the time of birth. There is gene:
cient nourishment in the breasts, for the child, f
few days. The mother may lie on one side or
and receive the child upon the arm of that u]
she is lying. If the nipple be not perfectly dra
that the child can grasp it in its mouth, the dif

be overcome by filling a porter bottle with hot water, emptying it, and then placing the mouth of the bottle immediately over the nipple. This will cause, as the bottle cools, a sufficient amount of suction to elevate the sunken nipple. The bottle should then be removed and the child substituted, a little sugar and water or sweetened milk being applied, if necessary, to tempt the child to take the breast.

The patient should be cleansed every *four or five hours*. A soft napkin, wet with warm soap and water, should for this purpose be passed underneath the bed-clothing, without exposing the surface to a draft of air. After using the soap and water, apply again the diluted claret wine and the goose grease. Much of the safety of the mother depends upon the observation of cleanliness. The napkin should not be allowed to remain so long as to become saturated with the discharges.

The patient should maintain rigidly the recumbent position for the first few days, not raising her shoulders from the pillow for any purpose, and should abstain from receiving visitors and from any social conversation for the first twenty-four hours.

For the first three or four days, until the milk has come and the milk fever passed, the mother should live upon light food—oatmeal gruel, tea and toast, panada, or anything else of little bulk and unstimulating character. Afterwards the diet may be increased by the addition of chicken, lamb, mutton or oyster broth, buttered toast and eggs. The object of light nourishment at first is to prevent the too rapid secretion of milk, which might be attended with evil local and constitutional effects. If, however, the mother be in feeble health, it will be necessary from the outset that she shall be supported with nourishing concentrated food. *Beef-tea* will then be found very serviceable, particularly if made according to the following recipe: Take a pound of fresh beef from the loins or neck. Free it carefully from all fat. Cut it up into fine pieces,

and add a very little salt and five grains of
black pepper. Pour on it a pint of cold water a
for forty minutes. Then pour off the l'quor
meat in a cloth, and after squeezing the juice f
the tea, throw it aside. Return to the fire an
ten minutes.

After the first week, the diet of the lying
should always be nutritious, though plain a
The development of the mammary glands, the
of the mammary secretion, and the reduction v
place in the size of the womb, all require incre
ishment that they may be properly performed

After the third or fourth day *the dress should*
The dress worn during labour, if our directions
carried out, will not have been soiled. Th
should be changed without uncovering the p
without raising the head from the pillow. Pu
gown from over each arm and draw it out fron
body. Then unfasten the chemise in front a
down underneath her, so that it can be remove
low, as it should not be carried over the head.
arms in the sleeves of the clean chemise, thro
over her head, and, without lifting her shoulde
bed, draw it down. Then change the bed-g
same manner.

In changing the upper sheet, it should be
from below, and the clean one carried down
from above, underneath the other clothing, w.
readily accomplished by plaiting the lower hal
ducing a clean under-sheet, one side of it shou
ed and placed under the patient, lying on her
when she turns on her back the plaits can ther
drawn out. These directions, though apparently
important. The object is to guard against the
ger to which the mother is exposed by sitting
for even a few minutes during the first week.

Cathartic medicine should not be admin

first, the third, or any other day after confinement, unless it is needed. If the patient is perfectly comfortable, has no pain in the abdomen, no headache, and is well in every respect, she should be let alone, even if her bowels have not been moved. If a laxative be called for, citrate of magnesia is much pleasanter and equally as efficacious as the castor-oil so frequently administered on this occasion.

TO HAVE LABOUR WITHOUT PAIN.

Is it possible to avoid the throes of labour and have children without suffering? This is a question which science answers in the affirmative. Medical art brings the water of Lethe to the bedside of woman in her hour of trial. Of late years chloroform and ether have been employed to lessen or annul the pains of childbirth, with the same success that has attended their use in surgery. Their administration is never pushed so as to produce complete unconsciousness, unless some operation is necessary, but merely so as to diminish sensibility and render the pains endurable. These agents are thus given without injury to the child, and without retarding the labour or exposing the mother to any danger. When properly employed they induce refreshing sleep, revive the drooping nervous system, and expedite the delivery.

They should never be used in the absence of the physician. He alone is competent to give them with safety. In natural, easy and short labour, where the pains are readily borne, they are not required. But in those lingering cases in which the suffering is extreme, and, above all, in those instances where instruments have to be employed, ether and chloroform have a value beyond all price.

MORTALITY OF CHILDBED.

The number of the pregnancy affects the danger to be expected from lying-in. It has been declared by excellent authority that the mortality of first labours, and of child-

bed fever, following first labours, is about twice the mor
ity attending all subsequent labours collectively. A
the ninth labour the mortality increases with the num
A woman having a large family, therefore, comes i
greater and increasing risk as she bears her ninth
successive children.

The age of the woman also affects the mortality acc
panying confinement. The age of least mortality is r
twenty-five years. On either side of this, morta
increases with the diminution or increase of age.
age of the greatest safety in confinement, therefore, cor
ponds to the age of greatest fecundity. And during
whole of child-bearing life, safety in labour is directl
fecundity, and *vice versa*. Hence modern statistics pr
the correctness of the saying of Aristotle, that "to
female sex premature wedlock is peculiarly danger
since, in consequence of anticipating the demands of
ture, many of them suffer greatly in childbirth, and m
of them die." As the period from twenty to twenty-
is the least dangerous for childbirth, and as first lab
are more hazardous than all others before the ninth,
important that this term of least mortality be chosen
entering upon the duties of matrimony. This we h
already pointed out in speaking of the age of nubility

The sex of the child is another circumstance affec
the mortality of labour. Professor Simpson, of Edinbu
has shown that a greater proportion of deaths occu
women who have brought forth male children.

The duration of labour also influences the mortalit
lying-in. The fatality increases with the length of
labour. It must be recollected, however, that the dura
of labour is only an inconsiderable part of the many ca
of mortality in childbirth.

WEIGHT AND LENGTH OF NEW-BORN CHILDREN.

The average weight of infants of both sexes at the

of birth is about seven pounds. The average of male children is seven and one-third pounds; of male, six and two-third pounds. Children which at full term weigh less than five pounds are not apt to thrive, and usually die in a short time.

The average length at birth, without regard to sex, is about twenty inches, the male being about half an inch longer than the female.

In regard to the relation between the size of the child and the age of the mother, the interesting conclusion has been arrived at, that the average weight and length of the mature child gradually increases with the age of the mother up to the twenty-fifth year. Mothers between the ages of twenty-five and twenty-nine have the largest children. From the thirtieth year they gradually diminish. The first child of a woman is of comparatively light weight. The first egg of a fowl is smaller than those which follow.

The new-born children in our Western States seem to be larger than the statistics show them to be in the various States of Europe, and apparently even than in our Eastern States. In the Report on Obstetrics of the Illinois State Medical Society for 1868, it is stated that Quincy, Ill., produced during the year six male children whose average weight at birth was thirteen and a quarter pounds, the smallest weighing twelve pounds, and the largest seventeen and a-half, which was born at the end of four hours' labour, without instrumental or other interference. A recent number of a western medical journal reports the birth, at Detroit, in February last, of a well-formed male infant twenty-four and a-half inches long, weighing sixteen pounds. The woman's weight, *after labour*, is stated as only ninety-two pounds. An English physician delivered a child by the forceps which weighed seventeen pounds twelve ounces, and measured twenty-four inches. These are the largest well-authenticated new-born infants on record.

DURATION OF LABOUR.

The length of a natural labour may be said [be-]
tween two and eighteen hours. The interva[ls between]
the pains are such, however, that the actual [time of]
suffering, even in the longest labour, is compara[tively]
short. The first confinement is much longer t[han subse-]
quent ones.

The *sex* of the child has some influence on t[he duration]
of labour. According to Dr. Collins, of the Ly[ing-in Hos-]
pital of Dublin, the average with *male* births [is three]
and four minutes longer than with *female*. [The size]
of the child also affects the time of labour. Child[ren weigh-]
ing over eight pounds average four hours and [some min-]
utes longer in birth than those of less than ei[ght pounds]
weight.

STILL-BIRTHS.

The statistics of nearly fifty thousand deliv[eries oc-]
curred at the Royal Maternity Charity, Lo[ndon, give]
a percentage of nearly five still-born, or one [in twenty-]
seven.

There are more boys still-born than girls. [We have]
already spoken of the fact that male births are m[ore painful,]
and that a larger number of males die in th[e first few]
years of life than females. This series of misf[ortunes has]
been attributed to the larger size which the [male child]
at birth possesses over the female.

IMPRUDENCE AFTER CHILD-BIRTH.

After the birth of the child at full term, or at [any]
period of pregnancy, the womb, which has att[ained its]
wonderful proportions in a few months, begins [to resume]
its former size. This process requires at least [a month]
after labour for its full accomplishment. Rest

during this period. A too early return to the ordinary active duties of life retards or checks this restoration to normal size, and the womb being heavier, exposes the woman to great danger of uterine displacements. Nor are these the only risks incurred by a too hasty renewal of active movements. The surface, the substance, and the lining membrane of the womb are all very liable, while this change from its increased to its ordinary bulk is occurring, to take on inflammation after slight exposure. The worst cases of uterine inflammation and ulceration are thus caused. A "bad getting up," prolonged debility, pain and excessive discharge, are among the least penalties consequent upon imprudence after confinement. It is a mistake to suppose that women in the lower walks of life and the wives of Indians attend with impunity to their ordinary duties a few days after confinement. Those who suffer most from falling of the womb and other displacements are the poor, who are obliged to get up on the ninth day and remain upright, standing or walking for many hours with an over-weighted womb. Every physician who has seen much of Indian women has remarked upon the great frequency of womb disease in the squaws, which is to be attributed to the neglect of rest, so common among them, after childbirth. If this be true of vigorous women accustomed to hardy life, how much more apt to suffer from this cause are the delicately nurtured, whose systems are already, perhaps, deteriorated, and little able to resist any deleterious influence.

A mother should remain in bed for at least two weeks after the birth of the child, and should not return to her household duties under a month; she should also take great pains to protect herself from cold, so as to escape the rheumatic affections to which at the time she is particularly subject. If these directions were generally observed, there would be less employment for physicians with diseases peculiar to women, and fewer invalids in American homes.

TO PRESERVE THE FORM AFTER CHILDBIRTH.

This is a matter of great anxiety with many w[omen] and it is proper that it should be, for a flabby, pend[ulous] abdomen is not only destructive to grace of movem[ent and] harmony of outline, but is a positive inconvenience.

To avoid it, be careful not to leave the bed too [soon.] If the walls of the abdomen are much relaxed, t[he bed] should be kept from two to three weeks. Gentle fri[ction] daily with spirits and water will give tone to the m[uscles.] But the most important point is to wear for s[ome] months a *well-fitting* bandage—not a towel pinned a[bout] the person, but a body-case of strong-linen, cut bia[s, fit]ting snugly to the form, but not exerting unpleasan[t pres]sure. The pattern for this has already been give[n.]

THE MOTHER.

It has been well said by Madame Sirey, that the women who comprehend well their rights and duties as mothers of families certainly cannot complain of their destiny. If there exists any inequality in the means of pleasure accorded to the two sexes, it is in favour of the woman. The mother who lives in her children and her grandchildren has the peculiar privilege of not knowing the grief of becoming old.

"So low down in the scale of creation as we can go," says Professor Laycock, of Edinburgh, "wherever there is a discoverable distinction of sex, we find that maternity is the first and most fundamental duty of the female. The male never in a single instance in any organism, whether plant or animal, contributes nutrient material."

Among the Romans it was enacted that married women who had borne three children, or, if freed women, four, had special privileges of their own in cases of inheritance, and were exempted from tutelage. Juvenal has recorded the reverence paid in Rome to the newly-made mother, and the sign by which her house was designated and protected from rude intruders—namely, by the suspension of wreaths over the door.

At various times and in various countries, legislators have made laws discriminating in favour of matrons, justly regarding the family as the source of the wealth and prosperity of the state.

Louis XIV. granted, by the edict of 1666, certain pensions to parents of ten children, with an increase for those who had twelve or more.

NURSING.

So soon as the infant is born it ought to be placed at the breast. From this source it should receive its *only* nourishment during the first four or six months, and in many cases the first year, of its life. The child which the mother has carried for nine months and brought with suffering into the world still depends upon her for its existence. At the moment of its birth her duties to her infant, instead of ceasing, augment in importance. The obligation is imposed upon her of nourishing it with her own milk, unless there are present physical conditions rendering nursing improper, of which we are about to speak. It is well known that the artificial feeding of infants is a prominent cause of mortality in early life. The foundlings of large cities furnish the most striking and convincing proof of the great advantages of nursing over the use of artificially-prepared food. On the continent of Europe, in Lyons and Parthenay, where foundlings are wet-nursed from the time they are received, the deaths are 33.7 and 35 per cent. In Paris, Rheims, and Aix, where they are wholly dry-nursed, their deaths are 50.3, 63.9, and 80 per cent. In New York City, the foundlings, numbering several hundred a year, were, until recently, dry-nursed, with the fearful and almost incredible mortality of nearly one hundred per cent. The employment of wet nurses has produced a much more favourable result. Therefore, if for any reason the mother cannot nurse her own child, a hired wet-nurse should be procured. This brings us to the consideration of

HINDRANCES TO NURSING, AND WHEN IT IS IMPROPER.

Women who have never suckled often experience difficulty in nursing, on   e sunken and flat cond

tion of the nipple. We have pointed out the causes of this depression, and how by early attention, before the birth of the infant, it may be prevented. If, however, these precautions have been neglected, and it is found that the nipple is not sufficiently prominent to be grasped by the child's mouth, it may be drawn out by a common breast-pump, by suction with a tobacco pipe, by the use of the hot-water bottle in the manner described, or by the application of a puppy, or of an infant a little older. Neither the child nor the mother should be constantly fretted in such cases by frequent ineffectual attempts at nursing. Such unremitting attention and continual efforts produce nervousness and loss of sleep, and result in a diminution of the quantity of the milk. The child should not be put to the breast oftener than once in an hour and a half or two hours. By the use of the expedients mentioned the whole difficulty will be overcome in a few days.

Delay in applying the child to the breast is a common cause of trouble. After it has been fed for several days with the spoon or bottle, it will often refuse to nurse. When nursing is deferred, the nipple also becomes tender. For these reasons, as well as the others detailed in our directions for the care of the new-born infant, the child should always, in say from two to three hours after labour, be placed at the breast.

Ulcerated and fissured nipples should be treated by the physician in attendance. As it is highly desirable and nearly always possible to avoid them, we would again call attention to the manner of doing so, indicated in a previous article. Fissured nipples sometimes do harm to the infant by causing it to swallow blood, disturbing in this way the digestion. But all these local interferences with nursing can generally be obviated in the course of a few weeks, and rarely entirely prevent the exercise of this maternal pleasure and duty.

But there are certain physical conditions which necessitate the employment of a hired wet-nurse, or weaning. If the mother belongs to a consumptive family, and is herself pale, emaciated, harassed by a cough, and exhausted by suckling, wet-nursing is eminently improper. A temporary loss of strength under other circumstances should not induce a mother at once to wean her child, for it is often possible, by the judicious use of tonics, nourishing food, and stimulants, to entirely restore the health with the child at the breast. It should always be recollected, however, that the milk of those in decidedly infirm health is incapable of properly nourishing the child. Professor J. Lewis Smith, of New York, quotes, in his recent work on Diseases of Children, several instructive cases, which show the danger sometimes attending suckling, and which may imperatively demand its discontinuance. "A very light-complexioned young mother, in very good health, and of a good constitution, though somewhat delicate, was nursing for the third time, and, as regarded the child, successfully. All at once this young woman experienced a feeling of exhaustion. Her skin became constantly hot; there were cough, oppression, night-sweats; her strength visibly declined, and in less than a fortnight she presented the ordinary symptoms of consumption. The nursing was immediately abandoned, and from the moment the secretion of milk had ceased, all the troubles disappeared." Again: "A woman of forty years of age having lost, one after another, several children, all of which she had to put out to nurse, determined to nurse the last one herself. This woman, being vigorous and well built, was eager for the work, and, filled with devotion and spirit, she gave herself up to the nursing of her child with a sort of fury. At nine months she still nursed him from fifteen to twenty times a day. Having become extremely emaciated, she fell all at once into a state of weakness, from which nothing could raise her, and two days after the poor woman died of exhaustion."

It does not always follow that, because the mother is sick

the child should be taken from the breast. It is only necessary in those affections in which there is great depression of the vital powers, or in which there is danger of communicating the disease to the child. In the city, where artificially-fed infants run great danger, extreme caution should be exercised in early weaning.

Inflammation of either of the breasts necessitates the removal of the infant from the affected side and its restriction to the other. As the inflammation gets well and the milk reappears, the first of it should always be rejected, as it is apt to be thick and stringy, after which nursing may be resumed.

RULES FOR NURSING.

The new-born child should nurse about every second hour during the day, and not more than once or twice at night. Too much ardour may be displayed by the young mother in the performance of her duties. Not knowing the fact that an infant quite as frequently cries from being overfed as from want of nourishment, she is apt to give it the breast at every cry, day and night. In this manner her health is broken down, and she is compelled, perhaps, to wean the child, which, with more prudence and knowledge, she might have continued to nurse without detriment to herself. It is particularly important that the child shall acquire the habit of not nursing more than once or twice at night. This, with a little perseverance, can readily be accomplished, so that the hours for rest at night, so much needed by the mother, may not be interfered with. Indeed, if the mother does not enjoy good health, it is better for her not to nurse at all at night, but to have the child fed once or twice with a little cow's milk. For this purpose, take the upper third of the milk which has stood for several hours, and dilute it with water, in the proportion of one part milk to two of water.

In those cases in which the milk of the mother habitually disagrees with the infant, the attention of the doctor should at once be called to the circumstance. A microscopic examination will reveal to the intelligent practitioner the cause of the difficulty, and suggest the remedy

It may be well here to mention—as, judging from the practice of many nurses and mothers, it seems to be a fact not generally known or attended to—that human milk contains all that is required for the growth and repair of the various parts of the child's body. It should therefore be the sole food of early infancy.

INFLUENCE OF DIET ON THE MOTHER'S MILK.

Certain articles of food render the milk acid, and thus induce colicky pains and bowel complaint in the child. Such, therefore, as are found, in each individual case, to produce indigestion and an acid in the mother, should be carefully avoided by her.

Retention of the milk in the breasts alters its character. The longer it is retained, the weaker and more watery it becomes. An acquaintance with this fact is of practical importance to every mother; for it follows from it that the milk is richer the oftener it is removed from the breast. Therefore, if the digestion of the child is disordered by the milk being too rich, as sometimes happens, the remedy is to give it the breast less frequently, by which not only is less taken, but the quality is also rendered poorer. On the contrary, in those instances in which the child is badly nourished and the milk is insufficient in quantity, it should be applied oftener, and the milk thus rendered richer.

The milk which last flows is always the richest. Hence, when two children are nursed, the first is the worst served.

INFLUENCE OF PREGNANCY ON THE MILK.

Menstruation is ordinarily absent, and pregnancy therefore impossible, during the whole course of nursing, at least during the first nine months. Sometimes, however, mothers become unwell at the expiration of the sixth or seventh month; in rare instances, within the first five or six weeks after confinement. When the monthly sickness makes its appearance, without any constitutional or local disturbance, it is not apt to interfere with the welfare of the infant. When, on the contrary, the discharge is profuse and attended with much pain, it may produce colic, vomiting, and diarrhœa in the nursling. The disturbance in the system of the child, ordinarily resulting from pregnancy in the mother, is such that, as a rule, it should be at once weaned so soon as it is certain that pregnancy exists. The only exceptions to this rule are those cases in the city during the hot months in which it is impossible either to procure a wet-nurse or to take the child to the country to be weaned. In cold weather, an infant should certainly be weaned if it has attained its fifth or sixth month, and the mother has become pregnant.

INFLUENCE OF THE MOTHER'S MIND OVER THE NURSING CHILD.

We have spoken, in treating of mother's marks, of the influence of the mother's mind upon her unborn offspring. The influence of the maternal mind does not cease with the birth of the child. The mother continues during the whole period of nursing powerfully to impress, through her milk, the babe at her breast. It is well established that mental emotions are capable of changing the quantity and quality of the milk, and of thus rendering it hurtful and even dangerous to the infant.

The secretion of milk may be entirely stopped by the action of the nervous system. Fear, excited on account of the child which is sick or exposed to accident, will check the flow of milk, which will not return until the little one is restored in safety to the mother's arms. Apprehension felt in regard to a drunken husband has been known to arrest the supply of this fluid. On the other hand, the secretion is often augmented, as every mother knows, by the *sight* of the child, nay, even by the *thought* of him causing a sudden rush of blood to the breast, known to nurses as the *draught*. Indeed, a strong desire to furnish milk, together with the application of the child to the breast, has been effectual in bringing about its secretion in young girls, old women, and even men.

Sir Astley Cooper states that "those passions which are generally sources of pleasure, and which, when moderately indulged, are conducive to health, will, when carried to excess, alter and even entirely check the secretion of milk."

But the fact which it is most important to know is that nervous agitation may so alter the *quality* of the milk as to make it poisonous. A fretful temper, fits of anger, grief, anxiety of mind, fear and sudden terror, not only lessen the quality of the milk, but render it thin and unhealthful, inducing disturbances of the child's bowels, diarrhœa, griping, and fever. Intense mental emotion may even so alter the milk as to cause the death of the child. A physician states in the *London Lancet*, that having removed a small tumor from behind the ear of a mother, all went on well until she fell into a violent passion. The child being suckled soon afterwards, died in convulsions. Professor Carpenter records in his Physiology two other fatal instances; in one, the infant, put to the breast immediately after the receipt of distressing news by the mother, died in her arms in the presence of the messenger of the ill-tidings; in the other, the infant was seized with convulsions on the right side and paralysis on the left, on sucking directly after the mother had met with an agitating occurrence. Another case of similar character may be mentioned. A woman while nursing became violently excited on account of a loss she had just met with from a theft. She gave her child the breast while in an intense passion. The child firs refused it, but subsequently nursed when severe iting occurred. In the course of some ho the child took the other breast, was attacked at once with violent convulsions, and died in spite of all that could be done for it.

The following cases are related by Professor Carpenter as occurring within his own knowledge. They are valuable as a warning to nursing mothers to avoid all exciting or depressing passions. A mother of several healthy children, of whom the youngest was a vigorous infant a few months old, heard of the death, from convulsions, of the infant child of an intimate friend at a distance, whose family had increased in the same manner as her own. The unfortunate circumstance made a strong impression on her mind, and, being alone with her babe, separated from the rest of her family, she dwelt upon it more than she otherwise would have done. With her mind thus occupied, one morning, shortly after nursing her infant, she laid it in its cradle, asleep and apparently in perfect health. Her attention was soon attracted to it by a noise. On going to the cradle she found it in a convulsion, which lasted only a few moments, and left it dead. In the other case, the mother had lost several children in early infancy, from fits, one infant alone surviving the usually fatal period. While nursing him, one morning, she dwelt strongly upon the fear of losing him also, although he appeared to be a very healthy child. The infant was transferred to the arms of the nurse. While the nurse was endeavouring to cheer the mother by calling her attention to the thriving appearance of her child, he was seized with a convulsion, and died almost instantly in her arms. Under similar circumstances, a child should not be nursed by its mother but by one who has reared healthy children of her own, and has a tranquil mind.

An interesting illustration of the powerful sedative action of the mother's milk—changed in consequence of great mental distress—upon the impressible nervous system of the infant, is furnished by a German physician. "A carpenter fell into a quarrel with a soldier billeted in his house, and was set upon by the latter with his drawn sword. The wife of the carpenter at first trembled from fear and terror, and then suddenly threw herself furiously between the combatents, wrested the sword from the soldier's hand, broke it in pieces, and threw it away. During the tumult, some neighbours came in, and separated the men. While in this state of strong excitement, the mother took up her child from the cradle, where it lay playing and in the most perfect health, having never had a moment's illness. She gave it the breast, and in so doing sealed its fate. In a few minutes the infant left off sucking, became restless, panted, and sank dead upon its mother's bosom. The physician, who was instantly called in, found the child lying in the cradle as if asleep, and with his features undisturbed, but all his resources were fruitless. It was irrevocably gone."

Professor William A. Hammond, of New York, mentions in a recent number of the "Journal of Psychological Medicine," several instances, from his own practice, of affections in the child caused by the mother's milk. "A soldier's wife, whilst nursing her child was very much terrified by a sudden thunder-storm, during which the house in which she was then quartered was struck by lightning. The infant, which had always been in excellent health was immediately attacked with vomiting and convulsions, from which it recovered with difficulty." "A lady three weeks after delivery, was attacked with puerperal insanity. She nursed her child but once after the accession of the disease, and in two hours subsequently it was affected with general convulsions, from which it died during the night. Previous to this event it had been in robust health."

Again, Dr. Seguin, of New York, relates, in his work on Idiocy, a number of cases of *loss of mind* produced by the altered state of the mother's milk. "Mrs. B. came out from a ball-room, gave the breast to her baby, three months old; he was taken with spasms two hours afterwards, and since is a confirmed idiot and epileptic."

"In a moment of great anxiety Mrs. C. jumped into a carriage with her suckling, a girl of fifteen months, so far very intelligent and attractive. The child took the breast only once in a journey of twenty miles, but before arriving at their destination she vomited several times, with no interruption but that of stupour, and after an acute fever the little girl settled down into the condition of a cripple and idiot."

The celebrated physician Boerhave mentions the milk of an angry nurse as among the causes of *epilepsy*.

These facts show the importance of a placid mind and cheerful temper in the mother while nursing.

POSITION OF THE MOTHER DURING NURSING.

The habit of nursing a child sitting up in bed, or half reclining upon a lounge, is a wrong one. Such a position is injurious to the breasts, hurtful to the woman's figure, and apt to cause backache. When in bed, the mother ought always to be recumbent while the child is at the breast, held upon the arm of the side upon which she lies. When out of bed, she should sit upright while nursing.

QUANTITY OF MILK REQUIRED BY THE INFANT.

The amount of milk furnished every day by a healthy woman has been estimated at from a quart to a quart and a half. An infant of one or two months of age takes about two wine-glassfuls, or three ounces every meal;—that is— as it nurses every two hours, excepting when asleep—in the neighbourhood of a quart and a quarter during the twenty-four hours. When it attains the age of three months, it thrives well on five meals a day, the quantity taken at each meal then—the stomach being more capacious—amounting to about half a pint. A child above three months of age ordinarily requires a quart and a half daily.

A healthy mother is fully capable of furnishing this quantity of milk per day, and of affording the child all the nourishment it needs until four or six months after birth.

The quantity of the mother's milk varies according to many circumstances. It is most abundant and also most nutritious in nursing women between the ages of fifteen and thirty; least so, in those from thirty-five to forty There is likewise a great difference in different women in this respect.

THE QUALITIES OF A GOOD NURSING-MOTHER

are well described by Professor J. Lewis Smith. "The best wet-nurses are usually robust, without being corpulent. Their appetite is good, and their breasts are distended, from the number and large size of the blood-vessels and milk ducts. There is but a moderate amount of fat around the gland, and tortuous veins are observed passing over it. Such nurses do not experience a feeling of exhaustion, and do not suffer from lactation. The nutriment which they consume is equally expended on their own sustenance and the supply of milk. There are other good wet-nurses who have the physical condition described, but whose breasts are small. Still the infant continues to nurse until it is satisfied, and it thrives. The milk is of good quality, and it appears to be secreted mainly during the time of suckling. Other mothers evidently decline in health during the time of nursing. They furnish milk of good quality and in abundance, and their infants thrive, but it is at their own expense. They themselves say, and with truth, that what they eat goes to milk. They become thinner and paler, are perhaps troubled with palpitation, and are easily exhausted. They often find it necessary to wean before the end of the usual period of lactation. There is another class whose health is habitually poor, but who furnish the usual quantity of milk without the exhaustion experienced by the class just described. The milk of these women is of a poor quality. It is abundant but watery. Their infants are pallid, having soft and flabby fibre."

OVER-ABUNDANCE OF MILK.

An excessive amount of milk often distends the breasts of those women who are prone to have long and profuse monthly sickness. It is also apt to occur in those subject to bleeding piles. It may be produced by any excitement of the womb or ovaries, and by over-nursing. In these cases there is usually a constant oozing away and consequent loss of milk. The mother is troubled by this overflow, because it keeps her clothing wet, and the child suffers because of the unnutritious, watery character of the milk under such circumstances.

This over-abundant supply may be moderated and the quality improved by diminishing the quantity of drink, and by the use of preparations of iron. Fifteen drops of the muriatic tincture of iron, taken three times a day in a little sweetened water, through a glass tube, will be useful. It will lessen the amount of the milk, and make it richer. So soon as these objects are accomplished, the medicine should be discontinued, as if taken too long it may so much diminish the milk as to necessitate weaning. The application of a cloth, wrung out in cold water, around the nipples, is also often of value. It is to be removed as soon as it becomes warm, and reapplied. In those cases in which the trouble seems to be not so much an oversupply as an inability to retain the milk, the administration of tonics addressed to the nervous system, and the local use of astringents and of collodion around the nipples, will overcome the difficulty; but these remedies can only be employed successfully by the physician. And to

THE MOTHER.

him alone should be intrusted the use of those medicines which directly diminish the amount of milk secreted within the breast. The expedients we have mentioned are the only ones which can be safely employed by the mother herself in this annoying affection.

SCANTINESS OF MILK.

Some mothers have habitually an insufficiency of milk. They are most numerous in large cities, and among working women, whose daily occupations require a separation from the infant. Indigestion and the want of a proper amount of nourishing food cause a diminution in the quantity of milk. So also do overfeeding and gormandizing. Age lessens the secretion of the milk, as has been already mentioned. Those who first bear children late in life have less milk for them than those who begin earlier. In some cases want of milk in the breasts seems to be due to its reabsorption. In such instances it may make its appearance at distant parts. Thus, a case has been recorded of the coughing up of milk following sudden arrest of the secretion, and others in which it presented itself as an exudation in the groins.

In the treatment of a scanty formation of milk, one of the best measures which can be resorted to is the frequent application of the child to the breast. In addition, the flow may be increased by milking the breasts by means of the thumb and finger, suction through a tobacco pipe, or the breast-pump, or by the use of the puppy, or of another infant.

Friction of the breasts and forcible drawing upon the nipples will make them sore, and so irritate them as to defeat the object in view. A change of scene, fresh air, and out-door exercise, attention to personal cleanliness, and the improvement of the general health, all increase the quantity and produce a favourable effect upon the quality of the milk. A sojourn at the seaside often pro-

causes an abundant secretion of milk. The diet should be regulated by the condition of the constitution. By those who are weak and pale, a large proportion of meat is required. On the contrary, those who are full-blooded and corpulent should restrict the amount of their animal food, and take more exercise in the open air. Oatmeal gruel enjoys a reputation for increasing the flow of milk. A bowl of it sometimes produces an immediate effect. The same is true of cows' milk. Porter or ale once or twice a day, in those with reduced systems and impaired digestion and appetite, will be found useful. Anise, fennel and caraway seeds, given in soup, act sometimes as stimulants upon the secretion of milk. The application of a poultice made from the pulverized leaves of the castor-oil-plant is a most efficient remedy when milk fails to make its appearance in the breast in sufficient quantity after confinement.

WET-NURSING BY VIRGINS, AGED WOMEN AND MEN.

As a rule the secretion of milk is limited to one sex, and in that is confined to a short period after childbirth. But there are many cases on record of the flowing of milk in women not recently mothers, in girls before the age of puberty, in aged women, and even in individuals of the male sex. In such instances, the secretion is induced by the combined influence, acting through the nervous system, of a strong desire for its occurrence, of a fixed attention towards the mammary glands, and of suction from the nipples.

Travellers among savage nations report many examples of such unnatural nursing. Dr. Livingstone says he has frequently seen in Africa a grandchild suckled by a grandmother. Dr. Wm. A. Gillespie, of Virginia, records, in the *Boston Medical and Surgical Journal*, the case of a widow, aged about sixty, whose daughter having died, leaving a child two months old, took the child and tried to raise it by feeding. The child's bowels became deranged, and being unable to procure a nurse, and her breasts being large and full, he advised her to apply the child in hopes milk would come. She followed his advice perseveringly; and to her astonishment, a plentiful secretion of milk was the result, with which she nourished the child, which afterwards became strong and healthy. A similar instance, still more remarkable, is recorded of a woman at seventy years, who wet-nursed a grandchild twenty years after her last confinement.

Cases of nursing in the opposite extreme of life are also well authenticated. The distinguished French physician, Baudelocque, has related that of a deaf and dumb girl, eight years old, who, by the repeated application to her breast of a young infant, which her mother was suckling, had sufficient milk to nourish the child for a month, while the mother was unable to nurse it on account of sore nipples. The little girl was shown to the Royal Academy of Surgery on the 16th of February, 1783. The quantity of milk was such, that by simply pressing the breast it was made to flow out in the presence of the Academy, and on the same day, at the house of Baudelocque, before a large class of pupils. Again an interesting case is known of a young woman who, in consequence of the habit of applying the infant of her mistress to her breast in order to quiet it, caused a free secretion of milk. In the Cape de Verde Islands, it is stated that virgins, old women, and even men, are frequently employed as wet-nurses. Humboldt speaks of a man, thirty-two years old, who gave the breast to his child for five months. Sir John Franklin saw a similar case in the arctic regions. Professor Hall presented to his class in Baltimore a negro, fifty-five years old, who had been the wet-nurse of all the children of his mistress.

Instances of powers of *prolonged nursing* in mothers are not uncommon. Indeed, it is the habit among some nations to suckle children until they are three or four years of age, even though another pregnancy may intervene, so that immediately one child is succeeded at the breast by another. In those who have thus unnaturally excited the mammary glands, an irrepressible flow sometimes continues after the demand for it has ceased. Dr. Green published some years ago, in the *New York Journal of Medicine and Surgery*, the case of a woman, aged forty-seven, the mother of five children, who had had an abundant supply of milk for *twenty-seven years* previously. A period of exactly four years and a half occurred between each birth; and the children were permitted to take the breast until they were running about at play. At the time when Dr. G. wrote, she had been nine years a widow and was obliged to have her breasts daily drawn, the secretions of milk being so copious. When, therefore, it is desirable, on account of the feebleness of the child, to protract the period of nursing, a wet-nurse should relieve the mother at the end of twelve or fifteen months.

RULES FOR CARE OF HEALTH WHILE NURSING.

From what we have previously said of the influence of the nervous system over the quantity and quality of the milk, and the instances we have adduced of the danger to the infant of all violent passions—such as anger, terror, anxiety, and grief—on the part of the mother, it will be apparent that it is of the greatest moment, during the whole course of nursing, to maintain a tranquil state of mind. Pleasing and peaceful emotions favour the normal secretion of milk, and go far towards securing the health of the child. When strongly affected by any powerful feeling, mothers should not give the breast, but should wait until they have calmed down to their usual tenor of temper. A case was related of a woman who was always excited by a highly electrical state of the atmosphere, and particularly during stormy weather. If when thus influenced she nursed her child, he was sure to fall into convulsions, while if she delayed doing so until this nervous excitement had passed, no unpleasant symptoms occurred But we have already dwelt at length upon this subject in speaking of the influence of the mind of the mother over the child at her breast, and need not, therefore, recur to it. The *food* while nursing must be nutritious and varied, though simple and unstimulating, and should consist both of meat and vegetables, soups, fish, flesh, and fowl, either in combination or succession. When the digestion requires aid. a glass of mild ale twice a day will be useful. Wines, brandy and whisky should not be taken without the advice of a physician. Moderate exercise in the open air and regular habits are necessary.

A defective or excessive diet, fatigue, loss of rest at night, and irregularities and excesses of all kinds, are unfavourable to mother and child. The proper methods of combating a tendency to over-abundance or to scantiness of milk have been alluded to. Medicines, unless prescribed by the medical attendant, should rarely or never be taken during this period, as many of them enter the milk and may thus affect the child.

RELATIONS OF HUSBAND AND WIFE DURING NURSING.

After natural and healthy confinement, the nurse usually remains with the mother for a period of four weeks. During the whole of this time the husband should occupy a separate apartment, and, accordimg to some physicians, this separation should be protracted during the entire period of nursing. But this is unusual, and in most cases unnecessary. Only those women who are warned by the recurrence of their monthly illness that they are liable to another pregnancy immediately, should insist on such an ascetic rule as this.

Unquestionably the quality of the milk is much deteriorated by a conception, and therefore, both in the inter

...of the mother and child, the husband should renounce his usual privileges at such times.

Most women do not have their periodical illness, and consequently are not liable to a second pregnancy, before seven months have elapsed after childbirth. There are however, numerous exceptions to this rule, and it is impossible to foretell who will and who will not be the exception.

Moreover, as any excitement of the passions alters, to some extent, the secretion of the breasts, often to the injury of the child, it is every way desirable that great temperance be exercised in all cases in the marital relations at these epochs.

SIGNS OF OVER-NURSING.

The symptoms of over-nursing may be enumerated as follows: Aching pain in the back; often pain across the shoulders, and on the top of the head or forehead; marked paleness of the face; inability to sleep; frightful dreams when sleep does come; great debility; extreme depression of spirits; disorders of the sight, and mental disturbances, which take on the form of melancholy, the delusions relating mostly to subjects of a religious character, to the effect that the unpardonable sin has been committed and the like. The headache is situated on the top of the head, and this spot may be noticed to be perceptibly hotter to the touch than other parts of the head. These symptoms indicate that the process of nursing is making too great a drain upon the system.

A woman in ordinary health will generally be able to suckle her child for twelve months without experiencing any bad effects. When the child is kept at the breast much beyond this time, most mothers render themselves liable to the injurious consequences we have mentioned. Some, indeed, cannot furnish the child all the nourishment it needs longer than three or four months without

detriment to themselves. In such cases, by feeding the child two or three times a day the mother may be relieved of the burden of its entire support, and may thus be enabled to continue nursing. The proper food for infants, under these circumstances, will be shortly mentioned. The prostrating effects of nursing upon the body and mind of the mother are in some, though comparatively rare, instances so marked as to render it altogether improper from the commencement.

The treatment of the condition of the system described as resulting from over-nursing is, if it cannot be remedied by partially feeding the infant and the use of tonics, to remove the child from the breast altogether, and either procure a wet nurse for it or wean it. The wet nurse is greatly to be preferred, and the preference is the stronger the younger the child. We have already alluded to the great difficulty of rearing children from birth by the hand. But after the infant has attained the age of several months, the danger of artificial feeding is much lessened, provided that the weaning does not take place during the hot weather. This brings us to the consideration of the regimen for the mother who cannot nurse her own child, of the rules of the selection of a wet nurse, of the directions for bringing up by hand, and of the proper method of weaning. These subjects we will now take up in the order mentioned.

DIRECTIONS FOR MOTHERS WHO CANNOT NURSE THEIR OWN CHILDREN.

There are many reasons why a mother should, if possible, nurse her own child. "One of the principal is," says the distinguished Dr. Tilt, of London, "that as nursing, generally speaking, prevents conception up to the tenth month, so it prevents the ruin of the mother's constitution by the too rapid bringing forth of children, and, we might even add, prevents a deterioration of the race, by the imperfect bringing up of this too-fast-got family." The same author appropriately adds: "But while advocating maternal nursing, we must not forget that woman is not the Eve of a primeval world; that human nature, wherever it is now met, in barbarous tribes or in civilized communities, is frequently so deteriorated, so diseased or prone to disease, that, by nursing, a mother may sometimes undermine her own frail constitution for the sake of giving an imperfect sustenance, and perhaps a poisonous heritage, to her babe."

Some mothers cannot nurse, however anxiously they may wish to do so. They are shut out from this charming and tender experience in the life of a woman. The milk that comes is not sufficient, and quickly disappears. Because of the influence of the mind of the mother over the child at her breast, to which we have before called attention, women who are very hysterical and nervous, subject to violent perturbations of the mind, should not, particularly if there be any family tendency to insanity, expose the child to the mischievous effects latent in their milk. So, also, the presence of certain diseases forbids wet-nursing. Thus it is ordinarily prohibited by consumption, scrofula, skin affections of long standing, and cancer. In consumption, all efforts to suckle are frequently equally fatal to the mother and child. Even a strong hereditary predisposition to this disease may render it advisable, in the opinion of the medical attendant—who should always be consulted in such a case,—to counteract the family taint by giving the milk of the healthiest nurse that can be procured. The condition of the nipples and of the breast may not permit of nursing. We have pointed out how best to guard against such an occurrence in treating of the care of the nipples during pregnancy.

She who is to be debarred from nursing her own child should take care that it is not allowed to approach her breasts, as sometimes the mental and physical excitement caused by such an approach is of an injurious and lasting character.

Ordinarily, if this direction be followed out, the mother will have little trouble in regard to herself. Under such circumstances the chief danger is to the child. Hence the importance of knowing

HOW TO SELECT A WET-NURSE.

The choosing of a wet-nurse is a matter of great moment and responsibility. She should not be over thirty years of age, and should, if possible, be one who has previously suckled and had charge of children. Her own infant should be under the age of six months, for when above that age the milk sometimes disagrees with her new-born charge. One who has had several children should be preferred, because her milk is richer than after the first confinement.

The doctor should always examine carefully into the condition of the nurse's health, and into the quality and quantity of the milk. Various diseases and taints of the system are so hidden, while yet communicable to the child, that the knowledge and skill of a professional expert are required for their detection and the protection of the nursling. In testing the quality of the milk, the experienced physician allows a little to rest on his finger nail, and by its examination readily decides as to its richness and fitness to nourish the little applicant for food. It is not necessary that the breasts should be large, as those of moderate size often furnish a sufficient amount of milk. But it is important that the nipples should be well developed. Those wet-nurses should be preferred in whom large blood-vessels are seen prominently passing in blue lines over the surface of the breasts. The possession of a vigorous, healthful infant is a good recommendation for a nurse, but care should be taken to ascertain that it is her *own*, as nurses have been known to borrow for such an occasion, and so obtain credit not justly their due.

The moral and mental as well as physical characteristics should be considered. Temperance and cleanliness are indispensable in a wet nurse, and the want of either should be an imperative reason for rejection. Equanimity of temper, cheerfulness, and an open, frank, affectionate disposition are, of course, greatly to be desired.

If the nurse becomes "unwell," shall the child be taken from her? Should the monthly sickness reappear early, and both nurse and child be in good health, suckling may be continued. But when the return happens about the ninth or tenth month, the child should be weaned or the nurse changed. There is no physiological reason for preventing the nurse from living matrimonially, but if pregnancy occurs, the child should be taken from her.

The same rules that we have laid down for the mother for the care of her health while nursing, are of course applicable to the hired wet nurse, and should be insisted on and enforced.

Changing a Nurse.—When it becomes necessary to change a nurse, for any of the reasons above mentioned, it may be done without injury to the child. For fear of the effect of the unwelcome tidings upon the mind of the nurse, and the possible influence upon the milk, she should not be informed of the projected change until a successor has been secured to take her place at once. In choosing the second nurse, the same precautions should be had as in the selection of the first.

BRINGING UP BY HAND.

We have already alluded to the great danger to the child, particularly in a city, that is artificially fed from birth. But as there are many mothers who are unable, on account of the expense, to have a wet nurse for the child they cannot suckle themselves, we will give such directions in regard to the diet as are best calculated to lessen the risk invariably incurred under such circumstances.

The child's food should be of the best quality, and prepared with the most scrupulous attention to cleanliness. The milk of the cow is preferable to that of the ass or of the goat, the former of which it is difficult to procure, and the latter having a disagreeable odour. For a child under three months of age, cows' milk should be used as the only food. It should be fresh, and if possible from one cow. When of the ordinary richness, it is to be diluted with an equal quantity of water or thin barley-water. If, however, the first milking can be obtained, which is more watery, and bears a closer resemblance in its chemical composition to human milk, but little dilution will be required. If green and acrid stools make their appearance, accompanied by emaciation and vomiting, the milk must be more diluted and given less frequently. If the symptoms of indigestion do not yield, milk containing an excess of cream should be used. To procure it, allow fresh milk to stand for two or three hours, and remove the upper third, to which add two or three parts of warm water or barley-water, after having dissolved in it a little sugar of milk. Should this food also disagree, any of the preparations we are about to mention may be prepared and tried.

Professor Falkland recommends the following method of preparing milk for infants, as affording a product more nearly like the natural secretion:—" One-third of a pint of pure milk is allowed to stand until the cream has risen. The latter is removed, and to the blue milk thus obtained, about a square inch of rennet is to be added, and the milk-vessel placed in warm water. In about five minutes the curd will have separated, and the rennet, which may again be repeatedly used, being removed, the whey is carefully poured off and immediately heated to boiling, to prevent

.t becoming sour. A further quantity of curd separates, and must be removed by straining through calico. In one quarter of a pint of this hot whey three-eighths of an ounce of milk sugar are to be dissolved; and this solution, along with the cream removed from the one third of a pint of milk, must be added to half a pint of new milk. This will constitute the food for an infant from five to eight months old for twelve hours; or more correctly speaking, it will be one-half of the quantity required for twenty-four hours. It is absolutely necessary that a fresh quantity should be prepared every twelve hours; and it is scarcely necessary to add that the strictest cleanliness in all the vessels is indispensable.

Dr. J. Forsyth Meigs directs the following article of diet, as one which he has found to agree better with the digestive system of the infant than any other kind of food:—"A scruple of gelatine (or a piece two inches square of the flat cake in which it is sold) is soaked for a short time in cold water, and then boiled in half a pint of water, until it dissolves—about ten or fifteen minutes. To this is added, with constant stirring, and just at the termination of the boiling, the milk and arrowroot, the latter being previously mixed into a paste with a little cold water. After the addition of the milk and the arrowroot, and just before the removal from the fire, the cream is poured in, and a moderate quantity of loaf sugar added. The proportions of milk, cream, and arrowroot must depend on the age and digestive powers of the child. For a healthy infant, within the month, I usually direct three or four ounces of milk, half an ounce to an ounce of cream, and a tea-spoonful of arrowroot to half a pint of water. For older children the quantity of milk and cream should be gradually increased to a half or two-thirds milk and from one to two ounces of cream. I seldom increase the quantity of gelatine or arrowroot."

The egg is a valuable article of food for infants and young children, especially in conditions of debility. It should be given nearly raw, and is best prepared by placing it in boiling water for two minutes. It is then easily digested.

Beef-tea prepared in the manner described already, is highly nutritious and useful as a food for infants; if it produces a laxative effect it should be discontinued. When the child shows signs of weakness or of a scrofulous condition, its condition will be improved by mingling with its food a small piece of butter or mutton suet.

During the first four or five months, the food should be thin, and taken through a teat, thus preventing the stuffing of the infant.

On attaining the age of twelve or fifteen months, infants are usually able to digest ordinary wholesome solid food, neatly and well cooked, when mashed or cut into fine pieces.

An article of food employed for the diarrhœa of infants is prepared as follows:—"A pound of dry wheat flour, of the best quality, is packed snugly in a bag and boiled three or four hours. When it is taken from the bag it is hard, resembling a piece of chalk, with the exception of the exterior, which is wet and should be removed. The flour grated from the mass should be used the same as arrow-root or rice."

Infants nourished by prepared food thrive well enough during cool weather; but during the warm months of the year they are exceedingly liable to bowel complaint, of which it is said one-half of the spoon-fed infants of New York City die each summer season. Hence the importance of taking them into the country, and keeping them there until the return of cool weather lessens the danger of city life.

WEANING.

This should take place when the child is about twelve months of age—sometimes a few months earlier, oftener a few later. If the mother's health be good, and her milk abundant, it may be deferred until the canine teeth appear between the fifteenth and twentieth month. The child will then have sixteen teeth, with which it can properly masticate soft, solid food.

Time of the year for.—The infant should not be taken from the breast during or immediately preceding warm weather. If the mother, either on account of sickness or failure in her breast-milk, is obliged during the summer to give up nursing, she should at once procure a wet nurse. If she cannot, the child must be sent into the country. To wean an infant in the city in hot weather is to expose it to almost certain death.

Proper Method.—The process of weaning should be a very slow one. No definite day should be fixed for it. Little by little, from week to week, the amount of spoon-food should be increased and the nursing lessened—being first given up at night. The breast should never be suddenly denied to a child unaccustomed to artificial food, but be displaced by degrees by the bottle and the spoon. This gradual change will neither fret the child nor annoy the mother, as sudden weaning always does.

The infant may begin to get accustomed to artificial food at the age of four months. At first only dilute cows' milk should be given it occasionally between the times of nursing. In a tumbler one-third full of water dissolve a tea-spoonful of sugar of milk; add to the sweetened water an equal quantity of fresh cows' milk; then, if the child's stools are at all green, mix this with two tea-spoonfuls of lime water. Instead of pure water, barley-water, made in the usual way, and boiled to the consistency of milk, may be employed in this preparation, being added while still warm, to an equal amount of milk. Or, toast water may be substituted as a diluter of the milk. Cows' milk should not be boiled if it can be preserved in any other way. As the infant advances in months, some solid food may be allowed. After six months, pap, made with stale bread and crackers, is proper, once or twice a day. Beef-tea, made according to the recipe we have given, and chicken, lamb, or mutton broth, may now also be occasionally taken. As the quantity of milk diminishes towards the close of the first year, the spoon-food should be resorted to more frequently to supply the want. Solid food ought not to be given before the child is a year old.

The breasts usually cause little trouble when the weaning is performed in the gradual manner which has been recommended. The mother should during this time drink as little as possible, refrain from stimulating food, and take occasionally a little cream of tartar, citrate of magnesia, or a seidlitz powder. If the breasts continue to fill with milk, *they should not be drawn.* The "drying up of the milk" may be facilitated by gently rubbing the breasts several times a day with a camphorated oil, made by dissolving over a fire, in a saucer of sweet oil, as much camphor as it will take up. Tea made from the marsh mallow has also been recommended for this purpose.

THE CARE OF INFANCY.

By infancy we mean that portion of the life of the child between birth and the completion of teething, about two and a half years. The care of this period of human life is entrusted to the mother. It forms an important era in the physical life of woman. Its discussion is therefore germane to our subject. In order that the young mother may fully appreciate the responsibilities of her position, she should know something of the liability of infants to sickness and death.

Out of one thousand children born, one hundred and fifty die within the first year, and one hundred and thirteen during the next four years. Thus two hundred and sixty-three, or *more than one-fourth die within five years after birth.* Between the ages of five and ten thirty-five die. During the next five years, eighteen more are recorded on the death list. Hence, at fifteen years of age only six hundred and eighty-five remain out of the one thousand born. When these figures are considered, and the additional fact that, out of those who survive, very many bear permanent marks of imperfect nourishment, or of actual disease, the consequence of maladies contracted in early life, the importance of our present inquiry, the care of infancy, will be apparent to all mothers.

The younger the infant the greater the danger of death. *One-tenth of all children born, die within the first month after birth,* and four times as many as during the second month.

The mortality is much larger in cities than in the country. In Dublin, during 1867, very nearly one-third of all the persons who died were under five years of age. In the same year, forty-three per cent. of those who died in the eight principal towns of Scotland were children below the age of five. In Philadelphia, during the same year, forty-five per cent. of all the deaths were of children under five years of age. In New York City fifty-three per cent. of the total number of deaths occur under the age of five years, and twenty-six per cent. under the age of one year.

The danger of death lessens as the period of puberty approaches. Yet, even in the last years of childhood, there is greater liability of disease and a larger proportionate loss of life than during youth or middle age.

What are the causes of this startling mortality of infant life? Why does one child out of ten die in the first month, and only three out of four live to be five years old? And what are the means of prevention?

Some of the causes which are active in producing this mortality among the little ones cannot be successfully opposed after birth. Such for instance, are imperfect and vicious developments of internal organs, existing when born. These malformations often result from inflammation while in the womb, excited by some taint of the mother's blood, or by some agitation of her nervous system. Means of prevention in those cases are therefore to be directed to the mother, in the manner indicated in treating of pregnancy. But other causes of death begin to act only after birth, and are to a greater or less extent avoidable. These are largely traceable to ignorance, negligence, and vice.

One cause of death to which infants are peculiarly liable, and which alone is said to have destroyed forty thousand children in England between the years 1686 and 1799, is being *overlain* by the parents. For this reason, some physicians caution the mother against having the infant in bed with her while she sleeps.

The frightful waste of life caused by bringing children up by hand has been mentioned, and the importance of avoiding it when possible.

The natural feebleness of the system of infants is the reason why they succumb so easily to any malady. Deaths from any given disease are more numerous among infants than children, and among children than adults. Hence the importance of timely corrective measures in infantile affections; hence, also, the need that mothers should know and practice the means best adapted to preserve the health of their frail charges.

These means we shall proceed to give in detail, commencing with

THE CLOTHING OF INFANTS AND YOUNG CHILDREN.

A fertile cause of disease and death is to be found in the negligence or ignorance displayed in regard to the dress of children. And it is not the poorly attired, but in many cases the fashionably robed child which suffers the most. To parental vanity can be traced the catarrh on the chest or the inflammation of the bowels which has resulted in death. Most mothers appear to be ignorant of the fact that children are exceedingly susceptible to the influence or cold. The returns of the Registrar-General of England show that a very cold week always greatly increases the mortality of the very young. While adults carefully protect themselves against every change of weather, and against currents of air, children, who most need such protection, are too often neglected.

The warmth of the infant's body is best secured by that of the nurse and by warm clothing. It is more effectually and healthfully provided for in this manner than by confining the child to a warm atmosphere. Young children should never be dressed décolleté—in low necks and short sleeves. That fashion is a dangerous one which leaves the neck, shoulders, and arms uncovered. To this irrational custom may be traced a vast amount of the suffering, and many of the deaths of early life; doubtless, also, in many cases it lays the foundation of consumption, which manifests itself a little later. But, it is said, the child will be "hardened" by having its chest and limbs thus exposed. The surest and safest way to harden a child is to so care for it that it shall pass through its first months and years of life without any ailment. Every mother should see to it that her charge is so clothed that every part of the body is effectually protected from dampness and cold. She can then best secure for it a hardened constitution by carrying it daily into the sunlight of the open air.

The material of the clothing should be such as will unite lightness with warmth. Flannel and calico are therefore to be preferred. At first, as the skin of the child is very delicate, a shirt of fine linen may be interposed between it and the flannel. But after the first few months, the gentle friction of soft flannel next the skin is desirable, as it stimulates the circulation of the blood on the surface of the body and promotes health. Flannel underclothing should be continued all the year; and during the summer months, a very light texture being used. When the dress of the child is shortened, care must be taken that the feet are well covered with soft stockings of

cotton or woollen (which in winte
above the knees), and with light leat

The *night-dress*, at least during co
made of flannel, thin or thick, accor
It has been recommended that after tl
advanced the night-clothes be constr
night-pants, so that it may not be
clothing be thrown off. Every articl
ing the day ought to be removed at n

The rule, in regard to the *quantity*
should be in sufficient amount to pi
It must therefore be regulated by th
and the state of the weather. We
fatal practice of leaving bare at all sea
upper part of the chest and arms of
the rest of the body is warmly clad
speak too emphatically nor too ofte
which the mother thus exposes that
duty to wisely and safely conduct tl
dependent infancy and childhood. It
for the child to be too closely envel
thus rendered highly susceptible to
cold. The prevalent error, however,
is in the direction of too scanty clothi

The make of the dress should be l
to permit of the free movement of all p
it should be cut high in the neck, an
wrists; its construction should be sir
be quickly put off and on; and the f
should be tapes, not pins.

BATHING.

Many advantages attach to the dail
infants. It secures cleanliness. It
vous system. It preserves from colds

We have already endeavoured to

mind of the reader the great susceptibility to cold which exists in early life. On this account the water for the bath should be warm (96° or 98°) for the first few weeks of infancy, especially during the winter season. Gradually the temperature may be reduced to that of the apartment, never to actual coldness. It is as foolish and hazardous to attempt to "harden" infants by plunging them into cold water, as it is by carrying them with uncovered necks, chests, and limbs, into the keen and damp air. Knowledge of these facts would bring safety to many children who now suffer because of the dangerous ignorance of mothers in regard to the susceptibility of the infant organization.

An infant should be immersed in its tub every morning. Besides the regular morning bath, it is often advisable to put the child for a few minutes in tepid water in the evening. This will quiet the nervous system and induce sleep. The bath should not be too long a one, for fear of exciting perspiration; nor, for the same reason, should the water be too warm. If the child be of a delicate constitution, the evening bath will be especially useful, and can be made more so by the addition of two tablespoonfuls of salt to the water necessary for the bath.

The time immediately after the nursing or feeding is not proper for bathing. An hour or two after a meal should be allowed to elapse. Neither should a bath ever be given in a cold room. Even in a warm atmospere, care should be taken, both after and during the ablution, that the wet skin of the infant be not exposed to the air. Its body should be completely immersed; it should not be held up out of the water, nor, if it be old enough, allowed to stand or sit in the tub. It is well also to have a warm blanket in which to receive the child as it comes dripping from the bath. It should be wrapped up in this for a few minutes to absorb a part of the moisture. Then a portion of the body should be uncovered at a time, and dried before exposing the rest.

Drying the skin.—For this purpose a piece of soft flannel will be found servicable. By gently rubbing the surface of the body with it the skin will be warmed and stimulated, and the resulting glow will be as agreeable to the child as is that in the adult which follows the Turkish bath. The actual grooming of the human body is very useful to improve the health of scrofulous children.

At first from three to five minutes will be a sufficiently long immersion. In a little while, however, this period may be lengthened, all the precautions mentioned against injurious exposure being observed.

The lukewarm daily bath, taken either in the morning or evening, ought to be continued until at least the age of four years. If, after the fourth or fifth year, ablutions of the entire body be resorted to only every second or third day, the practice should be commenced of sponging the chest every morning with cold, or alternately with cold and hot water, followed by brisk frictions.

Soap is to be used but sparingly in the bath of young children. It must be of the blandest and purest quality. Various eruptions are caused by the employment of impure soaps, and even by the excessive application of the best kind. In illustration of the importance of our present subject, we may state that Dr. Hufeland, to whose admirable work on the art of prolonging life we have before alluded, lays down, as one of the means which lengthen life, the care of the skin. , He dwells upon the benefit of paying such attention to it from infancy that it may be kept in a lively, active, and useful condition.

The power of the bath to ward off disease in childhood is not appreciated by parents. Properly managed, it soothes but never increases any internal irritation which may exist, and often does away with the necessity of resorting to the administration of drugs. If due attention were paid to the condition of the skin in early life, many of the most common ailments of childhood would be averted. The daily employment of the bath, and scrupulous attention to cleanliness of the person and clothing would materially lessen the demand both for purgative medicines and for soothing syrups.

One word more in regard to the washing of the infant. The mother herself, if she be in health, should always perform this office, and not entrust it to the child's nurse. Plutarch awards high praise to Cato, the censor, for his invariable custom of being present when his child was washed. Every mother, at least, would do well to follow the example of this old Roman. It will give her the opportunity to detect many incipient affections which would for a long while escape her attention if she saw the child only when dressed. The mother will also take pains to engage the mind of the little one, and render the bath a source of amusement to it.

After the fourth or fifth year, two or three baths a week during the colder seasons of the year will be sufficient to keep the skin clean and properly active. During the summer, however, a daily bath is of great advantage to children, and ought not to be neglected.

Swimming is very useful and very invigorating to the health of both sexes. It is desirable that children be taught this art.

The importance of the *culture of the skin* to the well-being of infancy and childhood cannot be brought too prominently to the notice of all mothers. We have, therefore, endeavoured to give some useful hints in regard both to the preservation of its cleanliness and to the prevention, by means of garments and warming, of its exposure to too great changes of temperature.

By proper attention to the skin, in the manner pointed out, many of the eruptions with which children are afflicted might be prevented. The appearance of these the mother ought to regard as a great calamity, for they are often difficult of cure and render the child an object of disgust. She ought also to look upon them as the mischievous consequences of the neglect of those laws of health which it is her duty to learn and observe.

THE FOOD OF INFANTS AND CHILDREN.

The diet of children is frequently improper either in regard to quantity, quality, or variety. In 1867, a committee, of which, Professor Austin Flint, Jr., was chairman, was appointed in New York City to revise the "Dietary Table of the Children's Nurseries on Randall's Island." In the record rendered, attention was forcibly called to the fact that in childhood "the demands of the system for nourishment are in excess of the waste, the extra quantity being required for growth and development. If the proper quantity and variety of food be not provided, full development cannot take place, and the children grow up, if they survive, into young men and women, incapable of the ordinary amount of labour, and liable to diseases of various kinds. This is frequently illustrated in the higher walks of life, particularly in females, for many suffer through life from improper diet in boarding schools, due to false and artificial notions of delicacy or refinement. After a certain period of improper and deficient diet in children, the appetite becomes permanently impaired, and the system is rendered incapable of appropriating the amount of matter necessary to proper development and growth."

Charlotte Bronte has drawn, in "Jane Eyre," a graphic and physiologically true picture of the effects upon young girls of long-continued insufficiency of food. Let mothers bear in mind that proper food cannot be too abundantly eaten by children, and that the greatest danger to which they are exposed arises from defective nutrition. We would again urge the value of a large amount of milk in the dietary of young people. The disorders of the bowels which are not uncommon in infancy and childhood, are due to errors in diet by which improper food is supplied and not to an excess of simple and proper nourishment.

We have already given some directions for the preparation of infants' food in treating of "bringing up by hand." In addition to the various substitutes for the mo-other's milk there mentioned we wish to note that known as *Liebig's soup*. This great chemist thus describes the method of making it.

"Half an ounce of wheat flour, half an ounce of malt-meal, and seven and a half grains of bicarbonate of potassa, are weighed off. They are first mixed by themselves, then with the addition of one ounce of water, and lastly of five ounces of milk. The mixture is then heated upon a slow fire, being constantly stirred until it begins to get thick. At this period, the vessel is removed from the fire and the mixture is stirred for five minutes, is again heated and again removed, when it gets thick, and lastly, it is heated till it boils. The soup is purified from bran by passing it through a fine sieve (a piece of fine linen) and now it is ready for use."

Barley-malt can be obtained at any brewery. First, it is separated from the impurities, and then ground in an ordinary coffee-mill to a coarse meal. Care should be taken to get the common fresh wheat flour, not the finest, because the former is richest in starch.

In practice, the troublesome weighing of the materials may be dispensed with, as a heaped tablespoonful of wheat flour weighs pretty nearly half an ounce, and a like tablespoonful of malt-meal not quite as heaped, weighs also half an ounce. The bicarbonate of potassa can be obtained from the druggist, put up in powders of seven and a half grains each, ready for use. The amount of water and of milk prescribed can be attained with sufficient accuracy by means of the tablespoon; two tablespoonfuls will give the quantity of water (one ounce), and ten tablespoonfuls the quantity of milk (five ounces). These directions will enable any mother to make the preparation without difficulty. The soup tastes tolerably sweet, and, when diluted with water, may be given to very young infants.

Although the method of preparing Liebig's soup is a

somewhat tedious one, yet as it is a combination so highly recommended by physicians of the largest experience for having visibly saved the life of many wasting children, it deserves a trial in all cases in which the ordinary kinds of food disagree.

Elsewhere are recorded the directions given by Dr. J. Forsyth Meigs, for an article of diet, consisting of gelatine and arrowroot, which he prefers to all other kinds of artificial infant food. Another method of preparing a useful arrowroot mixture is as follows:—

Place a teaspoonful of arrowroot into a porcelain vessel with as much cold water as will make it into a fine dough. Then add a cupful of boiling milk or of beef tea, stir the mixture a little and allow it to boil for a few minutes until the whole acquires the consistency of a fine light jelly.

The manner in which nutriment is administered to infants is not immaterial. The custom of feeding them from a small spoon or from a cup with a snout is objectionable. The use of a sucking-bottle most nearly imitates the way in which nature designed the nursling to obtain its nourishment. By the act of sucking, the muscles of the face are exercised in an equal manner, and the saliva is mixed with the food to an extent which is not possible if any other mode of feeding be resorted to. The bottle may be provided with mouth pieces of gold, silver, tin, ivory, bone, a prepared cow's teat, a piece of washed chamois leather, or a few folds of fine soft linen. Children drink very readily out of the perforated rubber nipples, which are now so popular for this purpose. They are made to fit over the mouth of any bottle, and are especially to be recommended on account of their cleanliness. The bottle should never be refilled until both it and the rubber cap have been thoroughly cleansed in hot water. A white glass bottle only should be employed, in order that any want of cleanliness may readily be detected. It should be recollected that milk very quickly sours when kept in this way in a warm room; it is therefore better always to empty the bottle and fill it afresh each time it is given to the child, rather than wait until its contents are exhausted before replenishing it.

We have hitherto been treating mainly of the diet proper for the first year of life. In the second year children may be permitted to have soft, finely-cut meat. Fresh ripe fruit in season ordinarily agrees excellently well. But boiled green vegetables and husk fruits are very apt to cause indigestion and diarrhœa. Fruit for the children should be freed from the seeds and skins, which are indigestible and often do harm.

As an example of a diet suitable for a child two years of age, we append the following:—In the mornings, between six and seven o'clock in the summer, or between seven and eight in winter, milk gruel; between nine and ten o'clock, a piece of wheat bread with a little butter on it. At twelve o'clock, well prepared beef-tea, or chicken, lamb, mutton, or oyster broth, or meat with a little gravy, or in place of the meat a meal broth prepared with eggs but with very little fat; green vegetables to be allowed very rarely, and in very small quantities. At this noon meal, a mealy, well-mashed potatoe is unobjectionable; so, also, is rice pudding, for a change. In the afternoon between three and four, bread and milk, with the addition in summer of fresh ripe fruit. In the evening, at seven, bread and milk.

It will be observed that this dietetic table calls for five meals a day. Should the child eat so frequently? We answer, yes. But the meals should be at regular intervals. A child, in order to replace the waste of the system and to furnish over and above sufficient material to build up the growing body, requires a much larger proportionate amount of food than an adult. It also requires its food at shorter intervals. By observing the hours for meals stated above, *regularity*, which is of so much importance to the health of the digestive organs, will be secured. If a young child be allowed only the three ordinary meals for the family, it will crave for something between times and too often have its cravings met with a piece of cake or other improper food. Its appetite for dinner or supper will in this manner be destroyed, and the stomach and the general health suffer.

After the third or fourth year children are able to eat all kinds of vegetables. They may then very appropriately be allowed to eat at the table with the family. It is only necessary to refuse them very salt, sour, and highly spiced victuals. Of all others they may partake in moderation. Neither wine nor any malt liquor should be given them. Tea and coffee are also unnecessary. They should have a regular luncheon between the meals which are farthest apart. This must be at a regular hour, and consist of bread and butter with milk or water.

Pains should be taken to see that children do not fall into the habit of eating too rapidly. Too often this pernicious habit, so destructive to healthy digestion, is formed in early life, and becomes the source of that dyspepsia which is the bane of so many lives. Food that is gulped down enters the stomach unmasticated and unmixed with the secretions of the mouth. A dog may bolt his food without injury, but a human being cannot.

A child should be taught to eat everything that is wholesome, and not permitted to become finical or fastidious in his appetite. It ought not, however, to be forced to eat any particular article for which it is found that there is an invincible dislike. Variety of diet is good for a child, after the second or third year.

The position of the child when fed.—An infant, no matter how young, should not receive its meals when lying. Its head should always be raised in the nurse's arm, if it be too young to support itself. The practice of *jolting* and *dandling* the infant after eating is a wrong one. Rest of the body should be secured by placing the child on a bed or holding it on the mother's knee for a half hour or so. Observe the inclination which all animals show for repose and sleep after a full repast, and respect the same inclination in the infant.

In our remarks upon bathing we pointed out the importance of the mother herself performing for her child this office. So again in connection with children's food, we must notice the necessity of the mother being always present at their meals, in order that they may be taught to take them quietly, with cleanliness and without hurry. Such advice is not needed by the poor, nor by women of moderate fortune, who, ordinarily, constantly have their children under their eyes. But affluence brings with it many occupations which are frequently deemed of more moment than presiding over a child's dinner.

CONCERNING SLEEP IN EARLY LIFE.

There is a natural desire for much sleep during infancy, childhood, and youth, and there is reason for its free indulgence. Infants pass the greater portion of both day and night in sleep. Children up to the age of six years require, as a rule, twelve hours of repose at night, besides an hour or more in the middle of the day. About the sixth year the noon nap may be discontinued, but the night sleep ought not to be abridged before the tenth year, and then only to a moderate extent until the age of puberty. From this time the period of slumber may be gradually reduced to nine or ten hours. No further diminution should be attempted until the completion of growth, when another hour or two may be taken away, leaving about eight hours of daily sleep as the proper amount during middle life.

It is wrong, therefore, to wake a child in the morning. It should be allowed to sleep as long as it will, which will be until the wants of the system are satisfied, if it be not aroused by noise or light.

When after a few months the infant is awake a considerable portion of the day, it should be brought into the habit of taking its second sleep near the middle of the day, say from eleven to one o'clock, and again from half an hour to an hour about three o'clock. It should not be permitted a nap later than this in the afternoon, as it would be very apt to cause a disturbed night. Although some physicians recommend that the sleep during the day be discontinued after the infant has attained the age of fifteen months, the wisdom of such advice may well be doubted. As soon as the child begins to walk, not only are its movements very constant and active, but its mind is busily employed and its nervous system excited. It therefore thrives better if its day be divided into two by sleep for an hour or two.

Should the infant sleep alone? We have mentioned the danger of being overlain, to which it is exposed when in bed with its mother or nurse. On the other hand, it must be remembered that an infant keeps warm with difficulty, even when well covered, and that contact with the mother's body is the best way of securing its own warmth. Hence, during the first months, the child had better be allowed to sleep with its mother. How, then, can the risk of being suffocated, which is no imaginary one, be lessened? The following rules are those given by an English physician of reputation to prevent an infant from being accidentally overlain:

"Let the baby while asleep have plenty of room in the bed. Do not allow him to be too near; or, if this be unavoidable from the small size of the bed, let his face be turned to the opposite side. Let him lie fairly either on his side or on his back. Be careful to ascertain that his mouth be not covered with the bedclothes. Do not smother his face with the clothes, as a plentiful supply of pure air is as necessary as when he is awake. Never let him lie low in the bed. Let there be *no* pillow near the one his head is resting on, lest he roll to it and bury his head in it. Remember a young child has neither the strength nor the sense to get out of danger; and, if he unfortunately either turn on his face or bury his head in a pillow that is near, the chances are that he will be suffocated, more especially as these accidents usually occur at night, when the mother or the nurse is fast asleep. Never entrust him at night to a young, giddy, and thoughtless servant. A foolish mother sometimes goes to sleep while allowing her child to continue sucking. The unconscious babe, after a time, loses the nipple and buries his head in the bedclothes. She awakes in the morning, finding to her horror a corpse by her side! A mother ought, therefore, never to go to sleep until her child has ceased sucking.

"When a couple of months have elapsed, the child, if a healthy one, may sleep alone. What the child sleeps in is not a matter of great moment, provided it has a sufficiency of clothing and not be exposed to currents of air. A large clothes basket will serve all the purposes of a crib. The mistake is often made of burying the child under too heavy a mass of bedclothes in a warm room when asleep. And this inconsistency is committed by the very mothers who scantily clad the child during the day in order to inure it to the cold. The great transition from its wrappings by night to those by day is injurious to the health and comfort of the infant.

"In arranging night coverings, the soft feather-bed is very often estimated as nothing; or, in other words, the same provision of blankets is considered indispensable, whether we lie upon a hard mattress or immersed in down. The mother, looking only to the covering laid over the child, forgets those on which it lies, although, in reality, the latter may be the warmer of the two. An infant deposited in a downy bed has at least two-thirds of its body in contact with the feathers, and may thus be perspiring at every pore, when, from its having only a single covering thrown over it, the mother may imagine it to be enjoying the restorative influence of agreeable slumber. In hot weather, much mischief might be done by an oversight of this kind."

It is of course essential to the health and comfort of the infant, that its bed and bedclothing be kept perfectly dry and sweet. They should frequently be taken out and exposed to the air.

A child should be accustomed early to sleep in a darkened room. Plutarch praises the women of Sparta, for, among other things, teaching their children not to be afraid in the dark. He says "they were so careful and expert that without swaddling-bands, their children were all straight and well-proportioned; and they brought them up not to be afraid in the dark, or of being alone, and never indulged them in crying, fretfulness, and ill-humour; upon which account Spartan nurses were often bought by people of other countries."

Position in sleeping.—It has long been a popular opinion that the position of our bodies at night, with reference to the cardinal points of the compass, has some influence on the health. This belief has recently been corroborated by some observations made by a prominent physician Henry Kennedy, A.B., M.B. In an essay on the "Acute Affections of Children," published in the *Dublin Quarterly Journal of Medical Science*, he states that for several years he has put in force in his practice a plan of treatment by means of the position of the patient, and often with very marked results. He asserts that in order to insure the soundest sleep the head should lie to the north. Strange as this idea may at first sight appear, it has more in it than might be supposed. There are known to be great electrical currents always coursing in one direction around the globe. In the mind of Dr. K. there is no doubt that our nervous systems are in some mysterious way connected with this universal agent, as it may be called, electricity. He relates several cases of acute diseases in children in which, by altering the position of the body so that the patient should lie from north to south, instead of from east to west, quiet sleep was induced. This plan of invoking sleep is often successful, but not always so, for all are not equally susceptible. It applies likewise to adults. It is not so striking in its effects on the poorer as on the richer classes of society. This is what might be expected, for it cannot be doubted that the nervous system in the middle and upper ranks is always in a much more sensitive state than with their poorer brethren. It is worth noting that even in healthy persons sleep will often be absent or of a broken kind from the cause of which we are now speaking. It is very common to hear people saying they can never sleep in a strange bed. Although many causes may conspire to this, Dr. Kennedy cannot doubt that amongst these ought to be placed the one to which we are now drawing attention.

VACCINATION.

This operation, to which every infant should be subjected, is one of the greatest practical importance. The attempt has been made of late to shake the public faith in its efficacy, and to revive the old fabulous stories and foolish notions as to the production of serious affections of the blood and skin in this manner. At the same time the increasing frequency and virulence of small-pox in this country are becoming only too evident. We therefore consider it our duty, in treating of the maternal management of infancy, to lay some stress upon the necessity for vaccination as a preservation of life and health. If observation and experience ever taught anything, they have taught the protective power of this operation against the most loathsome and one of the most fatal diseases that ever afflicted the human race. And that mother who is careless and indifferent in this matter, neglects for her children a means of preventing disfigurement and saving life, compared with which all other means are scarcely worthy of mention.

In order to appreciate the value of vaccination it is only necessary to consider what small-pox was before its discovery—to look at that disease through the eyes of our fathers and grandfathers. Until the close of the last century it was the most terrible of all the ministers of death. It filled the churchyards with corpses. When Jenner published his great discovery, about seventy years ago, the annual death-rate from small-pox in England was estimated at three thousand in the million of population. In other countries of Europe the rate reached as high as four thousand in the million. And these fatal cases must be multiplied by five or six to give the entire number of persons annually attacked by the disease. It spared neither high nor low. Macaulay informs us that Mary, the wife of William III., fell a victim to it. Those in whom the disease did not prove fatal, carried about with them the hideous traces of its malignity, for it "turned the babe into a changeling at which the mother shuddered and made the eyes and cheeks of the betrothed maiden objects of horror to the lover." Few escaped being attacked by this fell disease. Nearly one-tenth of all the persons who died in London during the last century, died of this one cause. Children were peculiarly its victims. In some of the great cities of England more than one-third of all the deaths among children under ten years of age arose from small-pox. Two-thirds of all the applicants for relief at the Hospital for the Indigent Blind had lost their sight by small-pox. The number of hopelessly deafened ears, crippled joints and broken down constitutions from the same cause cannot be accurately computed, but was certainly very large. *Vaccination is all that now stands between us and all these horrors of the last century.* To the mothers in the land is entrusted the care of this only barrier against their return.

Is the strength of this barrier doubted? Its efficacy is readily proved. In England, during the twelve years (1854-1865) in which vaccination has been, to a certain extent, compulsory, the average annual rate of deaths by small-pox has been two hundred and two in the million of population. Contrast this with the annual death-rate of three thousand to the million, which was the average of thirty years previous to the introduction of vaccination. John Simon, medical officer of Her Majesty's Privy Council, one of the best statisticians in England, has collected a formidable array of figures, "to doubt which would be to fly in the face of the multiplication table." From this mountain height of statistics Mr. Simon says: "Wheresoever vaccination falls into neglect, small-pox tends to become again the same fruitful pestilence as it was in the days before Jenner's discovery, and wherever it is universally and properly performed, small-pox tends to be of as little effect as any extinct epidemic of the Middle Ages."

Are other diseases ever produced by vaccination? The popular belief would answer the question in the affirmative. All affections of the skin and swellings of the glands noticed in children soon after vaccination, are attributed by parents in many cases to this operation. They forget that such diseases are met with constantly in infancy and childhood, as often among the unvaccinated as the vaccinated. Observation does not show that they occur with greater frequency among the vaccinated. An English physician has been at the trouble to examine and record a thousand cases of skin disease in children; he found no evidence whatever that vaccination disposes the constitution to such affections. It has been stated with apparent justness, that parental complaints of this kind frequently arise from their unwillingness to believe there is anything wrong in their offspring. Hence, when other diseases follow, vaccination gets blamed for what is really and truly due to other causes. So far from doing any harm to the system, it has been observed in those countries where vaccination has been most thoroughly practised, that leaving small-pox out of question, there have been fewer deaths from other maladies. This is especially true of two of the most important classes of diseases namely, scrofulous affections and low fever. For this reason some medical statisticians have attributed to vaccination an indirect protective influence against these disorders.

At what *age* should a child be vaccinated? If the health permit, the operation should always be performed in very early infancy. The chief sufferers from small-pox are young children. One-fourth of all who die from this fatal disease in England are children under the age of one year. In Scotland, where, until recently, vaccination has been much more neglected than in England, the proportion even amounted nearly to one-third; and of these one-fourth were under the age of three months. The great risk, particularly in large towns where small-pox is seldom absent, of delaying vaccination, is obvious. City children, if healthy, should be vaccinated when a month or six weeks old. Rarely or never ought it to be delayed beyond two or three months. This early period of life is also particularly suitable to vaccination, because the accompanying fever will then be over before the disturbing influence of teething begins.

Revaccination.—If the first vaccination be found imperfect in character, that is, if it has not properly "taken," the operation should be repeated at the earliest opportunity. It has been recommended in all cases, to perform a second vaccination not later than the sixth or eighth year. If small-pox be prevailing, it is proper to vaccinate all who have not been vaccinated within three or four years. In any event, revaccination at or after the period of puberty is of extreme importance. It will give additional security even to those whose original vaccination was perfect. In some cases, the susceptibility to small-pox is not wholly exhausted by one vaccination. Inasmuch as it is desirable for every one to escape this disease even in its most modified form, revaccination should always be performed, as it affords a very sure and reliable means of such escape. After successful revaccination, small-pox even in its mildest shape is rarely met with. In girls especially, in whom the changes which occur at puberty are most marked, revaccination should be performed about the age of fourteen.

AIR AND VENTILATION.

Fresh air is necessary for the robust development of infancy and childhood. Infants born in the summer season should be carried out daily when the weather is pleasant, from the second or third day after birth. Those born in the winter should be kept in the house for two or three months before being introduced to the outer world on some sunny noonday. Older children can scarcely pass too much time in the open air.

A change in the dress, must, of course, be made before exposing the child to the out-door air. The head should be covered, and the chest and limbs well protected from the cold.

As a rule, a child ought to be carried out, or permitted, when old enough, to walk out at least once every pleasant day during the year. The time of the day is to be varied with the season. In the winter the middle of the day is to be chosen; in summer, the early portion of the forenoon, a few hours after sunrise.

Children show very quickly, even when in ill-health, the beneficial effect of a ride or walk. It quiets the irritability to which they are liable, more effectually than any other procedure. For a delicate child, or one recovering from sickness, fresh air and sunshine are the best tonics that can be administered. A fretful, peevish child will soon learn to look forward to its daily jaunt on the street or road, and will be quieted by it for the rest of the day.

At all times of the year regard must be had to the state

of the weather. The infant ought never to be taken out on a wet day. Exposure to a damp atmosphere is one of the most powerful causes of catarrh on the chest and inflammation of the lungs, to which young children are so subject. A very high wind, even though the day be bright and dry, is injurious to a young infant, as it has been known to suspend his breathing for a time, which accident might, if not at once observed, bring about a fatal result.

Besides fresh air, *light* is an indispensable requisite to the health of children. Nothing can compensate for the absence of its beneficial effects. It is to be remembered, however, that during the first week or two the eyes of the new-born babe are not strong enough to bear the full glare of light. The first eight days of its existence should be spent in a half-darkened room. Gradually the apartment may be brightened, until finally, after about two weeks, the young eyes become entirely accustomed to the light, and may be exposed to it without injury. A neglect of this precaution is one of the most common causes of the bad inflammation of the eyes so frequently met with among young infants. After the sight has become quite strong, a bright room will strengthen the eyes, not weaken them, for light is the natural stimulant of the eye, as exercise is of the muscles, or food of the stomach.

Scrofulous diseases are the heritage of those children who are deprived of a plentiful supply of pure air and light. A distinguished English writer upon the laws of health ascribes to the careful avoidance of the salutary influence of air and light by so many young girls, who are fearful of walking out while the sun is powerful, much of their sickly appearance, the loss of consistency of their bones, and their being able to afford but a deformed temple to the immortal soul.

Humboldt states that during a five years' residence in South America, he   any natural deformity amongst the men or women belonging to the Cariff, Muyscas, Indian, Mexican, or Peruvian races. If parents in our own country were to accustom their daughters from an early age to daily exercise in the open air and sunlight, there would be fewer weak backs requiring the support of apparatus from the surgical instrument maker, and less pallor in lips and cheeks, to be remedied by iron, from the shop of the apothecary.

EXERCISE.

The first exercise which a child obtains is had, of course, in its nurse's arms. Are there any directions, then, to be noticed in regard to the *manner of carrying an infant?* Dr. Eberle gives the following useful advice upon this subject; "The spine and its muscles seldom acquire sufficient strength and firmness before the end of the third month, to enable the child to support its body in an upright position, without inconvenience or risk of injury. Until this power is manifestly acquired, the infant should not be carried or suffered to sit with its body erect, without supporting it in such a manner as to lighten the pressure made on the spine, and aid it in maintaining the upright posture of its head and trunk; therefore, at first (a few days after birth), the infant should be taken from its cradle or bed two or three times daily and laid on its back upon a pillow, and carried gently about the chamber. After the third or fourth week, the child may be carried in a reclining posture on the arms of a careful nurse, in such a manner as to afford entire support both to body and head. This may be done by reclining the infant upon the forearm, the hand embracing the upper and posterior part of the thighs, whilst its body and head are supported by resting against the breast and arm of the nurse. When held in this way, it may be gently moved from side to side, or up and down, while it is carefully carried through a well-ventilated room."

After the child is three months old, it will probably have become strong enough to maintain itself in a sitting position. It may then be carried about in this upright posture, with the spine and head carefully supported by the nurse, which aid ought not to be withdrawn until the age of six or seven months.

"In *lifting* young children," as has been well observed by Dr. Barlow, "the nurse should be very careful never to lay hold of them by the arms, as is sometimes thoughtlessly done; but always to place the hands, one on each side of the chest, immediately below the arm-pits. In infancy, the sockets of the joints are so shallow, and the bones so feebly bound down and connected with each other, that dislocation, and even fracture of the collar bone may easily be produced by neglecting this rule. For the same reason, it is a bad custom to support a child by one or even by both arms, when he makes his first attempt to walk. The grand aim which the child has in view, is to preserve his equilibrium. If he is partially supported by one arm, the body inclines to one side, and the attitude is rendered most unfavourable to the preservation of his natural balance; and consequently, the moment the support is in the least relaxed, the child falls over and is caught up with a jerk. Even when held by both arms, the attitude is unnatural and unfavourable to the speedy attainment of the object. To assist the child, we ought to place one hand on each side of the chest, in such a way as to give the slightest possible support, and to be ready instantly to give more if he lose his balance. When this plan is followed, all the attitudes and efforts of the child are in a natural direction; and success is attained not only sooner, but more gracefully than by any ill-judged support given to one side.

"There is one very common mode of exercising infants, which, we think, deserves particular notice—we mean the practice of hoisting or raising them aloft in the air. This practice is of such venerable antiquity, and so universal that it would be vain to impugn it. The pleasure, too, which most children evince under it, seems to show that it cannot be so objectionable as a cursory observer would be disposed to consider it. Still, there are hazards which ought not to be overlooked. The risk of accident is one of some amount; children have slipped from the hand and sustained serious injury. Some people are so energetic as to throw up children and catch them in descending. This rashness there can be no hesitation in reprobating; for, however confident the person may be of not missing his hold, there must ever be risks of injury from the concussion suffered in the descent, and even from the firmness of the grasp necessary for recovering and maintaining the hold. The motion of the body, too, has a direct tendency to induce vertigo; and when the liability of the infant brain to congestion and its consequences is considered, when the frequency of hydrocephalus in infants is borne in mind, an exercise which impels blood to the brain will not be regarded as wholly insignificant. There is one more objection which seems not to have attracted attention. The hold taken of a child in the act of hoisting him, is by the hand grasping the chest. The fingers and thumb placed on each side of the breast bone, compress the ribs, and any one with the hand so placed will at once perceive that if the pressure were strong and the resistance from the elasticity of the ribs weak, the impression on the chest resulting would correspond exactly with the deformity named chicken-breast. That any force is ever used, capable of inducing speedily such a change, is in the highest degree improbable; but that reiterated pressure of this kind, however slight, would, in a weakly child, have power to impress and distort the chest, few, we imagine, will doubt."

When two or three months old, the infant may be placed on a soft mattrass upon the floor or on the carpet. He can then toss his limbs about without danger, and develop the powers of his muscular system.

"The best mode of teaching a child how to walk," says Dr. Bull, "is to let it teach itself, and this it will do readily enough. It will first learn to crawl; this exercises every muscle in the body, does not fatigue the child, throws no weight upon the bones, but imparts vigour and strength, and is thus highly useful. After a while, having the power, it will wish to do more; it will endeavour to lift itself upon its feet by the aid of a chair, and though it fail again and again in its attempts, it will still persevere until it accomplish it. By this it learns, first, to raise itself from the floor; and secondly, to stand, but not without keeping hold of the object on which it has seized. Next it will balance itself without holding, and will proudly and laughingly show that it can stand alone. Fearful, however, as yet of moving its limbs, without support, it will seize a chair or anything else near it, when it will dare to advance as far as the limits of its support will permit. This little adventure will be repeated day after day with increased exultation; when, after numerous trials, he will feel confident of his power to balance himself, and he will run alone. Now, time is required for this gradual self-teaching, during which the muscles and bones become strengthened; and, when at last called upon to sustain the weight of the body, are fully capable of doing so."

It is not merely want of strength which prevents an infant from walking at first. The natural shape of the legs renders it impossible. The feet are turned in so that the inner sides look upwards. When placed upon its feet, therefore, the soles will not rest upon the ground. In a short time the position of the feet changes, and they become fitted for the purposes of support and locomotion. When he begins to walk, the child should have shoes with tolerably broad soles, which ought to be at least half an inch longer than the foot.

The first efforts of the little one to support and propel itself are to be carefully watched, but not unnecessarily interfered with, neither frightened by expressions of fear nor rendered timid by too frequent warnings.

The first seven years of life should be one grand holiday for all sports and amusements which will bring into play the muscles, and divert at the same time the mind. Time cannot be more usefully employed than in thus laying the foundation of health, upon which alone can rest the physical, mental, and moral well-being of after life.

TEETHING.

The period at which the teeth first make their appearance is not a fixed one. It varies considerably even within the limits of perfect health. It may be said, as a rule, that the babe begins to cut his teeth at the age of six or seven months. Quite frequently, however, the first teeth appear as early as the fourth month, or are delayed until the eighth. In some instances children come into the world with their teeth already cut. This is said to have been the case with Louis XIV., and with Mirabeau. King Richard the Third is another example. Shakespeare makes the Duke of York refer to this circumstance in these words:—

> "Marry, they say my uncle grew so fast,
> That he could gnaw a crust at two hours old;
> 'Twas full two years ere I could get a tooth."

It does not follow that children whose teeth show themselves early will have therefore a quicker general development. Such cases are merely instances of irregularity in the time of dentition, and carry with them no particular significance. Irregularities, in regard to the order in which the teeth are cut, are also of frequent occurrence.

While therefore it cannot be maintained that all healthy children cut their teeth in a certain regular order and time, yet it is certain that those children who follow the general rule which prevails in this respect, suffer least from the difficulties and effects of dentition. As all mothers desire to know at what time they may expect the teeth, we will state the rule of their development in the great majority of cases.

The lower teeth generally precede those of the upper jaw by two or three months.

The twenty milk teeth usually appear in the five following groups:—

First.—Between the fourth and eighth months of life the two lower middle front teeth appear almost simultaneously. Then a pause of from three to nine weeks ensues.

Second.—Between the eighth and tenth months of life the five upper front teeth appear, following shortly upon each other, the two central preceding the two on each side of them. Another pause of from six to twelve weeks succeeds.

Third.—Between the twelfth and sixteenth months of life, six teeth appear nearly at once. They are, first, the two first grinding teeth in the upper jaw, leaving a space between them and the front teeth which before appeared; next, the two lower front teeth situated one on each side of the central ones, which were the first to appear; and, lastly, the two front grinders of the lower jaw. A pause until the eighteenth month now ensues.

Fourth.—Between the eighteenth and twenty-fourth months of life the canine teeth cut through (the upper ones are called eye teeth). Again a pause until the thirtieth month.

Fifth.—Between the thirtieth and thirty-sixth months the second four grinders finally make their appearance.

This concludes the first teething. The child has now twenty milk teeth.

We have mentioned that children are sometimes born with teeth. It is also true sometimes they never acquire any. Instances are on record of adults who have never cut their teeth. Dentition has been known to take place very late in life. A case is related, on excellent authority, of an old lady aged eighty-five who cut several teeth after attaining that age.

APPEARANCE OF THE PERMANENT TEETH.

Between the fifth and sixth years of life the second dentition begins. The front grinders are the ones first cut through. Between the sixth and tenth years all the front teeth appear, followed by the canines before the twelfth year. At this time the second grinders show themselves; and, finally, between the sixteenth and twenty-fourth year,—the wisdom teeth complete the dental furniture of the mouth.

GROWTH AND DEVELOPMENT.

During infancy the body grows with great rapidity. About the end of the third year, one-half of the adult height of the body is attained. After this period growth is more gradual, for in order to reach the remaining half, about eighteen years more are required. At twenty years of age, the height is somewhat more than three and a half times that at birth, and the weight about twenty times. Development does not go on at an equal rate in all parts of the body. The lower limbs, small at birth, increase proportionately more rapidly, while the head, relatively large at birth, develops more slowly. The muscular system is gradually strengthened. At the end of the third month, the infant is able, if in good health, readily to support its head; at the fourth month it can be held upright; at the ninth month it crawls about the floor; before the end of the year it is able with assistance to step; and between one and two years, at different times, according to its vigour and activity, it acquires the power of standing and walking alone. The periods of greatest and least growth of the child are, on the one hand, spring and summer; on the other, autumn and winter. It has long been known that animals grow more rapidly in the spring than at any other season of the year. This has been attributed to the abundance of herbage they are then able to obtain. It has been ascertained by actual measurement that children grow chiefly in the spring.

At six months of age the child begins to lisp, and at twelve months it is usually able to utter distinct and intelligible sounds of one or two syllables. The development of the senses and of the mind proceeds gradually. The sense of hearing is more active and further advanced than that of sight. Sounds are appreciated sooner than light or bright-coloured objects. The next sense which is developed is, perhaps, that of taste; then follow smell and touch.

IS THE RACE DEGENERATING?

This is a question which perplexes some minds in our times. A German author of note has recently written a volume to prove that each generation is feebler than the preceding. Old physicians say that in their youth diseases of exhaustion were rarer than nowadays. For this our habits of life, the pressure on our nervous systems, the prevalence of hereditary diseases, and the excessive use of narcotics and stimulants are held responsible. "The fathers," say these crokers, "have eaten sour grapes, and the children's teeth are set on edge."

We attach little weight to these gloomy views. There are plenty of facts on the other side. The suits of old armour still preserved in Europe prove that, as a rule, we have slightly gained in weight and size. Tables of life insurance companies and reports of statistics show that the average length of human life is greater than it ever was. Dr. Charles D. Meigs used to state in his lectures that the size of the head of our American infants at birth is somewhat greater than in the Old World.

That there are more numerous diseases than formerly

is not true; but it is true that we know more, for we have learned to detect them more readily and to examine them more minutely. This is especially true of such as are peculiar to women. Within the last ten or twenty years so much that is of sovereign importance has been contributed to this department of medical science that it is hardly possible for one to become an expert in it unless he gives it his whole attention.

To avoid the tendency to debilitated frames and chronic diseases, woman should, therefore, learn not only the laws of her own physical life, but the relations in which she stands to the other sex. Thus she can guard her own health, and preserve from degeneracy her offspring. It is only by enlightenment and the extension of knowledge on the topics relating to soundness of body and mind, that we can found rational hopes of a permanent and widespread improvement of the race.

Some have maintained, not understanding the bearing of the facts, that such degeneracy is more conspicuous in the frame of woman than anywhere else. They quote the narratives of travellers who describe with what fortitude, we might almost say with what indifference, the Indian women, and those of other savage races, bear the pangs of childbirth, and how little the ordeal weakens them. A squaw will turn aside for an hour or two when on the march, bear a child, wash it in some stream, bind it on the top of her load, and shouldering both, quietly rejoin the vagrant troop. Our artificial life seems, indeed, in this respect to be to blame; but if we look closer, we can learn that these wild women often perish alone, that they are rarely fertile, that unnatural labours are not unknown, and that the average duration of their life is decidedly less than among the females in civilized States.

THE PERILS OF MATERNITY.

In the early part of this work we quoted some authorities to show that those women who choose single life as their portion, do not escape the ills of existence, nor do they protract their days, but, on the contrary, as shown by extensive statistics, are more prone to affections of the mind, and die earlier. While, therefore, Nature thus rewards those who fulfil the functions of their being, by taking part in the mysterious processes of reproduction, and perpetuating the drama of existence, it is true, also, that she associates these privileges with certain deprivations and suffering. We do not wish to throw around the married state any charms which are not its own. Rather is it our aim to portray with absolute, and therefore instructive, fidelity, all that this condition offers of unfavourable as well as favourable aspects.

Let us say at once, maternity has its perils apart from those of pregnancy and child-birth—perils as peculiar and as inevitable as those which pertain to single life. Our present purpose is to mention these, and by stating their nature and what are their causes, so far as known, to put married women on their guard against them. Some are almost trifling, at least not involving danger to life; others harassing to the sufferer and to her friends.

Of the latter character is that deplorable condition called by physicians puerperal mania. This is a variety of insanity which attacks some women shortly after child-birth, or at the period of weaning a child. The period of attack is uncertain, as it may manifest itself first in a very few days, or not for some months, after the confinement. Its duration is likewise very variable. In most instances a few weeks restore the patient to herself, but there are many cases where judicious treatment for months is required, and there are a few where the mental alienation is permanent, and the wife and mother is never restored to her sanity.

The question has been much discussed whether such a condition is to be imputed to a hereditary tendency to insanity in the family, and also whether a mother who has had such an attack is liable to transmit to her children, male or female, any greater liability to mental disease. We are well aware what deep importance the answers to these inquiries have to many a parent, and in forming our replies we are guided not only by our own experience but by the recorded opinion of those members of our profession who had given the subject close and earnest attention. To the first query the reply must be made that in one-half, or nearly one-half, of the cases of this variety of insanity there is traceable a hereditary tendency to aberration of mind. Usually one or more of the direct progenitors, or of the near relatives of the patient, will be found to have manifested unmistakable marks of unsoundness of mind. In the remaining one-half cases no such tendency can be traced, and in these it must be presumed that the mania is a purely local and temporary disorder of the brain. The incurable cases are usually found in the first class of patients, as we might naturally expect.

The likelihood of the children in turn inheriting any such predisposition depends on the answer to the inquiry we first put. If the mania itself is the appearance of a family malady, then the chances are that it will pass downward with their transmissible qualities. But if the mania arises from causes which are transitory, then there is no ground for alarm.

An inquiry still more frequently put to the physician by the husband and by the patient herself after recovery is, whether an attack at one confinement predisposes her to a similar attack at a subsequent similar period. There is considerable divergence of opinion on this point. Dr. Gooch, an English physician of wide experience, is very strenuous in denying any such increased likelihood, while an American obstetrician of note is quite as positive in taking the opposite view. The truth of the matter undoubtedly is, that where the mania is the exhibition of a hereditary tendency, it is apt to recur; but where it arises from transient causes, then it will only occur again if such causes exist.

Here, therefore, we perceive the importance of every woman who has had, or who fears to have, one of these distressing experiences, being put on her guard against disregarding those rules of health the neglect of which may result so disastrously. One of the most powerful of these causes is *exhaustion*. We mean this in its widest sense, mental or physical. In those instances where mania appears at weaning, it is invariably where the child has been nursed too long, or where the mother has not had sufficient strength to nourish it without prostrating herself. It should be observed as a hygienic law that no mother should nurse her children after she has had one attack of mania. The mere nervous excitement is altogether too much for her. She must once and for ever renounce this tender pleasure. We even go so far as to recommend that no woman in whose family a mental taint is hereditary shall nurse her children.

Anxiety, low spirits, unusual weakness from any cause, are powerful predisposing causes, and therefore in all cases, especially in those where the family or personal history leads one to fear such an attack, they should be avoided. The diet should be nourishing and abundant, but not stimulating. Cheerful society and surroundings should be courted, and indulgence in any single train of ideas avoided. As for directions during the attack they are unnecessary, as to combat it successfully often tasks the utmost skill of the physician, and it will be for him to give these directions.

Many, we may say most, married women whose health is broken down by some disease peculiar to their sex, refer the commencement of their suffering to some confinement or premature birth. This, therefore, we must also take into account in estimating the perils of maternity. Perhaps, in four cases out of five, this breaking down is one of the symptoms of a displacement of the internal organs, a malposition, in other words, of the uterus. This is familiarly known as an "inward weakness," and many a woman drags through years of misery caused by a trouble of this sort.

It is true that these mal-positions occur in unmarried women, and occasionally in young girls. But it is also true that their most frequent causes are associated with the condition of maternity. The relaxation of the ligaments or bands which hold the uterus in its place, which takes place during pregnancy and parturition, predisposes to such troubles. It requires time and care for these ligaments to resume their natural strength and elasticity after child-birth. Then, too, the walls of the abdomen are one of the supports provided by nature to keep all the organs they contain in proper place by a constant elastic pressure. When, as in pregnancy, these walls are distended and put on the strain, suddenly to be relaxed after confinement, the organs miss their support, and are liable to take positions which interfere with the performance of their natural functions. Therefore we may rightly class the greater tendency of married women to this class of diseases among the perils of maternity.

Within the last fifteen years, probably no one branch of medical science has received greater attention at the hand of physicians than this of diseases of women. Many hitherto inexplicable cases of disease, much suffering referred to other parts of the system, have been traced to local misfortunes of the character we have just described. Medical works are replete with cases of the highest interest illustrative of this. We are afraid to state some of the estimates which have been given of the number of women in this country who suffer from these maladies. Nor do we intend to give in detail the long train of symptoms which characterize them. Such a sad rehearsal would avail little or nothing to the non-medical reader. It is enough to say that the woman who finds herself afflicted by manifold aches and pains without obvious cause; who suffers with her head, and her stomach, and her nerves; who discovers that, in spite of the precepts of religion and the efforts of will, she is becoming irritable, impatient, dissatisfied with her friends, her family, and herself; who is, in short, unable any longer to perceive anything of beauty and of pleasure in this world, and hardly anything to hope for in the next; this woman, in all probability, is suffering from a displacement or an ulceration of the uterus. Let this be relieved, and her sufferings are ended. Often a very simple procedure can do this. We recall to mind a case described in touching language by a distinguished teacher of medicine. It is of an interesting young married lady who came from the Southern States to consult him in her condition. She could not walk across the room without support, and was forced to wear, at great inconvenience to herself, an abdominal supporter. Her mind was confused and she was the victim of apparently causeless unpleasant sensations. She was convinced that she had been and still was deranged.

The physician could discover nothing wrong about her system other than a slight falling of the womb. This was easily relieved. She at once improved in body and mind, soon was able to walk with ease and freedom, and once more enjoyed the pleasures of life. In a letter written soon after her return home, she said, "This beautiful world, which at one time I could not look upon without disgust, has become once more a source of delight." How strongly do these deeply-felt words reveal the difference between her two conditions.

There is one source of great comfort in considering these afflictions. It is, that they are in the great majority of cases traceable to causes which are avoidable. Most of them are the penalties inflicted by stern nature on infractions of her laws. Hence the great, the unspeakable importance of women being made aware of the dangers to which they are exposed, and being fully informed how to avoid them. This task we now assume.

There is, we concede, a tendency in the changes which

take place during pregnancy and parturition, to expose the system to such accidents. But this tendency can be counteracted by care, and by the avoidance of certain notorious and familiar infractions of the laws of health. It is not usually until she gets up and commences to go about the house that the woman feels any pain referable to a misplaced womb. Very frequently the origin of it is leaving the bed too soon, or attempting to do some work too much for her strength, shortly after a premature birth or confinement. Not only should a woman keep her bed, as a rule, for nineteen days after every abortion, and every confinement, but for weeks after she commences to move about she should avoid any severe muscular exertion, especially lifting, long walks, straining, or working a sewing machine. Straining at stool is one of the commonest causes. Many women have a tendency to constipation for weeks or months after childbirth. They are aware that it is unfavourable to health, and they seek to aid nature by violent muscular effort. They cannot possibly do a more unwise act. Necessarily, the efforts they make press the womb forcibly down, and its ligaments being relaxed, it assumes either suddenly, on some one well-remembered occasion, or gradually, after a succession of efforts, some unnatural position. The same reasoning applies to relieving the bladder, which is connected, in some persons, with undue effort.

Constipation, if present, must, and almost always can, be relieved by a judicious diet, and the moderate use of injections. These simple methods are much to be preferred to purgative medicines, which are rarely satisfactory, if they are continued for much time. When anything more is needed, we recommend a glass of some laxative mineral water, that, for instance from the Bedford or Congress Springs. This should be taken before breakfast.

For the difficulty with the bladder we mentioned, diet is also efficacious. It is familiarly known that several popular articles of food have a decided action in stimulating the kidneys; for instance, asparagus and water-melon. Such articles should be freely partaken, and their effect can be increased by some vegetable infusion, taken warm, as juniper tea, or broom tea. The application to the parts of a cloth wrung out in water, as hot as it can conveniently be borne, is also a most excellent assistant to nature.

Similar strains on the muscles of the abdomen are consequent on violent coughing and vomiting. Therefore these should be alleviated, as they always can be, by some anodyne taken internally. Any physician is familiar with many such preparations, so that it seems unnecessary to give any formula, particularly as it would have to be altered more or less to suit any given case.

Women of a languid disposition, and relaxed muscles, are frequently urged to "take exercise," and to "go to work." Their condition sometimes excites censure rather than commiseration, because it is thought that they do not exert and thus strengthen themselves as much as they should. We are quite as much in favour of work and vigorous muscles as any one. But often it were the foolishest advice possible to give a woman to tell her to seek active exercise. It is just what she should avoid, as it may ultimately give rise to that very trouble which, not only threatening, is the cause of her listlessness. Many instances are familiar to every physician of extensive experience, where a long walk, a hard day's work, a vigorous dance in the evening, or a horseback ride, has left behind it a uterine weakness which has caused years of misery. Especially after confinement or premature delivery, it is prudent for a woman to avoid any such exertion for months and months. Moderate employment of her muscles in any light avocation, short walks and drives, fresh air, with judicious exercise, these are well enough in every instance, but beyond them there is danger. We know too well that advice like this will sound like mockery to some who read these lines. They have to work, and work hard; they have no opportunity to spare themselves; the iron hand of necessity is upon them, and they must obey. We can but sympathize with them, and cheer them with the consolation that many a woman has borne all this and lived to a healthy and a happy old age. Nature has surrounded the infinitely delicate machinery of woman's organization with a thousand safeguards, but for all that, the delicacy remains, and it is because so many women are forced to neglect their duties to their own selves that so many thousands walk the streets of our great cities, living martyrs.

But no. We must modify what we have just written. In justice to our own sex, and in all truthfulness, we cannot allow the blame to be removed altogether from women themselves. They alone are responsible for one of the most fruitful causes of their wretchedness. The theme is a threadbare one. We approach it with hardly any hope that we shall do good by repeating warnings utterly monotonous and tiresome. But still less can we feel comfortable in mind to pass it over in silence. We refer to the foolish and injurious pressure which is exerted on the lower part of the chest and the abdomen by tight corsets, belts, and bands to support the underclothing: in other words, *tight lacing*. Why it is, by what strange freak of fashion and blindness to artistic rules, women of the present day think that a deformed and ill-proportioned waist is a requisite of beauty, we do not know. Certainly they never derived such an idea from a contemplation of those monuments of perfect beauty bequeathed to posterity by the chisels of Attic artists, nor from those exquisite figures which lend to the canvas of Titian and Raphael such immortal fame. Look, for instance, at that work of the former artist, now rendered so familiar by the chromo-lithographic process, called "Titian's Daughter." It is the portrait of a blonde-haired maiden holding aloft a trencher heaped with fruits. She turns her face to the beholder, leaning slightly backward to keep her equilibrium. Her waist is encircled by a zone of pearls, and it is this waist we would have our readers observe with something more than any æsthetic eye. It is the waist of health as well as beauty. Narrower than either the shoulders or the hips, it is yet anything but that "wasp-like waist" which is so fashionable a deformity. With such a waist, a woman is fitted to pass through her married state with health and pleasure. There is little fear that she will be the tenant of doctors' chairs, and the victim of drugs and treatments. Let women aim at beauty, let them regard it as a matter of very high importance, worth money, and time, and trouble, and we will applaud them to the echo. But let them not mistake deformity, vicious shapes, unnatural and injurious attitudes, and hurtful distortions for beauty. That not only degrades their physical nature, but it lowers their taste, and places them in æsthetics on a level with the Indian squaw who flattens her head and bores her nose, and with the Chinese woman who gilds her teeth, and compresses her foot into a shapeless mass. True beauty is ever synonymous with health, and the woman who, out of subservience to the demands of fashion, for years squeezes her waist and flattens her breast, will live to rue it when she becomes a mother. Away, then, with tight corsets and all similar contrivances.

Of a similar objectional character are many of the devices which ignorant men connected with the medical profession urge upon the public for the sake of remedying curvature of the spine, restoring the figure, or supporting the abdomen. Not a few of such braces and supporters are seriously dangerous. A good brace, well-fitting, carefully adjusted, suited to the particular case, is often of excellent service, but the majority of them do not answer this description. Our advice is, that no girl, and still more no mother, should wear one of these without it is fitted upon her by an experienced hand. We have known more than one instance where the binder put on after childbirth has been wrongly placed, and pinned so firmly that it has resulted in producing falling of the womb. This, too, should be sedulously looked after.

All these are causes which are strictly under the control of the woman herself. They are therefore such as she should have in mind and be on her guard against. There are others, but they are less frequent, which are beyond her power, and it would be labour lost, therefore, for us to mention them.

Equally vain would it be for us to speak of the various means by which difficulties of this nature are removed. Probably no one branch of medical surgery has been more assiduously cultivated than this, and the number of supporters, pessaries, braces, and levers which have been recently brought before the medical profession for this purpose is simply appalling. There are women and men who make it their business to carry them through the country and sell them on commission. We distinctly warn our readers against the class. They are almost invariably ignorant and unscrupulous, rich in promises and regardless of performances. She who patronizes them will be sure to lose her money, and will be lucky if she does not forfeit her health.

The most we shall do is to give some advice how to treat such complaints on principles of hygiene. And indeed this means nearly one-half the battle. For without these simple cases, treatment of any kind is useless and sure to fail; and with them, many complaints are remedied as well as avoided.

The first point we would urge is, that the woman who finds herself thus afflicted should seek to have such a position that she can rest. If she is burdened with family cares, let her, if possible, diminish or escape them for a time. A rest of a month or two, not at a fashionable watering-place nor at a first-class hotel in some noisy city, but in quiet lodgings, or with some sympathizing friend, will be of great advantage. This she should obtain without travelling too far. Prolonged motion in railway cars or carriages is in every instance injurious. If it must be undertaken, for instance, in order to consult a qualified physician, or to reach some friends, the modern appliances of comfort, such as air-cushions, foot-rests, and head-supports, should be provided. They cost but little, and to the invalid their value is great. No such journey should be undertaken at or near the time when the monthly illness might come on, as the suffering is always greater at these periods.

The pleasant associations which group themselves around a happy home are an important element in the treatment of diseases which, like these, are so intimately connected with the mind and nervous system. It will not do heedlessly to throw such advantages away. When the home *is* pleasant, and rest can there be had, the patient, in the majority of instances, will do well to abide there. But when, for any reason, be it domestic infelicities in which the husband has a share, be it disagreeable relatives, or importunate and tedious visitors, then the sooner such a mental weight is removed or avoided the better.

The diet is a very common subject of error. It is popularly supposed that everybody who is weak should eat a "strengthening" diet, meat three times a day, eggs, ale, and beef-tea to any extent. This is a great error. Frequently such a diet has just the contrary effect from what is expected. The patient becomes dyspeptic, nervous, and more debilitated than ever. The rule is that only that diet is strengthening which is thoroughly digested and taken up in the system. Frequently, we may say in the majority of cases, a small amount of animal food, especially game, fowls, fish, and soups, with *fresh* vegetables, and ripe fruits, will be far more invigorating than heavier foods. Pastry, cakes, and confectionery should be discarded, and great regularity in the hours of meals observed. Stimulants of all kinds are, as a rule, unnecessary, and highly-spiced food is to be avoided. There is an old German proverb which says, "Pepper helps a man on his horse, and a woman to her grave." This is much too strong, but we may avail ourselves in this connection of the grain of truth that it contains.

Cleanliness in its widest sense is an important element in the treatment. Not only should the whole surface of the body be thoroughly washed several times a week, but the whole person should be *soaked* by remaining in the water for an hour or more. This has an excellent effect, and is far from unpleasant. It was regarded in the days of ancient Rome as such a delightful luxury and such a necessity, indeed, that every municipality erected public bathing establishments, with furnaces to heat the water to such a temperature that persons could remain in it for several hours without inconvenience. The use of public baths is almost unknown in this country, but in place of them, every house of even moderate dimensions has its own bath-room, so that the custom of cleanliness might appear to be hardly less general among the better classes than in old Rome.

The difficulty is that so few people appreciate that to thoroughly cleanse the skin, still more for the bath to have a medicinal effect, it must be prolonged far beyond the usual time we allow it. The European physicians, who as a rule attach much greater importance to this than ourselves, require their patients to remain immersed two, three, four, and even ten or twelve hours daily! This is said to have most beneficial results; but who would attempt to introduce it in this country?

Local cleanliness is of equal importance. This is obtained by means of injections or irrigations of simple water, or of some infusion or solution. The use of the syringe, as an article of essential service in preserving the health of married women, should never be overlooked. Even when they are aware of no tendency to weakness or unusual discharge, it should be employed once or twice a week, and when there is debility or disease of the parts actually present, it is often of the greatest service.

There are many varieties of female syringes now manufactured and sold, some of which are quite worthless. Much the most convenient, cleanly, and efficient is the self-injecting rubber syringe, which is worked by means of a ball held in the hand, and which throws a constant and powerful stream. They come neatly packed in boxes occupying small space, and readily transported from place to place. Much depends on knowing how to apply them. The patient should be seated on the edge of a low chair or stool with a hard seat, immediately over a basin. The tube should then be introduced as far as possible without causing pain, and the liquid should be thrown up for five or ten minutes. About one or two quarts may be used, of a temperature in ordinary cases a little lower than that of the apartment. Water actually cold is by no means to be recommended, in spite of what some physicians say to the contrary. It unquestionably occasionally leads to those very evils which the judicious use of the syringe is intended to avoid.

No fluid but water should be used in ordinary cases. When, however, here is much discharge, a pinch of powdered alum can be dissolved in the water; and when there is an unpleasant odour present, a sufficient amount of a solution of permanganate of potash may be added to the water to change it to a light pink colour. This latter substance is most admirable in removing all unpleasant odours; but it will stain the clothing, and must, on that account, be employed with caution.

We will add a few warnings to what we have just said about injections. There are times when they should be omitted, as for instance during the periodical illness, when the body is either chilled or heated, and generally when their administration gives pain. There are also some women in whom the mouth of the womb remains open, especially those who have borne many children. In such cases the liquid used is liable to be thrown into the womb itself, and may give rise to serious troubles. These should either omit the use of the syringe altogether, or obtain one of those which throw the water backward and not forward. This variety is manufactured and sold by various dealers.

Irrigations are more convenient in some respects than injections. They are administered in the following manner: A jar holding about a gallon of water, simple or medicated, as may be advisable, is placed upon a table or high stand. A long rubber tube is attached to the bottom of the jar, ending in a metallic tube, and furnished with a stopcock. The patient seats herself on the edge of a chair over a basin, introduces the tube, and turns the stopcock. The liquid is thus thrown up in a gentle, equable stream, without any exertion on her part. No assistance is required, and the force and amount of the liquid can be exactly graduated by elevating or lowering the jar, or by turning the stopcock. When there is much debility, or when it is desirable to apply the liquid for a long time, this method is much preferable to syringing. The necessary apparatus can readily be obtained in any large city. It has, however, the drawback that the jar is large, and not convenient to carry on journeys.

THE SINGLE LIFE.

A few words, ere we pass to another branch of our subject, in the physical relations of her who by choice or other reason never marries. It is a common observation among physicians who have devoted themselves to the study of woman's physical nature, that in spite of these "perils of maternity," which we have taken no pains to conceal, the health of single women during the child-bearing period is, as a general rule, not better, nor even so good as that of their married sisters. Those insurance companies who take female risks, do not ask any higher premium for the married than the unmarried.

Various suggestions have been made to account for this unexpected fact. Some writers have pointed out that in many diseases marriage exerts a decidedly curative influence, especially in chronic nervous ailments. Chorea, for instance, or St. Vitus' dance, as it is popularly termed, has been repeatedly cured by marriage. As a rule, painful menstruation, which always arises from some defect or disease of the ovaries or adjacent organs, is improved and often completely removed by the same act. There are, as is well known, a whole series of emotional disorders, hysteria, and various kinds of mania and hallucination, which are almost exclusively confined to single persons, and only occur in the married under exceptional circumstances. An instance has lately been detailed in the medical journals by a Prussian physician of a case of undoubted hereditary insanity which was greatly bene fited, indeed temporarily cured, by a fortunate nuptial relation. Few who have watched a large circle of lady acquaintances, but will have observed that many of them increased in flesh and improved in health when they had been married some months. An English writer of distinction accounts for these favourable results in a peculiar manner. "Success," he says, "is always tonic, and the best of tonics. Now, to women, marriage is success. It is their aim in social life, and this accomplished, health and strength follow." We are not quite ready to subscribe to such a sweeping assertion, but no doubt it is applicable in a limited number of cases. Our own opinion is that nature gave to each sex certain functions, and that the whole system is in better health when all parts and powers fulfil their destiny.

Common proverbs portray the character of the spinster as peevish, selfish, given to queer fancies and unpleasant eccentricities. In many a case we are glad to say this is untrue. Instances of noble devotion, broad and generous sympathy, and distinguished self-sacrifice, are by no means rare in single women. But take the whole class, the popular opinion, as it often is, must be granted to be correct. Deprived of the natural objects of interest, the sentiments are apt to fix themselves on parrots or poodles, or to be confined within the breast or wither for want of nourishment. Too often the history of those sisterhoods who assume vows of singleness in the interest of religion presents to the physician the sad spectacle of prolonged nervous maladies, and to the Christian that of a sickly sensibility.

In this connection, we may answer a question not unfrequently put to the medical attendant. Are those women who marry late in their sexual life, more or less apt to bear living children than the married of the same age, and are they more or less likely to prolong the bearing period by their deferred nuptials? To both these inquiries we answer, no. On the contrary, the woman who marries a few years only before her change of life, is almost sure to have no children who will survive. She is decidedly less apt to have any than the woman of the same age who marries young. If, therefore, love of children and a desire for offspring form, as they rightly should, one of the inducements to marry, let not the act be postponed too long, or it will probably fail of any such

THE CHANGE OF LIFE.

AFTER a certain number of years, woman lays aside those functions with which she has been endowed for the perpetuation of the species, and resumes once more that exclusively individual life which had been hers when a child. The evening of her days approaches, and if she has observed the precepts of wisdom, she may look forward to a long and placid period of rest, blessed with health, honoured, yes, loved with a purer flame than any which she inspired in the bloom of youth and beauty. Those who are familiar with the delightful Memoirs of Madame Swetchine or Madame Racamier will not dispute even so bold an assertion as this.

But ere this haven of rest is reached, there is a crisis to pass which is ever the subject of anxious solicitude. Unscientific people, in their vivid language, call it *the change of life;* physicians know it as the *menopause*—the period of the cessation of the monthly flow. It is the epoch when the ovaries cease producing any more ova, and the woman becomes, therefore, incapable of bearing any more children.

The age at which it occurs is very variable. In this country, from forty to forty-six is the most common. Instances are not at all unusual when it does not appear until the half century has been turned, and we have known instances where women past sixty still continued to have their periodical illness.

Examples of very early cessation are more rare. We do not remember to have met any, in our experience, earlier than thirty years, but others have observed healthy women as young as twenty-eight in whom the flow had ceased.

The physical change which is most apparent at this time is the tendency to grow stout. The fat increases as the power of reproduction decreases. And here a curious observation comes in. We have said that when the girl changes to a woman, a similar deposit of fat takes place (though less in amount), which commences at the loins. This is the first sign of puberty. In the change of life the first sign is visible at the lower part of the back of the neck, on a level with the bones known as the two lowest cervical vertebræ. Here commences an accumulation of fat which often grows to form two distinct prominences, and is an infallible index of the period of a woman's life.

The breasts do not partake of this increase, but become flat and hard, the substance of the gland losing its spongy structure. The legs and arms lose their roundness of outline, and where they do not grow fat, dry up, and r semble those of the other sex. The abdomen enlarg even to the extent occasionally of leading the wife to believe she is to be a mother—a delusion sometimes strengthened by the absence of the monthly sickness. Finally, a perceptible tendency to a beard often manifests itself, the voice grows harder, and the characteristics of the female sex become less and less distinct.

Some who are more fortunate than their neighbours do not experience the least discomfort at the change of life. They simply note that at the expected time the illness does not appear, and forever after they are free from it. These are the exceptions. More commonly marked alterations in the health accompany this important crisis, and call for sedulous hygienic care. It is gratifying to know nearly all these threatening affections can be avoided by such care, as they depend upon causes under the control of the individual. Another fact, to which we have already referred, is full of consolation. It is an unexpected fact, one that we should hardly credit, did it not rest on statistical evidence of the most indisputable character. The popular opinion, every one knows, is that the period of the change of life is one peculiarly dangerous to women. If this is so, we might expect that if the number of deaths between the ages of forty and fifty years in the two sexes be compared, we should find that those of females far exceed those of males. This is, however, not the case. On the contrary, the deaths of the males exceed in number those of the females.

Hasty readers may draw a false conclusion from this statement. They may at once infer that the change of life merits little or no attention, if it thus in nowise increases the bills of mortality. This is a serious error. All intelligent physicians know that there are in very many cases a most unpleasant train of symptoms which characterize this epoch in the physical life of woman. They are alarming, painful, often entailing sad consequences, though rarely fatal. All physicians are, however, not intelligent, and there are too many who are inclined to ridicule such complaints, to impute them to fancy, and to think that they have done their full duty when they tell the sufferer that such sensations are merely indicative of her age, and that in a year or two they will all pass away. Such medical attendants do not appreciate the gravity of the sufferings they have been called to relieve. Says a distinguished writer on the subject, after entering into some details in the matter: " I would not dwell on things apparently so trivial as these, had I not seen some of the worst misery this world witnesses induced thereby." Such a conviction should be in the mind of the physician, and lead him to attach their full weight to the vague, transitory, unstable, but most distressing symptoms described by him.

We shall speak of the various signs and symptoms which occur at and mark the change, and in commencing so to do, we call attention to an interesting illustration of the rhythm which controls the laws of life. As in old age, when we draw near the last scene of all, we re-enter childhood, and grow into second infancy, so the woman, finishing her pilgrimage of sexual life, encounters the same landmarks and stations which greeted her when she first set out. She obeys at eve the voice of her own nature which she obeyed at her prime. The same diseases and disorders, the same nervous and mental sensations, the same pains and weaknesses which preceded the first appearance of her monthly illness will, in all probability, precede its cessation. Even those affections of the skin or of the brain, as epilepsy, which were suffered in childhood, and which disappear as soon as the periodical function was established, may be expected to re-appear when the function has reached its natural termination. Therefore, if a woman, past the change, notices that she suffers from bleeding at the nose, headache, boils, or some skin disease, let her bethink herself whether it is not a repetition of some similar trouble with which she was plagued before the eventful period which metamorphosed her from a girl into a woman.

So true is what we have just said, that in detailing the symptoms which frequently occur at the change of life, we could turn back to the previous pages where we discussed the dangers of puberty, and repeat much that we there said as of equal application here. For instance, the green-sickness, *chlorosis*, is by no means exclusively a disease of girls. It may occur at any period of child-bearing life, but is much more frequent at the *beginning* and the *end* of this term. Hardly any one has watched woman closely without having observed the peculiar tint of skin, the debility, the dislike of society, the change of temper, the fitful appetite, the paleness of the eye, and the other traits that show the presence of such a condition of the nervous system in those about renouncing their powers of reproduction. The precautions and rules which we before laid down can be read with equal profit in this connection

In addition to these symptoms, which in a measure belong to the individual's own history, there are others of a general character which betoken the approaching change. One of them is an increasing irregularity in the monthly appearance. This is frequently accompanied with a sinking sensation, a "feeling of goneness," as the sufferer says, at the pit of the stomach, often accompanied by flushes of heat, commencing at the stomach and extending over the whole surface of the body. The face, neck, and hands are suffused at inopportune moments, and greatly to the annoyance of the sufferer. This is sometimes accompanied by a sense of fulness in the head, a giddiness, and a dulness of the brain, sometimes going so far as to cause an uncertainty in the step, a slowness of comprehension, and feeling as if one might fall at any moment in some sort of a fit.

This is not the worst of it. These physical troubles react upon the mind. An inward nervousness intensely painful to bear, is very sure to be developed. She fears she will be thought to have taken liquor, and to be overcome with wine; she grows more confused, and imagines that she is watched with suspicious and unkind eyes, and often she worries herself by such unfounded fancies into a most harassing state of mental distress. Society loses its attractions, and solitude does but allow her opportunity to indulge to a still more injurious extent such brooding phantasms. Every ache and pain is magnified. Does her heart palpitate, as it is very apt to do? Straightway she is certain that she has some terrible disease of that organ, and that she will drop down dead some day in the street. Is one of her breasts somewhere sore, which, too, is not unusual? She knows at once it is a cancer, and suffers an agony of terror from a cause wholly imaginary.

Vibrating between a distressing excitement and a gloomy depression, her temper gives way, and even the words of the Divine Master lose their influence over her. She becomes fretful, and yet full of remorse for yielding to her peevishness; she seeks for sympathy without being able to give reasons for needing it; she annoys those around her by groundless fears, and is angered when they show their annoyance. In fine, she is utterly wretched, without any obvious cause of wretchedness.

This is a dark picture, but it is a true one, inexorably true. Let us hasten to add that such a mental condition is, however, neither a necessary nor a frequent concomitant of the change. We depict it, so that friends and relatives may better appreciate the sufferings of a class so little understood, and so that women themselves, by knowing the cause of such complaints and the sad results which flow from them, may make the more earnest efforts to avoid them.

Other symptoms are a sense of choking, a feeling of faintness, shooting pains in the back and loins, creepings, and chilliness, a feeling as if a hand were applied to the back or the cheek, a fidgety restlessness, inability to fix the mind on reading or in following a discourse, and a loss of control over the emotions, so that she is easily affected to tears or to laughter. All these merely indicate that Nature is employing all her powers to bring about that mysterious transformation in the economy by which she deprives the one sex for ever of partaking in the creative act after a certain age, while she only diminishes the power of the other.

Those women especially may anticipate serious trouble at this epoch in whom the change at puberty was accompanied by distressful and obstinate disorders, those in whom the menstrual periods have usually been attended with considerable pain and prostration, and those in whose married life several abortions or several tedious and unnatural labours have occurred. Also those who from some temporary cause are reduced in health and strength, as from repeated attacks of intermittent fever or disorders of the liver and digestive organs. Still more predisposed are they who are subject to some of those displacements or local ulcerations which we have mentioned among the "perils of maternity." It becomes of great consequence that any such deviation from the healthy standard shall be corrected before a woman reaches this trying passage in her career.

In rather more than one out of every four cases the change of life is either ushered in or accompanied by considerable flooding. When this occurs at the regular period, is not in sufficient quantity to cause debility, and is not associated with much pain, it need not give rise to any alarm. It is an effort of nature to relieve the impending plethora of the system, to drain away the excessive amount of blood which would otherwise accumulate by the cessation of the flow. When it is remembered that every month for some thirty years of life the woman of forty-five has been moderately bled, we need not wonder that suddenly to break off this long habit would bring about plethora, which would in turn be the source of manifold inconveniences to the whole system. Therefore, this flooding may be regarded as a wise act of nature, and as such, allowed to take its course so long as it is not attended with the symptoms mentioned above. When this is the case, however, the physician should be consulted as then the bleeding may be from inflammation, or ulceration, or even from that dreaded foe to life, cancer.

Instead of finding this exit, the blood occasionally is thrown off by bleeding at the nose, or is spit up from the lungs, or is passed from bleeding piles. Due caution must be used about stopping such discharges too promptly. Rest, cool drinks, and the application of cold to the parts, are generally all that is needed.

We have just spoken of cancer. This is a subject of terror to many women, and their fears are often increased and deliberately played upon by base knaves who journey about the country calling themselves "cancer doctors," and professing to have some secret remedy with which they work infallible cures. It should be generally known that all such pretensions are false. It is often a matter of no little difficulty, requiring an experienced eye, to pronounce positively whether a tumour or ulcer is cancerous. These charlatans have no such ability, but they pronounce every sore they see a cancer, and all their pretended cures are of innocent, non-malignant disorders. Cancers are more apt to develop themselves at this period. Their seat is most frequently in the womb or the breast, and they are said to be especially liable to arise in those women who have suffered several abortions or unnatural labours. Undoubtedly they are more frequent in the married life than in the unmarried, and they evidently bear some relation to the amount of disturbance which the system has suffered during childbirth, and the grief and mental pain experienced. For this reason a celebrated teacher of obstetrics insists upon classing them among nervous diseases. The surgeon alone can cure them, and he but rarely. Medicine is of no avail, however long and painstaking have been its researches in this direction. A touching story is related in this connection of Raymond Sully, the celebrated philosopher. When a young man he was deeply impressed with the beauty of a lady, and repeatedly urged his suit, which she as persistently repelled though it was evident she loved him. One day, when he insisted with more than usual fervour that she should explain her mysterious hesitation, she drew aside the folds of her dress and exposed her breast partly destroyed by a cancer. Shocked and horrified, but unmoved in his affection, he rushed to the physicians and demanded their aid. They replied they could give none. He determined to find a cure if he had to seek in all parts of the earth. He visited the learned doctors of Africa and Asia, and learned many wonderful things, even it was said, the composition of the philosopher's stone itself, but what he did not find and what has never yet been found, was what he went forth to seek—a cure for cancer.

At this time, too, or swellings of the ovaries

are apt to commence. They are nearly always preceded by scanty or painful menstruation, and this, therefore, it is the duty of every woman, as she values the preservation of her future health, to remedy by every means in her power.

Generally, from the commencement of the change of life, commences also a steady diminution of the sexual passions, and soon after this period they quite disappear. Sometimes, however, the reverse takes place, and the sensations increase in intensity, occasionally exceeding what they even were before. This should be regarded with alarm. It is contrary to the design of nature, and can but mean that something is wrong. Deep-seated disease of the uterus or ovaries is likely to be present, or an unnatural nervous excitability is there, which, if indulged, will bring about dangerous consequences. Gratification, therefore, should be temperate, and at rare intervals, or wholly denied.

To guard against the dangers of this epoch, those general rules of health which we have throughout insisted upon should be rigidly observed. If during the whole of her sexual life the woman has been diligent in observing the laws of health, she has little to fear at this period. Some simple remedies will suffice to allay the disagreeable symptoms, and the knowledge that most of them are temporary, common to her sex, and not significant of any peculiar malady, will aid her in opposing their attacks on her peace of mind. When plethora, flooding, or congestion is apparent, the food should be light, chiefly vegetable, and moderate in quantity. Liquors, wines, strong tea, coffee, and chocolate should be avoided; an occasional purgative or a glass of some laxative mineral water should be taken, and cool bathing regularly observed. Exercise should be indulged in with caution, and care taken to avoid excitement, severe mental or bodily effort, and exhaustion. If the system is debilitated, and the danger is rather from a want of blood than too much blood, nourishing food, tonic

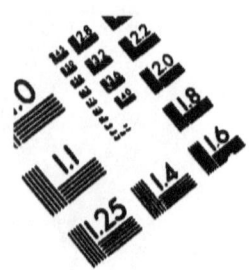 

**IMAGE EVALUATION
TEST TARGET (MT-3)**

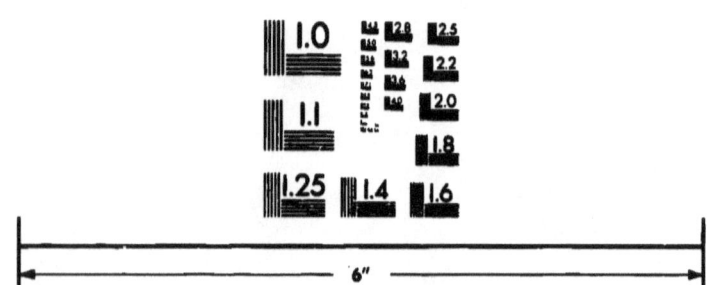

Photographic
Sciences
Corporation

23 WEST MAIN STREET
WEBSTER, N.Y. 14580
(716) 872-4503

medicines, and perhaps some stimulant are called for. When the perspiration is excessive, flannel should be worn next to the skin in the daytime, and a flannel night-dress at night. A tepid bath before retiring is also useful. The "goneness" and other unpleasant sensations referred to the pit of the stomach may be much relieved by wearing a well-made spice-plaster over the stomach, or binding there a bag of gum camphor, or if these fail, an opium plaster will hardly fail to be of service. Internally, we think nothing at all is needed; but as something must be taken, let it not be spirits or wine, but half a teaspoonful of aromatic spirits of ammonia in a few tablespoonfuls of water. There is too much of a tendency among some women to seek alleviation in intoxicating compounds, "bitters," "tonics," and so forth, at such times. They can only result in injury, and should be shunned. The pains in the back and loins often experienced can be removed by rubbing the parts with hot mustard-water, and taking a gentle purgative, or by placing against the lower part of the spine a hot brick wrapped in a flannel cloth wrung out in warm water or laudanum and water.

Once safely through this critical period, the woman has a better chance for long life and a green old age than the man of equal years. Tables of human life show this conclusively. With the sweet consciousness of duty performed, she is now prepared to assist others by intelligent advice, cheerful counsel, and tender offices; she can now surround herself with that saintly halo of kind words and good works which wins a worthier love than passion offers; and, passing onward to the silence of eternal rest, she will leave in the memory of all who knew her pleasant impressions and affectionate reminiscences.

NOTES.

P. 19. HERMAPHRODITES AND ASEXUALISM.—Rokitansky decides Hohmann to be a case of *hermaphrodita vera lateralis*, and all who examine her say the same. See *Wiener Medecin, Wochenschrift*, October, 1868, and the *Medical and Surgical Reporter*, vol. xix. p. 487. A marked case of asexualism, proven so by a *post-mortem* examination, is reported in the Buffalo *Medical and Surgical Journal* for April, 1869, p. 338; and another in the London *Medical Times and Gazette* of about the same date. We might refer to many less recent but less authentic cases.

P. 23. AGE OF PUBERTY.—See case by Dr. T. H. Twiner, in the *Richmond and Louisville Medical Journal*, March, 1869; Raciborski, *De la Menstruation et de l'Age Critique chez la Femme*, p. 130. The quotation is from Dr. Edward Smith, *Cyclical Changes in Health and Disease*—a profound work. Raciborski is the principal authority for this and the following section. Our own inquiries fully confirm his statements.

P. 29. INFLUENCE OF THE MOON ON MENSTRUATION.—On this question, see the researches of M. Parchappe, *Comptes Rendus de l'Académie des Sciences*, tom. xvi. p. 550. See also Dr. Shrye, *Tractatus de Fluxu Menstro* in the *Acta Lipsiensia* for 1686, p. 111; Dr. W Charleton, *Inquisitio Physica de Causis Catameniorum*, p. 78; and Galen, *De Diebus Decretoriis*, lib. iii., for other curious particulars.

P. 32. CHLOROSIS.—For the pathology of this disease, see Dr. Gaillard Thomas, *Diseases of Women*, p. 625; and Dr. C. H. Baner, in the *Wiener Medicin Zeitung*, No. 33, 1868. Occasionally the change at puberty leads to an affection very closely resembling typhoid fever, but which is strictly due to the sexual crisis, and often goitre commences at this period. See a review of Raciborski in the *Bulletin de Thérapeutique*, June, 1869.

P. 34. MASTURBATION IN GIRLS.—See Miss Catherine E. Beecher, *Letters to the People on Health and Happiness*, p. 159. The latest medical literature on the subject is abundant. See *Uber die Behandlung der Masturbation bei kleinen Mädchen, Journal für Kinderkrankheiten*, Bd. li. p. 360 ; H. R. Storer, *Western Journal of Medicine*, July, 1868 ; and *Journal of the Gynecological Society*, vol. i. No. 1.

Pp. 38, 39. PREMATURE MARRIAGES.—See Dr. Duncan, *Fecundity, Fertility*, etc., p. 241 ; Reich, *Natur und Gesundheitslehre des Ehelichen Lebens*, p. 518.

P. 41. HOLY LOVE.—The distinction between $αγαπη$, and $ερως$ is too familiar to all scholars to need extended mention. See Trench, *Synonyms of the New Testament*, sub voce.

Pp. 44, 45. SINGLE LIFE IN ITS RELATION TO SANITY AND MORTALITY.—The extraordinary statements in the text are vouched for by Dr. Casper, *Medicinische Statistik*, vol. ii. p. 164 ; and Dr. Reich, *Geschichte Natur, und Gesundheitslehre des Ehelichen Lebens*, pp. 510, 511. We have compared the reports of a number of American asylums for the insane, and find the proportions very nearly as great as stated by these authorities.

Pp. 55, 56. INTERMARRIAGE OF RELATIVES.—The view we advocate on this point, we know, is neither the received nor the popular one. In the middle ages it was forbidden to intermarry within the seventh degree of consanguinity. But this and all other regulations were based on theological and political, not physiological, grounds. Quite recently, Dr. Nathan Allen, of Massachusetts, has insisted on the danger of consanguineous marriages (*Journal of Psychological*

Medicine, April, 1869). But other very careful and recent students adopt the view of our text ; for instance, D. F. J. Behrend, *Journal für Kinderkrankheiten*, December, 1868, p. 316 ; Dr. A. Voisin, in the reports of the Paris *Académie de Médecine* 1864, 1865, and 1868; and Dr. H. Gaillard, in the last edition (1868) of the *Dictionnaire de Médecine et de Chirurgie Pratique*. All the statements in the text are supported with incontrovertible evidence by these writers. If we are asked how we meet the seemingly alarming array of allegations by Dr. Bemiss, the Kentucky physician referred to, in the *Transactions of the American Medical Association*, for 1859, we beg to refer to Dr. Behrend's articles, where the researches of Bemiss are severely, and, to our mind, justly criticised. For Dr. Edward Smith's assertion, see his *Essay on Consumption*, p. 244. (Philadelphia, 1865.)

Pp. 63, 64. COMMUNICATION OF VENEREAL DISEASES.—Many instances are recorded where a drinking-glass, a spoon, a fork, or a handkerchief has infected innocent persons with these terrible diseases ; see Cullerier, *Atlas of Venereal Diseases*, p. 43. They are communicated from the male to the female, or from the female to the male with equal facility, and either parent can transmit them to the children. The physician in Pennsylvania referred to is Dr. Sigmond, in the *Humboldt Medical Archives*, 1868.

P. 65. SYMBOLISM.—See Dr. Carus, *Symbolik der Menschlichen Gestalt*, the most scientific work ever written on physiognomy, phrenology, and allied subjects.

Pp. 71, 72. Vide Raciborski, *De la Puberté et de l'Age Critique chez la Femme*, p. 133 ; Tilt, *Uterine Therapeutics*, p. 315 (Am. ed., 1869.)

P. 74. See Dr. William A. Hammond's *Treatise on Hygiene*, p. 438, for air-space required by a healthy person. The contagion of phthisis is maintained by many authorities, among others Dr. W. Gerhard of this city ; vide Pennsylvania Hospital Reports for

1868, p. 266. Professor Castan has recently collected, in the *Montpelier Médicale*, a variety of facts which seem to show that tuberculosis may be communicated from a diseased to a healthy person by transpiration, breathed air, and living together (London *Press and Circular*, March 10, 1869). In regard to the inoculation of tubercle we have reference to the well-known experiments of M. Villemin, of the Hôpital Val-de-Grâce, Paris. In this connection we may record an instance of recent medical heroism. M. Lespiaud, attached to the surgical department of the Val-de-Grâce, in presence of several of his colleagues, extracted granular matter from the body of a phthisical subject, and introduced it under his own integument. This zealous investigator into the etiology of tuberculosis has thus exposed himself, in a courageous way, for the benefit of science, to the effects of a most dangerous and merciless disease. See *New Orleans Journal of Medicine* for January, 1869, quoted from the London *Lancet*.

P. 76. THE DIGNITY AND PROPRIETY OF THE SEXUAL INSTINCT.—Dr. Edward John Tilt, of London, is the Medical writer referred to; vide *Uterine Therapeutics*, pp. 95, 313. See also Bosquet, *Nouveau Tableau de l'Amour Conjugal*, vol. ii. p. 2, etc.; Roussel, *Système Physique et Moral de la Femme*, p. 211; Menville, *Histoire Médicale et Philosophique de la Femme*, vol. i. p. 36 *et seq.*; Raciborski, *De la Puberté*, etc., p. 45.

P. 78. ON THE INDULGENCE AND RESTRAINT OF SEXUAL DESIRE.—Menville, vol. ii. p. 91; Bosquet, vol. ii. p. 280; *Economy of Life; or Food, Repose and Love*, by George Miles (London, 1868). Dr. Edward Smith, in his valuable work on *Cyclical Changes in Health and Disease*, has collected extensive statistics showing the effect of the time of conception on the viability of the fœtus. The quotation is from Carpenter's *Human Physiology*, p. 753. (Am. ed.)

P. 81. See London *Lancet* for March 6, 1869, p. 337, for report of discussion in the Pathological Society of London upon the physical degeneracy resulting from procreation during intoxication. Authorities could be cited at length upon this subject, but it is not necessary. See Hufeland's *Art of Prolonging Life*, p. 207. (Am. ed., 1876.)

P. 82. Quotation from Dr. T. Gaillard Thomas's excellent work on *Diseases of Women*, p. 55.

Pp. 83-89. STERILITY.—For statistics referred to, see Dr. Matthews Duncan, *Fecundity, Fertility and Sterility* (Edinburgh, 1866), p. 181 *et seq.*; Dr. Tilt, *Uterine Therapeutics*, p. 291; Dr. Edward Reich, *Gesundheitslehre des Ehelichen Lebens*, Th. ii.

Dr. J. Marion Sims, *On the Microscope as an Aid in the Diagnosis and Treatment of Sterility*, New York Medical Journal, January, 1869, p. 406; Charles Darwin, *The Variation of Animals and Plants under Domestication*, vol. ii. p. 198 (Am. ed.); Philadelphia *Medical and Surgical Reporter*, November 2, 1867, p. 384; A. Debay, *Hygiène et Physiologie du Mariage*, p. 228 (Paris, Quarante-quatrième edition); Raciborski, *De la Puberté*, etc., p. 451; Virey, *De la Femme sous ses Rapports Phys.*, etc., p. 332; Dr. Gunning S. Bedford, *The Principles and Practice of Obstetrics*, p. 107.

P. 90. THE LIMITATION OF OFFSPRING.—We have taken great pains to avoid giving false or dangerous impressions in this section. The references in the order of quotation are :—Dr. Tilt, *Hand-Book of Uterine Therapeutics*, p. 317 (Am. ed.); Dr. Duncan, *Fecundity, Fertility and Sterility and Allied Topics*, pp 289, 290; Dr. Hillier, *Diseases of Children*, p. 114; John Stuart Mill, *Principles of Political Economy*, p. 591 (Eng. ed., 1866); Dr. Drysdale, London *Medical Press and Circular*, December, 1868, p. 478; Raciborski, *De l'Age Critique chez la Femme*, p. 484; *The Nation*, June, 1869; Dr. Ed. Reich, *Natur und Gesundheitslehre des Ehelichen Lebens*, p. 493; Boston *Medical and Surgical Journal*, February, 1867; Philadelphia *Medical and Surgical Reporter*, vol. xix. p. 305; Sismondi, *Principles of Political Economy*, book vii. chap. v.; Dr. MacCormac, in London *Medical Press and Circular*, March, 1869, p. 244 ; Dr. Gaillard Thomas, *Diseases of Women*, p. 58 ; Leavenworth *Medical Herald*, April, 1867 ; Dr. N. K. Bowling, in the Nashville *Journal of Medicine and Surgery*, October, 1868. We have rather let others speak than spoken ourselves, and have collected the opinions of many most distinguished physicians and statesmen, who thus pronounce against excessive child-bearing. Any intelligent physician will acknowledge the weight to be assigned to such names.

P. 102. Quotation from Philadelphia *Medical and Surgical Reporter*, August 8, 1868, p. 106.

P. 102. SIGNS OF FRUITFUL CONJUNCTION.—Carpenter, *Human Physiology*, p. 772 ; Dr. Gunning S. Bedford, *Principles and Practice of Obstetrics*, p. 304 ; Menville, vol. i. p. 295 ; Montgomery, *Signs and Symptoms of Pregnancy*, p. 90.

P. 105. INHERITANCE.—Darwin, *Animals and Plants under Domestication*, pp. 42, 473 (Am. ed.); Sir Henry Holland's *Medical Notes and Reflections*, p. 30 ; Pritchard, *Researches into the Physical History of Mankind*, vol. ii. p. 551 ; Carpenter, *Human Physiology*, p. 779 ; A. Debay, *Hygiène et Physiologie du Mariage*, p. 173 ; Flourens, *De la Longevité Humaine et de la quantité de Vie sur le Globe*, p. 256 (Paris, 1860); Hufeland, *Art of Prolonging Life*, pp. 91, 206 ; *Hammond's Hygiène*, p. 116 ; *American Journal of Medical Science*, July, 1865, p. 82 ; Francis Galton on *Hereditary Talent and Character*, in *Macmillan's Magazine*, vol. xii. pp. 157 and 318 ; Madden, *The Infirmities of Genius*, vol. ii. p. 107 ; London *Lancet*, December, 22, 1868, p. 825 ; the *British Medical Journal*, January 11, 1868, p. 25 ; Dr. Prosper Lucas, *Traité de l'Hérédité Naturelle;* Victor Hugo, *L'Homme Qui Rit*, le second chapitre préliminaire ; *Watson's Practice*, p. 1153 ; Dr. Daniel G. Brinton, *Guide Book to Florida and the South*, Pt. iii.

Dr. J. V. C. Smith, *Physical Indications of Longevity in Man.*

P. 122. Boston *Medical and Surgical Journal*, April 2, 1868.

P. 129. Dr. Arthur Mitchell, London *Medical Times and Gazette*, November 15, 1862.

P. 130. Duncan, *Fecundity, Fertility, and Sterility*, p. 69 ; Ramsbotham, *System of Obstetrics*, p. 461 (Am, Ed.) ; Philadelphia *Medical and Surgical Reporter*, vol. xix. p. 506 : xx. p. 98.

P. 132. London *Medical Press and Circular*, August 28, 1867 ; *Journal de Bruxelles*, July, 1867, p. 48.

P. 133. Menville i. p. 299 ; Dr. Gunning S. Bedford, *System of Obstetrics*, p. 144 *et seq.* ; Montgomery, *Signs and Symptoms of Pregnancy* ; Dr. Edward Rigby, *System of Midwifery*, p. 47.

P. 143. MOTHERS' MARKS.—See a very interesting article by Professor Wm. A. Hammond in *The Quarterly Journal of Psychological Medicine and Medical Jurisprudence*, January, 1868, p. 1, in which he says, in regard to the influence of the maternal mind over the fœtus *in utero*, " The chances of these instances, and others which I have mentioned, being due to coincidence, are infinitesimally small ; and though I am careful not to reason upon the principle of *post hoc ergo propter hoc*, I cannot, nor do I think any other person can, no matter how logical may be his mind, reason fairly against the connection between cause and effect in such cases. The correctness of the facts only can be questioned ; if these be accepted, the probabilities are thousands of millions to one that the relation between the phenomena is direct." See also Dr. J. Lewis Smith, *Diseases of Infancy and Childhood*, 1869, p 27 ; Philadelphia *Medical and Surgical Reporter*, vol. xix. p. 359.

Pp. 153-157. Raciborski, *De La Puberté*, etc., p. 491 ; Dr. Gunning S. Bedford, *System of Obstetrics*, p. 442 ; *Dict. des Sciences Médicales*, t. L. iii. ; London *Lancet*, August, 1856, p. 131 ; Carpenter, *Human Physiology*, p. 779 ; *Beck's Elements of Medical Jurisprudence*, Art. Superfœtation ; Rokitansky, *Pathological Anatomy* ; Philadelphia *Medical and Surgical Reporter*, May 1, 1859, p. 335 ; Professor

Pancoast removed some years since from the cheek of a child some months old, a rudimentary second child.

P. 158. Dr. Bedford, *Obstetrics*, p. 264; London *Lancet*, January 23, 1869.

P. 158. IS IT A SON OR A DAUGHTER ?—Philadelphia *Medical and Surgical Reporter*, vol. xvii. p. 495; Dr. Frankenhauser, in the *Monatschrift für Geburtskunde*; Dr. Packman on *Impregnation*, London *Lancet*, July 18, 1863.

P. 162. Dr. Bedford, *System of Obstetrics*, p. 299.

P. 162. Taylor, *Medical Jurisprudence*, p. 586; *Report of Proceedings against the Rev. Fergus Jardine*, Edinburgh, 1839.

P. 155. Churchill, *On Women*, p. 451 (Am. ed.); Menville, ii. 114; Tilt's *Elements of Health*, p. 271.

P. 189. TO HAVE LABOUR WITHOUT PAIN.—Professor T. Gaillard Thomas says, "The rule should be to employ an anæsthetic in every case of labour, *during the second stage*, unless some contra-indication exists. After a delivery under its influence, patients recover more rapidly, are freer from complications, and show fewer signs of prostration." Vide *Lecture on the management of Women after Parturition*, in the *Richmond and Louisville Medical Journal*. February, 1869, p. 145.

P. 190. Philadelphia *Medical and Surgical Reporter*, vol. xix. p. 388; Carpenter, *Human Physiology*, p. 810; Ramsbotham, *Obstetrics*, p. 111; *Detroit Review of Medicine and Pharmacy*, March, 1869, p. 150.

P. 195. THE MOTHER.—Dr. J. Lewis Smith, *A Treatise on the Diseases of Infancy and Childhood*, 1869, p. 28 et seq.; Dr. Thomas Hillier, *Clinical Treatise on the Diseases of Children*, p. 17 (Am. ed., 1868); Dr. Edward Smith, *Cyclical Changes in Health and Disease*; Dr. John Marshall, *Outlines of Physiology, Human and Comparative*.

pp. 761, 765, 998 (Am. ed., 1868); Dr. Charles A. Cameron, *Lectures on the Preservation of Health*, London, 1868, p. 174; Dr. Charles J. B. Williams, *Principles of Medicine*, p. 480 (Am. ed., 1868); Dr. J. Forsythe Meigs, *Diseases of Children*; Dr. E. J. Tilt, *Elements of Health and Principals of Hygiene*, p. 50 et seq. (Am. ed., 1853); Dr. Andrew Coombe, *The Management of Infancy*, p. 73 et seq. (Ninth ed., Edinburgh, 1860); *Report of Board of Health of Philadelphia*, for 1868, p. 43; *British and Foreign Medica-Chirurgical Review*, April, 1868, pp. 382, 454; *Southern Journal of the Medical Sciences*, November, 1865, p. 555; Dr. Thomas Hawkes Tanner, *Practice of Medicine*, p. 108,(Am. ed., 1866; Dr. Wm. A. Hammond, *Treatise on Hygiene*, p. 95 et seq.; Philadelphia *Medical and Surgical Reporter*, vol. xvi. p. 530; xix. pp. 36, 59, 119, 134, 382.

INDEX

	PAGE
Abdomen, changes in	137
pain in	175
Abortion, crime of, how to stop	93
evils of	98
Anger, effect on the milk	203
Appetite, depraved	139
Arrowroot, how to prepare it for children	219, 232
Atavism explained	106
Bath, hour of, for infants	226
drying skin after	228
use of soap in	228
value of, in infantile diseases	229
Bathing	169
Beautiful children, how to have	112
Beauty, value of	107
Bed, for married persons	73
most healthful	75
clothing of	75
in confinement	178
Body, symbolism of	65
Boys, more born than girls	123
Blondes, age of puberty of	26
Braces, abdominal	262
Breasts, changes in	125, 175

	PAGE
Bringing up by hand	217
Brunettes, age of puberty of	24
Celibacy, not chastity	44
results of	45
Change of life, regimen and perils of	271
Child, attention to	185
education before birth	152
can one cry before birth	155
Childbearing, excessive	56
Childbed, mortality of	189
Childbirth, imprudence after	192
to preserve form after	194
Children, decreased number of	58
diet for	230
new-born, weight and length of	190
three at a birth	130
four at a birth	131
five at a birth	131
Chlorosis	32
Cleanliness, curative influence of	265
Climate, effect on menstruation	25
Clothing during pregnancy	166
at confinement	177
of infants	224
Cold, effect of, on infants	225
Colour of infant	145
Complexion	108
Conception, nature of	99
signs of	102
Confinement, preparations for	175
bed for	181
dress for	177

	PAGE
Constipation	175
Constitution, effect on puberty	45
Consumption	56
Continence demanded from husbands	35
Courtship	51
Cousins, shall they marry	55
Daughters influenced by fathers	115
Deformities, hereditary	111
Degeneracy, cause of	82
of the human race, a query	252
Diet for infants	218
for children	230
Disease, transmission of	118
Diseases, hereditary	91
Divorce, its propriety	49
Education, influence of	117
of child in womb	152
Emotion, influence on child	147
Emotions, stimulation of	26
Engagement, the	67
Epilepsy, cause of	97
Eruptions of childhood, how to prevent	229
Exercise at puberty	37
during pregnancy	167
Falling of the womb	258
Fathers' influence on Daughters	115
Feeding of infants, manner of	230, 232
Fertility, hereditary	110
laws of	85
Flirtation	48

INDEX.

	PAGE
Food, during pregnancy	165
of infants and children	230
bill of fare, for	233
Foreigners, shall American women marry	58
Form, to preserve	194
Frigidity	86
Galen, anecdote of	101
Gardner, Lord, story of	161
Gotfr, story of	132
Green sickness	32
Growth of children	251
Hair, its significance	65
transmission of	109
Hardening infants, best way of	225
Husband, age of	59
temperament of	61
character of	63
how to choose	54
how to retain affections of	103
Husband and Wife	172, 212
Husbands, plurality of	50
Hysterics	34
Imagination, influence of, on child	148
Infancy, care of	222, 243, 245
deaths in	222
Infants' food	230
Infants, manner of carrying	243
how to lift	246
Inheritance	105
effects of	120
how to avoid	121
of talent	113

INDEX.

	PAGE
Injections	267
Intemperance, of several kinds	92
Irrigations	267
Knowledge, safety in	17
Labour, signs of approaching	179
symptoms of	179
false and true	180
cause of	180
duration of	192
dress during	182
how to calculate	164
how to have without pain	189
long	192
Late marriages, offspring of	269
Longevity, hereditary	110
Longings in pregnancy	149
Love, its power on humanity	40
what is it	42
differs from lust	43
is a necessity	44
is eternal	47
at first sight	53
Manner of feeding infants	230, 231, 232
Mania, puerperal	254
Marital relations, times to suspend	81
when painful	82
Marriage, time of year for	69
time of month for	69
Marriages, second	49
Maternity, perils of	253

		PAGE
Men as wet-nurses		210
Menstruation explained		22
Milk, influence of diet on		200
	influence of pregnancy on	200
	poisonous	202
	effect of anger on	205
	quantity required by infant	205
	over-abundance of	207
	scantiness of	208
	value as food	37, 230
Miscarriage		140
	causes and prevention of	142
Mind, changes in, in pregnancy		139
	influence of	102
	influence on nursing child	201
	of mother, influence on child	145
	the, during pregnancy	145, 171
Morning sickness		134
Mortality of infant life		222
	causes of	223
Mother, the		184, 195
	position in nursing	205
Mothers' influence on sons		115
Mothers' marks		143
Mutilations inheritable		119
Neck, form of		108
	its significance	66
Night-dress of children		226
Night-covering of children		226
Night, the wedding		71
Nipples, to harden		176
Nubility, the age of		35

INDEX.

	PAGE
Nursing	196, 210
care of health during	211
when improper	196
rules for	199
prolonged	210
position during	205
Nursing mother, qualities of good	206
Offspring, the limitation of	90
influenced by the mind	100
Over-nursing, signs of	213
Overlaying children, deaths from	224
how to prevent	224
Over-production, evils of	91
remedies for	95
Parr, Thomas	111
Perils of maternity	253
Perspiration, fetid	105
Plurality of wives or husbands	50
Pregnancy	133, 140
effect on health	172
signs of	134, 140
diseases of	173
double	153
length of	159
care of health during	165
causes of protracted	163
influence on the milk	200
Puberty, the age of	22, 23
what hastens and retards	25
the changes it works	27
mental changes	29

	PAGE
Puberty, completion of	29
dangers of	31
hygiene of	36
Qualities transmitted by parents	109
Quickening	136
Races, mixture of	56
Religion, mistaken notions of	94
Revaccination	242
Second marriages	49
Secret bad habits	34
Sex of child, how to predict	158
Sexes, distinction of	18
persons of both	19
production of, at will	125
Sexual desire, indulgence and restraint of	78
moderation in	79
Sexual instinct, dignity and propriety of	76
false notions about	78
influence on offspring	80
Sexuality, what it implies	18
Single life, the	268
Skin, culture of, in infancy	229
Sleep, at puberty	37
amount required in early life	235
during pregnancy	170
position in	170
Small-pox, death rate from	246
Soup, Liebig's	231
Spinal disease	32
Spring-time	69

	PAGE
Sterility	83
how to remedy	89, 90
Stillbirths	192
Stilling, Jung, anecdote of	53
St. Pierre, anecdote of	62
Sully, Raymond, anecdote of	278
Swimming, benefit of	229
Symbolism of the human body	45
Syringes	265
Talent, hereditary	113
Teething, period of	249
Temperament, transmission of	110
Temperaments explained	61
influence of	80
Tight lacing	261
Toilet, arts of, recommended	105
Tour, the wedding	69
Twins, how to predict	158
why born	129
Twin-bearing	128
Thury, Prof., his discovery	126
Vaccination, importance of	239
age for	242
Ventilation	169, 243
Virgins, wet-nursing by	209
Voice, change in puberty	28
Wedding	220
Wedding tour, the	69
night, the	71
Wet-nurse, how to select	216
Wet-nursing by virgins and men	209

	PAGE
Wives, plurality of	50
Woman, physical difference from man	19
sphereal	20
to be sought	51
Women, why redundant	122
diseases peculiar to	256
treatment of	258
Zurich, curious customs in	74

Parturition Without Pain:

A

Code of Directions

FOR

Escaping from the Primal Curse.

EDITED BY

M. L. HOLBROOK, M.D.,

Editor of the "Herald of Health."

"Neither shall there be any more pain, for the former things are passed away."
—Rev. xxi. 4.

Toronto:
ROSE PUBLISHING COMPANY.

PREFACE.

ORIGINALITY has not been sought in this work. All that has been attempted is, to set forth briefly and clearly the nature and importance of child-bearing, the slightness of its real dangers, and the best methods of alleviating its discomforts and sufferings.

The subject is itself extensive, and an immense range of related topics have a direct and important bearing on it. The difficulty has accordingly been, not to find what to say, but to decide what to omit.

It is believed that a healthful regimen has been described; a constructive, preparatory, and preventive training, rather than a course of remedies, medications, and drugs. The cooling, soothing, and nutritious Fruit Diet system is the central idea of the book, and it is believed that every recommendation in it is in harmony with that system.

Among the authorities who have been consulted and quoted or used, are the following: Bull, Dewees, Duncan, Gleason, Lozier, Montgomery, Napheys, Pendleton, Shew, Storer, Tilt, and Verdi.

CONTENTS.

CHAPTER I.
Healthfulness of Child-bearing 307

CHAPTER II.
Danger of Preventions.—Celibacy by the Diseased 312

CHAPTER III.
Opinions on Painless Childbirth.—Cases 317

CHAPTER IV.
Preparation for Maternity 322

CHAPTER V.
Exercise during Pregnancy 329

CHAPTER VI.
The Sitz-Bath, and Bathing generally, in Pregnancy .. 334

CHAPTER VII.
Painless Parturition by Fruit Diet.—Food generally... 337

CHAPTER VIII.
The Mind during Gestation.—"Longings."—"Mother's Marks" 350

CHAPTER IX.
The Ailments of Pregnancy and their Treatment 359

CHAPTER X.

Anæsthetics during Labour.—Female Physicians 367

Summary 371

APPENDIX.

The Husband's Duty—Small Families—Best Age for Procreation—Shall Sickly People Raise Children?—Importance of Physiological Adaptation—Celibacy—Tobacco and Alcohol—Determining the Sex of Children—Father's vs. Mother's Influence—Shall Pregnant Women Work?—Intellectual Activity and Parentage—Mrs. Stanton's Testimony..372–385

PARTURITION WITHOUT PAIN.

CHAPTER I.

HEALTHFULNESS OF CHILD-BEARING.

CHILDREN are a good and not an evil. A human being who is not to some extent fond of children, who does not to some extent desire to have children, is defective—maimed; just as a person is who is unable to take pleasure in music, or who is incapable of distinguishing between right and wrong, or cannot feel sympathy with the pleasure or pain of other people.

Accordingly, the cases of men, and still more of women, who do not desire children, are comparatively few, and are exceptions. They have always been, and still are, recognized as unfortunate instances of sickly or deformed natural constitution, or of the harmful influence of unhealthy social condition.

The whole range of history, the whole range of to-day's unperverted human nature, shows a profound love for offspring in the human race. A long series of cases might be cited, it is true, where infanticide has been practised. Yet the number, though great in itself, shrinks out of sight in comparison with the number of cases where it has not been practised. And, furthermore, it would be easy to show that this seeming ferocity is very often the perverted or rather inverted manifestation of the natural affection itself. That is, for instance, vast numbers of the infanticides practised by heathens upon their female children are perpetrated on the theory—either conscious or implied—that it is a kindness to put the little unfortunate things quickly out of a world where they have only unhappiness and servitude to expect.

Except such violations of natural law as this, it will be found that no more powerful motives, unless it be the instinct of preserving one's own life, shape the lives and govern the conduct of human beings than those which impel us to have children. Dr. S. G. Howe, the eminent physician and philanthropist, places but one motive above that of desire for reproducing our species in point of power over human beings. He says, in a discussion upon the treatment of feminine wrong-doers; "As with the FIRST great instinct of nature—to support and prolong our individual life at whatever cost to others—even so with the SECOND, which leads us to renew and extend our existence by transmitting it to others."

The Bible, unerringly true in its psychology, is full of this motive. It may even be said that the powerful protection of this profound instinct was used by the Almighty as the impregnable hiding-place in which the plan of human redemption was slowly evolved and human thought habituated to it. Every thoughtful student of Bible psychology will perceive that the two inseparable motives—love of offspring, and hope of motherhood of the Messiah—lay in the very heart of hearts of the Jewish national life.

But the point needs no argument. Few indeed are those who will seriously deny that children are a source of happiness. Helpless as an infant is, troublesome as are the fantastic tricks and naughtinesses of childhood, painful as are parental anxieties over the critical eras of youth—in spite of all, a home without children is inexpressibly dreary; a heart without children is sad and lonesome beyond expression; a life without children is felt by one of the deepest of instincts to be an imperfect life, shorn of one of the broadest and most vital and vivid portions of emotion and enjoyment.

The money value of a child has been calculated by one philosophical observer. He concludes, in a manner that reminds one somewhat of a slavetrader's computations, that, on an average, a healthy boy fifteen years old, is equivalent to fifteen hundred dollars cash. This is no doubt a sum not to be despised. But it becomes invisible when we compare it with an estimate of the affectional, social, and ethical value of children. The exercise of so much patience, forbearance, kindness and love, as their training requires, reacts with infinite power upon the heart of the parent. Constant thoughtfulness, prudence, foresight, and contrivance are indispensable in managing them; and this discipline in like manner reacts upon the character of the manager. The future of children is one of the most powerful considerations in restraining parents from carelessness or indiscretion in economical matters, in their ordinary walk and conversation, in the whole conduct of life. Many a man or woman has been held back from folly or from shame by the recollection of what the children would know of it, or would hear of it.

In truth, the whole fabric of society is keyed upon these feeblest and most imperfect of its members. Remove their influences, and the chief bond of matrimony disappears; and with it disappear the home, the family, and a whole vast circle of forces indispensable to individual self-control, to general morality, to the very existence of society and of nations. The individual, thus loosed, stands without ties to any of his kind, without recollections of ancestors, responsibilities to his fellows, or expectations towards a future generation. Our civilized and organized frame of society, a body instinct with healthy life, would drop at once into a mere collection of ultimate atoms, by putrid decomposition.

Truths inosculate. It is in accordance with what has

been said of the inestimable importance of children in society and as instruments for the development of character, that the office of bearing children should be not merely a natural but a positively healthful office.

As in all other respects whatever, a compliance with the natural laws of human existence in this particular, promotes the total significance—*i. e.*, the extent, the efficiency, the enjoyableness—of that existence. To suppose the case otherwise is to suppose the Creator other than wise. But it is an old paradox, that it is an absurdity which is the "thing impossible to God."

No doubt there are exceptions to the rule. But unless there are special reasons to the contrary, married persons live longer than unmarried; and as a general rule it is absolutely true that long life is happy life. This is the case with both men and women; and writers on longevity accordingly habitually prescribe matrimony as one important means. But the mother's office in the production of offspring is beyond all comparison a greater element in her life—it occupies an infinitely greater proportion of her time, her head, her heart, her physical strength and vitality, than in the case of the father. And as might be supposed, the influence of marriage and child-bearing upon the duration of women's lives is decidedly more distinct and easy to determine than the influence of marriage and paternity upon men.

Among the numerous elaborate statistical tables which have been prepared during the last half century, are many which show that of the women who die between the ages of twenty and forty-five, more are single than married. History affords no instance of a single woman who has lived to a remarkably great age. Of women who commit suicide, from two-thirds to three-fourths are single. Of women confined in lunatic asylums, from three-fourths to four-fifths are single. There is a startling list of diseases which either actually originate from celibacy strictly observed by persons possessing the average qualities of humanity, or which are very greatly developed and intensified by it. The proverbial eccentricities of "old maids" are no mere imaginations. They are neither more nor less than the unavoidable consequences of an unnatural way of living. So immediate and important is the influence of celibacy or marriage on health, that we find medical authorities of the highest rank treating it as a matter of hygienic importance, as obvious and as weighty as food or exercise or climate. Thus the great French physician, Pinel, says that medicine is helpless in cases where " the immutable necessities of fecundity and reproduction are perverted. When therefore a young marriageable maiden exhibits symptoms of the approach of *any disease*, she should if possible be united to the object of her affections." And the physician who quotes this language adds, "this treatment has often proved very successful in averting diseases that would have rendered her life one of misery."

Thus it appears that the process of child-bearing is essentially necessary to the physical health and long life, the mental happiness, the development of the affections and whole character of women individually (of men also), and to the very existence, not only of the human race but of civilised society.

CHAPTER II.

DANGER OF PREVENTIONS.

In like manner as it was shown that the healthfulness of child-bearing accords with natural indications, so does the doctrine that frustrations of child-bearing are unhealthful accord with the same indications. The invasion and devastation of a great province of life cannot but weaken the whole. The function of child-bearing diverts to its purposes and absorbs in its offices such a vast share of the physical frame, of the blood, of the nervous system, of the whole vitality of the mother, that to meddle with it meddles with her very existence.

The vast importance of the maternal office is strikingly shown in estimates of the influence of the female reproductive system upon the whole life which have been made by distinguished medical writers. "*Propter uterum est mulier*," asserts one of them—" Woman exists for the sake of the womb." And Professor Hubbard, of New Haven, in an annual discourse before a medical society during 1870, spoke as follows: "The sympathies of the uterus with every other part of the female organism are so evident, and the sympathetic relations of all the organs of woman with the uterus are so numerous and complicated, so intimate and often so distant, yet pervading her entire being, that it would almost seem, to use the expression of another, ' as if the Almighty, in creating the female sex, *had taken the uterus and built up a woman around it.*'" And again, he calls this organ "the great central *pivotal* organ of her existence."

Even when brought on without special violence—even when merely resulting from general or local imperfections previously existing, miscarriages are recognised as perilous to an exceptional and even mysterious degree. All the standard writers on the subject are as strenuous as language will permit in their warnings against causing miscarriages, in requiring the extremest delicacy of precaution for avoiding them, and in depicting not only their temporary and immediate consequences, but the terrible danger that they will cause—the utter ruin of all health and happiness during whatever is left of life. Thus Dr. Thomas Bull observes: " There is no accident befalling female health which forms a greater source of dread, anxiety, and subsequent regret to a married woman than miscarriage. When this occurrence becomes habitual, there is no circumstance the consequences of which are productive of more serious injury to the constitution, blasting the fairest promises of health, and oftimes laying the seeds of fatal disease."

This intrinsic danger is frightfully increased when drugs or violence are used in order to break up the natural course of gestation by the destruction of the unborn child. Much attention has, especially of late years, been called to the wide prevalence of such practices, and the assertion has been extensively and often made that American women are peculiarly addicted to it, and those of New England more than any other. Whatever may be the exact statistics of the subject, and while the practice itself is as bad as it can be called, yet it is extremely probable that in this case, as in many others, publicity and prevalence are confounded. No evil can be exposed by thorough local investigation without apparent proof that the locality best investigated was worst conditioned—which is a fallacious mode of reasoning.

However, the practice of deliberately procuring abortions is no doubt quite frequent, awfully dangerous, and awfully wicked. Recent publications on the subject, by Dr. Storer, Dr. Todd, Bishop Coxe, and others, have so powerfully attacked this wicked practice, from physiological, moral, and religious considerations, that no extended discussion of it is necessary here, even did space permit it. A summary of considerations must suffice.

It is hardly necessary to remind the reader that the common sense of mankind has been expressed in numerous laws inflicting fine, imprisonment, or death, upon the principals and accessories in procuring an abortion, as upon those guilty of a felony. In like manner, a stigma of horror and contempt is always set upon a known abortionist like that which used to brand the slave-trader. If he be a physican, his brethren reject him; if a quack, all society rejects him. Neither hundreds of thousands of dollars, limitless magnificence, a fine house on Fifth Avenue, the possession of the most dangerous secrets, eager ambition, nor unfailing energy, has been able to secure a respectable social position to the best known female abortionist in New York.

For this shame and horror there is overwhelming cause. The procuring of an abortion is putting to death a human being—that is, it is murder—unless there exist reasons as weighty and as urgent as those which prevent the taking of adult life from being murder.

It is, morever, self-murder also in many cases, for the number of deaths resulting directly and quickly from it is very great, and still greater is the destruction of life by shortening and sickening the subsequent existence of the mother. "Miscarriages," says Dr. Storer, "are often a thousand-fold more dangerous in their immediate consequences than the average of natural labours. ... They are not only frequently much more hazardous to life at the time, but to subsequent health; their results in some instances remaining latent for many years, at times not showing themselves until the so-called turn of life, and then giving rise to uncontrollable and fatal hemorrhage, or to the development of cancer or other incurable disease."

Among the results to the mother other than death, from what may be called natural, still more from artificial miscarriage, are all the numerous and varied miseries of displacement and falling of the womb; leucorrhœa; ovarian disorders, liable to end in tumour or dropsy; dangerous inflammations of the reproductive organs and of others from sympathy with them; fistulæ, perhaps the most horrible of surgical diseases; adhesions, degenerations, and numerous other permanently distressing results of these inflammations; subsequent inability to produce any but sickly or deformed children; total barrenness; and last, but not least, insanity.

Besides that it is murder to the child-victim, frequently suicide, murder, or physiological ruin to the mother, and a felony in all engaged in perpetrating it, the habitual practice of procuring abortions, like the habitual practice of any crime, saps the life and strength of the community, as well as of the individuals who compose it; and Storer aptly quotes from Granville on Sudden Death, the impressive warning: "Let the legislator and moralist look to it; for as sure as there is in any nation a hidden tampering with infant life, whether frequent or occasional, systematic or accidental, so surely will the chastisement of the Almighty fall upon such a nation."

Both celibacy and frustrated fruitfulness are unnatural and perilous. There are, however, as has been observed, exceptional cases when the enforcement of both one and the other may be justified. There may be cases where a miscarriage ought to be produced, just as there are cases where a living child must be put to death in the very act of delivering the mother. It is, however, the physician's duty to pass and execute such judgments; and he is bound, in doing so, to act from the motives of his profession, and not to consult the patient's fear of shame, nor her desire to avoid the care of maternity. There are cases where peculiarities of organization or disposition indispose or unfit individuals for matrimony; and such persons do rightly to live single. But such cases do not at all interfere with the principles above set forth as generally true.

A more difficult question is that sometimes raised, whether inheritable disease should prevent the person infected with it from marriage? On this point, it is believed that most opinions can be ranked in two groups: one starting from the belief that the requisite self-denial for such avoidance of marriage is practicable; and the other that it is not. The truth is, that in the present state of our knowledge about the real nature of diseases and of transmissibility of qualities from parent to offspring, the materials for an authoritative decision of this question do not exist; and no such, applicable to all cases, can be given. At the same time it is clear that to a high-minded person the fact of being tainted with a disorder likely to ruin the health and happiness of offspring would be a very powerful motive for refraining from marriage. And yet, on the other hand, the recuperative energies of the human organism, both individually and as a succession of generations, are so indefinite and so wonderful, that great excuse could be found for almost any one who should marry and have children, notwithstanding such an objection. It is an obvious suggestion, that when persons having inheritable disease become parents, mere justice as well as natural affection, require that they should bestow special and untiring pains and care to counteract the evil tendency in the children by the healthiest possible training, in order that the natural forces may be helped as far as may be to eject or overcome the malignant influences

CHAPTER III.

OPINIONS ON PAINLESS CHILDBIRTH.

THE accounts given by travellers of the marvellous ease, quietness, painlessness, and freedom from disablement, with which many savage women bring forth children, are well known. There is great reason for believing that among some savage races neither pregnancy nor labour interrupts the usual avocations and movements of the mother, except, perhaps, for an hour or two at the birth itself. It is not, however, so generally known that the records of medical observation contain accounts of a number of cases of almost equally complete contradictions of what is commonly considered a primal and universal curse upon humanity.

Dr. Tuke, a high authority, says: " Parturition itself, according to the general testimony of travellers, interferes much less, and for a shorter period, with the healthy action of the body and mind than among the luxurious daughters of artificial life."

Dr. Dewees, one of the best authorities in obstetrics, has argued in one of his publications, that "*pain in childbirth is a morbid symptom;* that it is a perversion of nature caused by modes of living not consistent with the most healthy condition of the system; and that such a regimen as should insure such a completely healthy condition might be counted on with certainty to do away with such pain." The account of the Fruit Diet system, given in our subsequent Chapter VII., demonstrates, it is believed, an entire fulfilment of this prediction of the eminent Philadelphia physician.

In like manner we find the great English scientist, Professor Huxley, saying in his paper on "Emancipation.

Black and White," "We are, indeed, fully prepared to believe that the bearing of children may, and ought to become, as free from danger and long disability to the civilized woman as it is to the savage."

The following paragraphs, from one of the essays in Dr. Montgomery's classical work on Pregnancy, are interesting as giving circumstantial details of cases in illustration of the belief in the practicability of painless parturition:

"In a letter to me, dated 5th November, 1832, Dr. Douglas states that he was called about six o'clock A. M., on the 26th of September, 1832, to attend Mrs. D., of the County of W——, but then residing in Eccles Street. On his arrival he found the house in the utmost confusion and was told that the child had been born before the messenger was despatched for the doctor; and from the lady herself he learned that, about half an hour previously, she had been awakened from a natural sleep by the alarm of a daughter about five years old, who had slept with her for some nights before, and this alarm had been occasioned by the little girl feeling the movements and hearing the crying of an infant in the bed. To the mother's great surprise, she found that she had brought forth her child without any consciousness of the fact. . . In the *London Practice of Midwifery*, a work generally ascribed to a late very distinguished practitioner, we find the following account:

"'A lady in great respectability, the wife of a peer of the realm, was actually delivered once in her sleep: she immediately awaked her husband, being a little alarmed at finding one more in bed than was before.' . . . .

"I have elsewhere mentioned the case of a patient of mine who bore eight children without ever having labour pain; and her deliveries were so sudden and void of sensible effort, that in more than one instance they took place under most awkward circumstances, but without any suffering. . . Dr Wharrie relates the case of a primipara (*i. e.*, a woman bearing children for the first time), aged twenty-one, who had been in labour about six hours; she complained of no pain, and the child was born without effort or consciousness."

A case is known of a lady in New England who had five children, and who, unless at her first delivery, experienced no pain; and another case is known of a lady whose reputation is high as a writer and speaker, who asserted that it was her own experience that the so-called pains of childbirth were no more entitled to the name than the sensations attendant upon other natural processes which are ordinarily entirely painless.

All these cases, it should be noted, were of women in good health; and the two latter, at any rate, were persons of exceptionally fine and strong constitutions. In like manner, those women of savage nations who bear children without pain, live much in the open air, take much exercise, and are physically active and healthy to a degree greatly beyond their more civilized sisters.

These instances tend directly to prove that parturition is likely to be painless in proportion as the mother is physically perfect and in a perfect condition of health. They certainly tend even more strongly to prove that pain is not an absolute necessary attendant of parturition.

As for the announcement of Genesis iii. 16, "In sorrow thou shalt bring forth children," it may judiciously be compared with the accompanying announcement to the man, that he should earn his bread by the sweat of his brow. This latter does not prohibit the ameliorations of associated effort, or of labour-saving machinery; not even if at some future time these should, as seems not improbable, elevate mankind above the necessity of yielding the greater part of life to mere drudgery. Nor does the former prediction prohibit the use of means to diminish the suffering which it foretells. It would be a misrepresentation of the Almighty, indeed, to assert that in prophesying evil He had meant to refuse escape from it. God is good, and does not do so. If He prophesies evil it is not in order to perpetuate it, but if possible to prevent or cure it. Indeed, the language may properly be considered as a prediction merely. As such it has already been abundantly fulfilled. There has been suffering enough in childbirth to satisfy, not merely a God, but a devil. There is enough within every day that passes over our heads. For the great majority of women in civilized nations, parturition is a period of intense pain. Doubtless the total of its sufferings are the greatest single item of every-day human misery. Dr. Storer says: "There is probably no suffering ever experienced which will compare, in proportion to its extent in time, with the throes of parturition." And he quotes from Dr. Meigs, who says: "Men cannot suffer the same pain as women. What do you call the pains of parturition? There is no name for them but Agony."

The course of modern scientific investigation, however, has gone far to justify a belief that this terrific burden upon humanity can be almost entirely removed; that the pain of parturition can be as completely done away with as the danger and disfigurement of small-pox, for instance. It is the object of the following chapters to set forth briefly the substance of the best principles and rules that have been arrived at for this purpose, up to the present time.

At the same time, this immeasurable benefit to humanity cannot be obtained without the proper use of means, and the continuance of such use for a considerable period. The doctrines of the ablest thinkers on the subject will be found to agree in this; that it is the previous life of the mother—*the whole of it*, from her own birth to the birth of her child—which almost entirely determines what her danger, her difficulty, and her pain during childbirth shall be. Her easy or difficult labour, in fact, is almost entirely her own work. Her conduct during gestation, it is true, is more immediately influential in the decision than that of remoter periods, and is or may be greatly more influential upon the future life of her offspring than even upon herself. But the suggestions to be given in these pages about the *whole* previous life of the mother, although at first they may seem too indirectly concerned with the subject, are not so by any means.

CHAPTER IV.

PREPARATION FOR MATERNITY.

It is not too much to say that the life of woman before marriage ought to be adjusted with more reference to their duties as mothers than to any other one earthly object. It is the continuance of the race which is the chief purpose of marriage. The passion of amativeness is probably, on the whole, the most powerful of all human impulses. Its purpose, however, is rather to subserve the object of continuing the species, than merely its own gratification.

As, however, this little treatise does not discuss either physiology, hygiene, education, or social ethics, what is to be said on the general subject of this chapter is only a series of reminders or hints, each of them meant to be reinforced by a special reference to their importance in the preparation for maternity.

The mother needs to be strong, healthy, sensible, well-informed, well-mannered, refined, accomplished, kind, pure, and good. The girl, accordingly, needs to be brought up to be such.

Girls should be brought up to live much in the open air, always with abundant clothing against wet and cold. They should be encouraged to take much active exercise; as much, if they want to, as boys. It is as good for little girls to run and jump, to ramble in the woods, to go boating, to ride and drive, to play and "have fun" generally, as for little boys.

All their physiological and hygienic habits should be watched and formed as early in life as possible. It is next to impossible to change after adult years are reached; it only requires steady care to form the habits of a child so that they shall need no change.

Sleep should be regular and plentiful; in airy rooms; at early hour; each child in a separate bed. After-life will afford all that is necessary in the way of late hours, bad air, and broken rest. As for habitually sleeping two in a bed, while no absolute rule can be laid down on the subject, it is coming to be believed by many sensible thinkers, that even among married people it is by no means always the most healthful practice.

Children should be carefully prevented from using their eyes to read or write, or in any equivalent exertion, either before breakfast, by dim daylight, or by artificial light. Even school studies should usually be such that they can be dealt with by daylight. Lessons that cannot be learned without lamp-light study are almost certainly excessive. This precaution should ordinarily be maintained until the age of puberty is reached. When the girl begins to study with the sense of a self-conducting intellect, she has reached an age when her physical as well as mental training should by right be intrusted as far as possible to her own guidance; and she must, in a great measure, take charge of her own eyes as well as her own thoughts and conduct.

The food should be healthful, plain, cooked with as much care as if the process were chemical, and almost always nutritious merely, and cooling, rather than stimulant, in quality. Coffee and tea, alcoholic fluids and spices, rich cake and pastry, had better be put off until adult age. If they are used then, it is on the recipient's own responsibility. Abundance of luxuries for the palate may be allowed not only without harm, but with advantage, by selecting among good, fresh, and preserved fruits and nuts; by choosing confectionary made only of clean good sugar and clean good flavours, *and by giving it exclusively as a dessert*, in moderate quantities. Thus associated with other food, it will be found as harmless as the brown sugar or molasses eaten with buckwheat cakes.

Bathing should be enforced according to constitutions, not by an invariable rule, except the invariable rule of keeping clean. Not necessarily every day, nor necessarily in cold water; though those conditions are doubtless often right in case of abundant physical health and strength.

The teeth should be closely watched, and the irksome task of brushing them should be personally supervised by the parent every day. It will often be the case that no less watchfulness than this will assure the performance of the duty up to the time when the girl begins to care for her own personal attractions.

The habit of daily natural evacuations should be solicitously formed and maintained. Words or figures could never express the discomforts and wretchedness which wrong habits in this particular have locked down upon innumerable women for years and even for life.

Attitude should be regarded, so far as not merely to cultivate habitually decorous manners in sitting and moving, but as to firmly establish habitually healthy postures of body. It is seldom necessary to use such deformity-cures as back-boards, braces, &c. They usually follow upon previous neglect. Few, indeed, are the girls who, if brought up with sufficient open-air exercise, good food, proper sleep, healthful costume, and correct hygienic habits, will poke out their chins, round their shoulders, or develop a curvature of the spine. As in mind, so in body—human beings are a pretty fair average, after all, if we let nature have a fair chance.

Dress should be warm, loose, comely, and modest rather than showy; but it should be good enough to satisfy a child's desires after a good appearance, if they are reasonable. Children, indeed, should have all their reasonable desires granted as far as possible; for nothing makes them reasonable so rapidly and so surely as to treat them reasonably.

The requisites just named for children's dress are quite as important during youth and married life. Dr. Verdi. in his work on Maternity, traces in a very striking way the influence of dress upon the children of the *next* generation. What he says exhibits the following chain of causes and effects, and is worthy to be set forth in whole discourses and volumes by itself, though it must here be compressed—like a misdressed young lady—perhaps too much for the greatest utility. It is thus:

Children and young persons should be dressed with equal warmth throughout, so that shoulders, arms, lower body, legs, and feet should be as well defended against cold and wet as the body from waist to shoulders. That exposure of legs and lower body, which is so extremely common for children, chills the skin. This clogs and impedes the circulation, and especially drives away the blood from the abdomen. This obstructs digestion, even causes the bowels to almost cease their functions, and causes a habitually constipated condition. This condition is one of the most usual causes of subsequent displacements of the womb, leucorrhœa, ulceration, and other local disorders extremely painful and wearing. These, lastly, are wellnigh fatal to the prospect of healthy children, and in many cases leave the mother who has grown up thus disordered actually incapable of carrying a child of full term, and condemned to miscarriages at the sixth or eighth week, with all their miserable concomitants.

At school, girls should not be forced to excessive study. Great harm is every year done in such forcing-houses as Miss Mary Lyon's famous school, and even in such comparatively low-pressure machines as Vassar College, by over-stimulation of girls' minds and deficient hygienic physical training, exactly at the delicate, critical period when they are changing from girls to women. The proportion between book-work and mental labour on the one hand, and physical training on the other, should be adjusted, that if either mental or physical progress must be temporarily neglected, *it shall not be the latter*; for at the school-girl age, a few months of ill-health or neglected symptoms may seriously compromise all the rest of life.

and life's happiness. This consideration is of greater importance than a hundred years of "schooling."

The young lady period—as perhaps that season may be called, between the close of school years and the time of marriage—has also its peculiar needs. However, what has been said of young girls is true, with the requisite qualifications, of marriageable maidens also. They must be allowed more elaborateness and adornment of attire. They range, with more or less of freedom, through some circuit of entertainments and company. They read novels; they are out late; they swallow solid or liquid trash; they dance, they flirt, they court—until marriage comes to close the last scene of this strange, eventful history— and then to re-open it, as soon as the birth-cry of the first-born thrills the mother's heart.

Great harm is often done to maidens for want of knowledge in them, or wisdom and care in their parents. The extremes of fashions are very prone to violate not only taste, but physiology. Such cases are, tight lacing, low necked dresses, thin shoes, heavy skirts. And yet, if the ladies only knew it, the most attractive costumes are not the extremes of fashions, but those which conform to fashion enough to avoid oddity, which preserve decorum and healthfulness, whether or no; and here is the great secret of successful dress—vary the fashion so as to suit the style of the individual.

A sensible girl and her sensible mother can accomplish all this. Indeed, let such a pair as that consult confidentially and unreservedly, and that girl is safe every way. She will dress beautifully, and yet comfortably; she will enjoy herself completely, and yet without disordering her stomach, killing the roses in her cheeks, or draining her life out in fatigues and sleeplessness; she will read extensively and abundantly, yet without slip-slopping her mind away with novels of the foolish sort, or inflaming and disorganizing it with such printed erysipelas as Braddon's and Ouida's books.

Last of all, parental care is the use of whatever influence can be exerted in the matter of courtship and marriage. Maidens, as well as youths, must, after all, choose for themselves. It is their own lives which they take in their hands as they enter the marriage state, and not their parents'; and as the consequences affect them primarily it is the plainest justice that with the responsibility should be joined the right of choice.

The parental influence, then, must be indirect and advisory. Indirect, through the whole bringing up of her daughter; for if they have trained her aright, she will be incapable of enduring a fool, still more a knave; her feminine instincts and intuitions, cultivated and sanctified by the purity and the intelligent thought of a refined home, will have become capable of giving great light upon any question of liking or disliking that may arise, and the truthful unreserve of a good daughter with a good mother will usually supply all the further guidance that is necessary. If a sensible matron and a sensible maiden together cannot conclude pretty safely in any case where a young man is concerned, the question may about as well be decided by tossing up a cent.

Yet there are some points respecting the intercourse of young women with young men that are worth referring to. They come pretty much within one general rule:

A young woman and a young man had better not be alone together very much until they are married.

This will be found to prevent a good many troubles. It is not meant to imply that either sex, or any member of it, is worse than another, or bad at all, or anything but human. It is simply the prescription of a safe general rule. It is no more an imputation than the rule that people had better not be left without oversight in presence of large sums of other folks' money. This does not mean that people are thieves—it means only that they are human; and it will be found in practice that the more thoroughly honest a man is, the more careful he is to avoid any pecuniary temptation himself, and to provide for constant and stringent oversight upon himself.

It is not good for a young man and a young woman to be left much alone together either in a dimly-lighted room or a brightly-lighted one; nor anywhere, except where they are liable to the ordinary interruptions of the household. The close personal proximity of the sexes is greatly undesirable before marriage. Kisses and caresses are most properly the monopoly of wives. Such indulgences have a direct and powerful physiological effect. Nay, they often lead to the most fatal results.

At some time before marriage, those who are to enter into it ought to be made acquainted with some of the plainest common-sense limitations which should govern their new relations to each other. Ignorance in such matters has caused an infinite amount of disgust, pain, and unhappiness. It is not necessary to specify particulars here; but if the mother of every bride would instruct her daughter in what a woman should comply with her husband, and when and how she ought to seek to decline compliance; and if the father of every bridegroom would instruct his son as to the just limits of indulgence, as to a gentleman's duty of self-control and respect toward a lady, and as to the proper occasions for exercising such self-control in the marital relations, this is all that could be done and it would be a great deal.

CHAPTER V.

EXERCISE DURING PREGNANCY.

IN considering how the mother can adjust her ways of living during pregnancy in such a manner as to insure the termination of the process in the safest and easiest manner possible, the question of bodily exercise may be first discussed.

It is, no doubt, almost needless to argue that some such general preparation, by careful living during pregnancy, is best. But much more than such a mere general careful living is best. The period of gestation should be solicitously employed for the purpose in question, on system, regularly, and under the best accessible instructions.

It may not be generally known that before the performance of many important surgical operations, it is the practice to carry patients through a course of training on purpose to prepare their bodies to endure the expected strain upon them. This training differs, of course, from that by which pugilists prepare their bodies for the immense exertion of a fight; but its purpose is just the same —to prepare the body to endure, with the least possible pain and injury, an unusual and violent exertion or strain. Dr. Storer (*Gynæcological Journal*, ii. 19), thus refers to this training for surgical purposes:

"Preparation of the patient before an operation, by weeks or months of careful general regimen, or of special care. . . . . depuration of the blood and its enrichment preparatory to the tax upon it—these were matters of cardinal importance."

There are, undoubtedly, cases in which great care need to be taken to avoid motion during pregnancy. These cases are, where there is danger of miscarriage. This is a misfortune which, for some unknown reason, grows into what may be called a constitutional habit more quickly, and becomes confirmed more surely and permanently, than almost any other. Where it has once taken place, the danger of its happening again is greatly increased; and the utmost care is usually necessary to bring the system back again to its natural condition. One of the most important precautions for this purpose is to be as nearly motionless as possible; for the local weakness which exists in such cases seems to depend greatly upon an inability to resist what may be called the mechanical results even of the ordinary exertions of every-day life; and the restoration of the healthy local conditions seems to depend greatly upon the avoidance of such exertion.

Leaving out, however, such exceptions, the general rule is, not that indolence promotes the health and the easy parturition of the mother, and the health and safety of her offspring, but exactly the contrary. From the beginning of pregnancy, even more care than usual should be taken to use regular, abundant, and healthful (N.B., not excessive nor violent) exercise, particularly during the first months of the period. As its termination approaches, more and more repose may be sought, as circumstances shall indicate.

Dr. Thomas Bull, an experienced and sensible English obstetrical practitioner, gives the following clear and useful directions on this point:

"During the first six or seven months, frequent and gentle exercise in the open air and domestic occupations *which require moderate exertion*, are exceedingly desirable; both have a beneficial influence on the health of the mother, and, through her, upon the child. The former invigorates health, the latter contributes, by its regular return and succession of duties, to employ her time, and thus insures that ease and serenity of mind so essential to her happiness. On the other hand, excessive effeminacy is highly injurious. The female whose time is spent in indolence, continually reclining on a softly-cushioned sofa, in the unwholesome atmosphere of an over-heated apartment, who never breathes the fresh and pure air of heaven, but is fearful of even putting her foot to the ground, and who yet, perhaps, at the same time indulges pretty freely an immoderate appetite, under such circumstances, is not likely to preserve her health, much less to improve it; in fact, it must suffer serious injury. Unfortunately the evil will not stop here; for by such improper and injudicious conduct the nutrition and growth of the child must, as a natural consequence, be much interfered with, and when born, it will be feeble, perhaps emaciated, and will be reared with difficulty.

"During the last few weeks exercise should still be taken in the open air; but as walking, with some, is now attended with inconvenience, and so quickly with fatigue, that it is injurious instead of useful, exercise in a convenient and easy carriage becomes indispensable. Domestic duties must be almost altogether given up; and the recumbent position ought to be resorted to for at least two or three hours in the course of the day; and it should never be forgotten that throughout the whole period of pregnancy, every kind of agitating exercise, such as riding in a carriage with rapidity on uneven roads, dancing much and frequently, lifting or carrying heavy weights, ought to be avoided; in short, all masculine and fatiguing employments whatever."

Dr. Verdi, in his *Maternity*, devotes but little space to general hygiene, as his work is a detailed enumeration of maladies and their remedies. The half-dozen lines in which he condenses his recommendations on this question of exercise are very solid sense. He says:

"Take daily exercise in the open air; do not lace; do not run; do not jump; do not drive unsafe horses; give up dancing and riding" [*i. e.*, on horseback]; "do not plunge into cold water. Many women in your condition will tell you they have done these things, and no harm befell them; still, do none of them. Sponging your body will answer for cleanliness, and a happy heart for the dancing and riding."

"A gently active life," is the still briefer and very judicious phrase used by another authority, who adds that even the strongest must be careful to practise moderation in this activity.

Moderate, gentle, agreeable exercise daily, then, is the rule; some of it in the open air always, if possible; and to include, where it is otherwise expedient, a share of the housework. This exercise to be taken more especially during the first seven months or thereabouts of pregnancy, and to be gradually diminished as health and comfort require, until confinement. Good exercises are: walking, but not to fatigue; driving, but over smooth roads, at a moderate speed, and with safe horses.

The things to be avoided are: fatigue, and sudden strains and exertions; and things that ought not to be done, as liable to produce those results, are: riding on horseback; driving rapidly, or so as to be jolted, in a carriage; riding in railway cars; dancing; running; jumping; reaching aloft (as in hanging out clothes, or putting up curtains); carrying weights (as a pail of water, a heavy basket, etc.); standing or kneeling for a long time; singing much while in either of these postures.

In all this, moreover, it should be remembered that the forenoon is the best part of the day for exercise; the afternoon the second best only; the evening the worst; and early going to bed highly expedient. Exercising in the morning, and avoiding it in the latter part of the afternoon and evening, will secure two advantages: *first*, the use of the best physical strength, and thus avoiding the additional risks from exertion when the body is more or less fatigued with the results of the day's occupation; and *second*, the use of the best of the sunshine and air, which are always more vital and inspiring in the forenoon; while toward evening there is risk of harm from dampness, dew, and cold.

One caution should here be added, which has become necessary only of late years. During pregnancy, even more care than usual should be observed to avoid doing *treadle work*, either on a sewing-machine or on a melodeon or other similarly operated musical instrument. This is a point of much importance.

The usual bathing for cleanliness, it is taken for granted, will be kept up during pregnancy, of course. That use of cold or tepid water which has been found suitable for this purpose will not be less agreeable, healthful, or restful, at this period than at others.

Of the use of the sitz-bath in particular, Dr. Shew speaks as follows:

"Pregnant women receive much benefit from a constant use of this bath. A small tub of sufficient size, set upon a very low stool, or anything by which it may be raised a few inches, is quite sufficient. Unpainted wood is the best material, metal being unpleasant and cold. The water is used from one to five or six inches deep. The length of time this bath is used varies from a few minutes to two hours or more. To avoid exposure to cold it is best to uncover only the part of the person to be exposed to the water. This bath has the effect of strengthening the nerves, or drawing the blood and humours from the head, chest, and abdomen, and of relieving pain and flatulency; and is of the utmost value to those of sedentary habits. It is sometimes well to take a foot-bath, tepid or cold, at the same time. If a large quantity of cold water were used in this bath, it would remain cold too long, and thus drive the blood to the head and upper parts of the body, which might be very injurious; but the small quantity of water used at once becomes warm, and thus admits of speedy reaction. In some local diseases of the lower parts, where there is inflammation, and the cold water feels most agreeable, the water is frequently changed. If there is any inclination to headache, or too much heat in the head, a cold bandage upon the forehead or temples is good. It is often well to rub the abdomen briskly during this bath. The sitz-bath may be used by any person, whether in health or otherwise, without the slightest fear of taking cold. Let those subject to giddiness, headaches, or congestion of blood in the upper regions try this, and they will at once perceive its utility."

CHAPTER VI.

THE SITZ-BATH, AND BATHING GENERALLY, IN PREGNANCY.

BATHING, like eating, should be agreeable. For healthy people, and properly managed, it is agreeable. It is an error to insist upon one particular mode of applying water to everybody alike. Strength, constitution, present physical condition, previously acquired habits, should all be considered. It would be inconsiderate if not quackish, for instance, to prescribe a full bath in cold water immediately upon getting out of bed, for everybody, men, women, and children, sick or well, all alike. Some persons of abundant vitality and great and prompt reactive power, would find a daily thorough plunge and swim agreeable, even if they had to cut in the ice to make room enough to swim in; while others, of weaker physique, might be so chilled by the process as to experience dangerous internal congestions or other affections of the circulation and vital processes.

Accordingly, the bath should be cold, tepid, warm, or hot; full or partial; by plunge, sponge, douche, sitz., etc; at rising, before meals, or at bed-time, and so on, as the condition and characteristics of the individual require.

These suggestions are especially important, of course, in regulating the use of the bath during pregnancy. As in the case of physical exercise, a proper allowance of it is of great importance and advantage, while excess or error in employing it may do much harm.

The milder of the modern methods of hydropathic practice afford very sensible directions for managing the application of baths for medical or physiological purposes; and such suggestions as are here offered are believed to be in accordance with those mild methods.

The tub or bath used for this purpose should be large enough to admit of rubbing the person, if desirable. It will be found a great convenience to raise it a few inches from the floor. Care should be taken not to use the sitz-bath while the stomach is fully occupied in digestion, as the effect made upon the skin and circulation by the bath diverts too much of the vital power from the stomach In his *Water Cure Manual*, Dr. Shew thus sums up the uses of the sitz-bath:

"As a tonic to the stomach, liver, bowels, womb, spine, etc., this bath is highly useful. In constipation and other irregularities it is famous. Those of sedentary habits will find its use of rare service. For the tonic effect, it is taken for from ten to twenty-five minutes or more. If it is continued some length of time, the water is to be changed once or more, as it would otherwise become too warm.

"In pregnancy, besides general ablutions, the semi-daily use of this bath is productive of great good. In those troublesome itchings (*pruritus pudendi*), this application should be made as often as the symptoms occur, and the remedy will be found a sovereign one.

"In piles and hemorrhoids the cold hip bath is used, and in all acute diseases of the genital organs."

The best time in the day for the sitz-bath is just before retiring for the night. Probably the best temperature for the water is 90° F. No shock should be given to the system, and the bath should be so arranged as to be entirely comfortable. It is well, while in the bath, to have an attendant rub thoroughly but gently the back, from the shoulders down to the hips, with the bare hand, and also the sides and abdomen. Besides the general tonic effect upon the whole system, this practice, strengthens all the muscles of those parts greatly, and relieves any congestion that may have been caused by clothing or other means. We have never known a woman who used the sitz-bath properly during pregnancy but found great benefit from it.

CHAPTER VII.

PAINLESS PARTURITION BY FRUIT DIET.

In 1841, there was privately printed in England, a small pamphlet of twenty-two pages, in which a gentleman, who was a chemist, gave an account of an experiment he himself tried in the case of his wife, whose labours had been so excessively painful that there was much reason to fear she would not survive the next one. The result was so favourable that he felt it his duty to publish it with his name and residence, and a reference to "the ladies, No. 27 Charlotte Street, Portland Place, London," where inquiries might be made by others wishing to verify the experiment; and where, it was requested, might be left accounts of other successful results of the plan of action.

A few experiments were made in Boston and vicinity with distinguished success; when the discovery of ether rather threw it into the shade. As, however, there are persons, especially out of New England, who do not use ether, the following extracts are made from the pamphlet in question, which has now become very scarce, and, indeed, practically inaccessible. It will be best to begin by stating the principle of the system, with which the experimenter ends his account, viz.: "In proportion as a woman subsists during pregnancy upon aliment which is free from earthy and bony matter, will she avoid pain and danger in delivery; hence the more ripe fruit, acid fruit in particular, and the less of other kinds of food, but particularly of bread or pastry of any kind, is consumed, the less will be the danger and sufferings of childbirth."

The subject of this experiment had within three years given birth to two children; and not only suffered extremely in the parturition; but for two or three months previous to delivery her general health was very indifferent; her lower extremities exceedingly swelled and painful; the veins so full and prominent as to be almost bursting; in fact, to prevent such a catastrophe, bandages had to be applied; and for the few last weeks of gestation, her size and weight were such as to prevent her from attending to her usual duties. She had on this occasion, two years and a half after her last delivery, advanced full seven months in pregnancy before she commenced the experiment at her husband's earnest instance; her legs and feet were, as before, considerably swelled; the veins distended and knotty, and her health diminishing.

She began the experiment in the first week of January 1841. She commenced by eating an apple and an orange the first thing in the morning and again at night. This was continued for about four days, when she took just before breakfast, in addition to the apple and orange, the juice of a lemon mixed with sugar, and at breakfast two or three roasted apples, taking a very small quantity of her usual food, viz., wheaten bread and butter. During the forenoon she took an orange or two and an apple. For dinner took fish or flesh in a small quantity, and potatoes, greens and apples—the apples sometimes peeled and cut into pieces; sometimes boiled whole, along with the potatoes; sometimes roasted before the fire, and afterward mixed with sugar. In the afternoon she sucked an orange or ate an apple or some grapes, and always took some lemon-juice mixed with sugar or treacle. At first the fruits acted strongly on the stomach and intestines, but this soon ceased and she could take several lemons without inconvenience. For supper she had again roasted apples or a few oranges, and rice or sago boiled in milk; sometimes the apples, peeled and cored, were boiled along with the rice and sago. On several occasions she took for supper apples and raisins, or figs with an orange cut among them, and sometimes all stewed together. Two or three times a week she took a teaspoonful of a mixture made of the juice of two oranges, one lemon, half a pound of grapes, and a quarter of a pound of sugar or treacle. The sugar or treacle served mainly to cover the taste of the acids, but all saccharine matter is very nutritious. The object in giving these acids was to dissolve as much as possible the earthy or bony matter which she had taken with her food in the first seven months of her pregnancy.

She continued in this course for six weeks, when, to her surprise and satisfaction, the swelled and prominent state of the veins, which existed before she began, had entirely subsided; her legs and feet, which were also swelled considerably, had returned to their former state; and she became so light and active, she could run up and down a flight of more than twenty stairs with more ease than usual when she was perfectly well. Her health became unwontedly excellent, and scarcely an ache or a pain affected her up to the night of her delivery. Even her breasts, which at the time she commenced the experiment, as well as during her former pregnancies, were sore and tender, became entirely free from pain, and remained in the very best condition after her delivery also, and during her nursing.

At nine o'clock on the evening of March 3rd, after having cleaned her apartments, she was in the adjoining yard shaking her own carpets, which she did with as much ease as any one else could have done. At half-past ten she said she believed her "time was come," and the accoucheur was sent for. At one o'clock the surgeon had left the room. He knew nothing of the experiments being made, but on being asked, on paper, by the husband two days afterward, if he "could pronounce it as safe and as easy a delivery as he generally met with," he replied, on paper, "I hereby testify that I attended Mrs. Rowbotham, on the 3rd instant, and that she had a safe labour, and more easy than I generally meet with." On his asking the female midwife if she thought it as easy as usual, she replied, "Why! I should say that a more easy labour I never witnessed—I never saw such a thing, and I have been at a great many labours in my time."

The child, a boy, was finely proportioned and exceedingly soft, *his bones being all in gristle*, but he became of large size and very graceful, athletic, and strong, as he grew up. The diet of his mother was immediately changed on his birth, and she eat bread and milk and all articles of food in which phosphate of lime is to be found, and which had been left out before. She also got up from her confinement immediately and well. After her last delivery, July, 1838, full ten days elapsed before she could leave her bed, and then she swooned at the first attempt; on this occasion, March, 1841, she left her bed the fourth day, and not only washed but partly dressed herself. Had she not been influenced by custom, and somewhat timid, she might have done so sooner. To be assisted appeared like a burlesque to her, not to say annoyance. She had no assistance from medicine; only one bottle had been sent by the surgeon, and this she refused to take.

In the former pregnancy she had subsisted very much on bread, puddings, pies, and all kinds of pastry, having an idea that solid food of this kind was necessary to support and nourish the fœtus—and it is quite right to suppose that nutritious food is necessary for this purpose; but nutritious food can be had without that hard and bony matter, which is so large an ingredient in wheaten flour, for instance. The West Indian grains—sago, tapioca, rice, etc.—have little of it; and Mr. Rowbotham made a table of substances, with the proportion of phosphate of lime in each, so that it may be avoided in the food during pregnancy, and used afterwards in nursing, when the bones and teeth of the child are made. Wheat contains most earthy matter. [In Parke's *Chemical Catechism*, page 194, he quotes La Grange as saying that a person who eats a pound of farina a day, swallows in a year three ounces, four drachms, and forty-four grains of phosphate of lime.]

Beans, rye, oats, barley, *have not so much earthy* matter as wheat. Potatoes and peas not more than *half as much*; flesh of fowls and young animals *one-tenth*; rice, sago, fish, eggs, etc., *still less*; cheese, *one-twentieth*; cabbage, savory, broccoli, artichokes, coleworts, asparagus, endives, rhubarb, cauliflower, celery, and fresh vegetables generally; turnips, carrots, onions, radishes, garlic, parsley, spinage, small salad, lettuce, cucumbers, leeks, beet-root, parsnips, mangel-wurzel, mushrooms, vegetable marrows, and all kinds of herbs and flowers, average less than *one-fifth*; apples pears, plums, cherries, strawberries, gooseberries, raspberries, cranberries, blackberries, huckleberries, currants, melons, olives, peaches, apricots, pineapples, nectarines, pomegranates, dates, prunes, raisins, figs, lemons, limes, oranges, and grapes, on the average are *two hundred times less* ossifying than bread or anything else prepared of wheaten flour.

Some articles, as honey, treacle, sugar, butter, oil, vinegar and alcohol, if unadulterated, are quite free from earthy matter. But still worse than wheaten flour is common salt, and nearly as bad are pepper, cinnamon, nutmeg, cloves, ginger, coffee, cocoa, Turkey rhubarb, liquorice, lentils, cinchona or Peruvian bark, cascarilla, sarsaparilla and gentian.

With regard to drinks, no water except rain and snow as it falls, and distilled water, is free from earthy matter, and every family should have a distilling apparatus; and perhaps it would pay capitalists to form a company for the purpose of distilling water on a large scale. Filtering water is not sufficient to purify it of earthy matter, because a filter can only remove such particles as are mechanically mixed, and mere boiling produces no beneficial change. Spring water, pure and limpid as it appears to the eye, is found, upon chemical examination, to contain a very large proportion of calcareous earthy matter; so much indeed that it has been calculated that a person drinking an average quantity of water per day for forty years, will, in that time, take into his body as much as would form a pillar of marble as large as an average-sized man. As it evaporates from the body, it leaves behind the earthy matter which it holds in solution, and thus tends to choke up or incrust the blood-vessels and nerves; in short, to harden and petrify the whole system, in the same manner as we find it incrust vessels from which water is evaporated (for this incrusting only takes place where the water goes off in the form of steam or vapour). Water from rivers and pits, in addition to calcareous earthy matter, generally contains putrid or vegetable substances.

But drink of any kind is foreign to human nature in its original capacity. If men ate every day as much fruit as they ought, they would never be thirsty, and so need no drink at all.

Before adding to the above account of the experiment others made in consequence of it, by well-known persons in England and America, we may copy Mr. Rowbotham's account of the origin of his idea. It was from reading, in the *Penny Cyclopedia*, the following paragraph:

"When first the human embryo becomes distinctly visible it is almost wholly fluid, consisting only of a soft gelatinous pulp. In this gelatinous pulp solid substances are formed, which gradually increase and are fashioned in organs. These organs in their rudimentary state are soft and tender; but in the progress of their development constantly acquiring a greater number of solid particles, the cohesion of which progressively increases, the organs at length become dense and firm. As the soft solids augment in bulk and density, bony particles are deposited, sparingly at first and in detached masses, but accumulated by degrees; these too are at length fashioned into distinct osseous structures, which, extending in every direction until they touch at every point, ultimately form the connected bony framework of the system. This bony fabric, although soft, solid, and tender at first, becomes by degrees firm and resisting.'

Upon the above remarks he reasoned thus:

"If the first visible state of the human being is that of a fluid, or soft gelatinous pulp; and if the embryo or fœtus gradually consolidates, or increases in firmness and density by the accumulation of bony particles, will it not, at any given period of its existence, be more or less firm according to the bony matter which has been deposited?

"And is not the mother's blood the source of this bony matter, since it builds, supports, and nourishes the fœtus?

"And is not the mother's blood derived from her food and drink? and, according to the proportion of bony matter existing in them, will not the fœtus become more or less firm and resisting?"

Moreover, he knew that it made all the difference whether the fœtus were in gristle or not, at birth, with respect to the pain of labour; and that it was better for the future size and beauty of the child, and even its strength, that it should be born with gristle, and not with the bones hardened, but that the latter process should be the consequence of its own food taken after birth. Hence he very philosophically concluded to try the experiment of having his wife feed during gestation on substances which did not hold a large proportion of phosphate of lime, which is the hard ingredient of bone, but take those substances during her period of nursing, and feed the child upon them during its growth.

The experiment succeeded in a partial trial in this morbid case, and it has succeeded in every normal case in which it has been tried, as far as is now known. The first case that is reported personally, was that of an English lady who had learned from the pamphlet. She brought to America a most beautiful child, which attracted everybody's attention; looking, as one person said, "like a young god." She said that from the first moment she thought she was pregnant, she lived without eating any bread, potatoes, or milk; but subsisted on sago, tapioca, rice, young meat—when she took meat—fruits of all kinds and vegetables; and drank tea and lemonade made with distilled water. She said she never had an hour of nausea or discomfort during her pregnancy; had so easy a labour that she thought it not worth dreading; and her boy, small and soft at birth, became unusually large, hard, and strong at six months. When born, he, like Mr. Rowbotham's, was covered from head to foot with a downy substance that could only be seen when held against the light, superior to the finest velvet, and of a beautiful feathery appearance.

An American lady, who usually suffered terribly in labour, immediately procured the pamphlet and governed her diet by it partially, and had the easiest labour she had ever had. Another, who governed herself *wholly* by it, from the first moment she was aware of being pregnant, like the English lady, never experienced a moment's discomfort before delivery. She had taken nothing made of our grains, but confined herself to the West Indian ones—rice, sago, tapioca; and taking a disgust to our summer fruits, subsisted largely on oranges, tamarinds, marmalade, and also took a great many lemons. At first, the fruits made her bowels too loose, but she did not abandon them on that account, but took mutton broth with rice in it, to correct this effect. She also took fish and sardines, and the young of meats; for the older animals are, the greater quantity of earthy matter is contained in their secretions, and so it is even with milk. She had so little thirst that she drank nothing but a little tea made with distilled water. This lady and her husband were neither of them very young—she was thirty-five and he forty at the birth of their eldest child; and she had been an invalid in her chamber from fifteen to thirty years of her life, though very well at the time of her pregnancy, and for the first time of her life taking much exercise in the open air.

Consequently, and because of her extreme nervous delicacy, she did not escape pain in the labour the first time, and the process was several hours. But in the two succeeding times, at the last of which she was forty, the labours were very short and not at all severe. In all the cases she rigidly adhered to the diet, without a single day's exception; and her three children were perfectly splendid instances of large, healthy, strong, and beautiful *physique*. The youngest of them is now eighteen years of age. Only one ever had any important illness, and that from extraneous cause, surmounted, as the physician said, by her perfect constitution. The teeth of all these children are very hard, like rocks.

No other case is now known of such exact compliance with the conditions as this one, but in very many cases of partial compliance, with corresponding success; and it is worthy of observation that in all those countries where tropical grains, rather than those of the temperate zones, are the food, and where vegetables and fruits predominate in the diet, as in the south of Europe, among the negroes of the Southern United States, among the Hindoos, and tropical nations generally, parturition is nearly painless. Combe says; "The very easy labours of native American negresses are not explicable by any prerogative of physical formation, for the pelvis is rather smaller in these dark-coloured races than in the European and other white people."

Nor is it to be referred to habits of greater exercise: "The Hindoo and other females, whose habits are anything but laborious, have always very easy labours."

In short, *the diet* is the only cause to which easy or difficult labour may be referred in general. In twenty-five years there has been known no mother who tried this experiment who has not blessed the knowledge of it; and it has saved many a young mother needless terror.

Thus far the pamphlet of Mr. Rowbotham.

A few additional observations on the subject of diet,

appetite, and the stomach during pregnancy, may not be out of place.

Derangement of the stomach, to greater or less extent, is one of the most common and trustworthy signs of pregnancy. The extent and troublesomeness of this ailment will, however, be found very greatly diminished by the vegetable and fruit regimen above described, by the use of the bath, judicious, open-air exercise, etc.; in short by living in a wise, active, cheerful and healthful manner.

A common error is that during gestation, the mother needs to "eat for two;" that is, that more food is necessary to support properly herself and her growing infant than at other times. This is a thorough delusion. On this point, and on diet during pregnancy generally, Dr. Bull, the very sensible and experienced English physician who has been already referred to, says:

"We habitually take more food than is strictly required for the demands of the body; we therefore daily make more blood than is really wanted for its support. A superfluity amply sufficient for the nourishment of the child is thus furnished—for a very small quantity is requisite—without the mother, on the one hand feeling the demand to be oppressive, and, on the other, without a freer indulgence of food being necessary to provide it. Nature herself corroborates this opinion; indeed, she solicits a reduction in the quantity of support rather than asks an increase of it; for almost the very first evidence of pregnancy is the morning sickness, which would seem to declare that the system requires reduction rather than increase, or why should this subduing process be instituted? The consequences, too, which inevitably follow the free indulgence of a capricious, and what will afterward grow into a voracious, appetite, decidedly favour this opinion; for the severest and most trying cases of indigestion are by these means induced, the general health of the female disturbed and more or less impaired, and through it the growth and vigour of the child. . . .

"If the appetite in the earlier months, from the presence of morning sickness, is variable and capricious, let her not be persuaded to humour and feed its waywardness from the belief that it is necessary so to do; for if she does, she may depend upon it, from such indulgence, it will soon require a larger and more ample supply than is compatible with her own health or that of her little one.

"If the general health, before pregnancy, was delicate and feeble, and, as a consequence of this state, becomes invigorated, and the powers of digestion increase, a larger supply of nourishment is demanded, and may be met in such case without fear; for instead of being injurious it will be useful. . . .

"Lastly, a female, toward the conclusion of pregnancy, should be particularly careful not to be persuaded to eat in the proportion of two persons, for it may not only bring on vomiting, heartburn, constipation, etc., but will contribute, from the accumulation of impurities in the lower bowel, to the difficulties of labour."

A few figures given by Dr. Dewees, whose discussion of this subject is exactly in harmony with Dr. Bull's, show very clearly the absurdity of the idea that it is necessary to "eat for two." They are in substance as follows:

On an average, a new-born child, together with all the accompanying materials expelled at birth, weighs not more than ten pounds, viz., eight pounds for the child itself, and two pounds for the placenta, etc. A table of 7077 births in Paris gave an average of about two pounds less than this, being for the child itself just over six pounds. Now, a daily supply of less than three-quarters of an ounce, during the average two hundred and eighty days of pregnancy, will amount to this ten pounds; and this daily supply is decidedly less than the average quantity of unnecessary food which is usually eaten. Since, therefore, we almost always eat too much, and since the ordinary overplus is more than enough to supply the requirements of pregnancy, and particularly since the natural symptoms of that state usually indicate less food rather than more, it is mere common sense to conclude that pregnant women neither *want* nor *need* to " eat for two." The fact is more likely to be the seeming paradox that enough for one is too much for two; *i.e.*, that less food than usual, rather than more, is best during pregnancy.

Regularity in hours of eating is advantageous to the health; and more care even than usual should be taken during pregnancy to observe this practice. Another almost or quite equally important rule is, to eat nothing for four hours, or at least for three hours, before going to bed.

Eating should also be—as, indeed, it should always be—in moderation. It should be deliberate, and it should be cheerful. Deliberation is almost indispensable to moderation; for it is the sense of satisfaction of hunger that tells us when to stop eating, and this sense is blunted and almost useless when the food is swallowed rapidly and without thorough chewing. And the appetizing effect and healthful stimulus of cheerfulness at meals is too well known to require any detailed enforcement in this place.

CHAPTER VIII.

THE MIND DURING GESTATION.

The process of gestation produces a kind of revolution in the organism of the mother, frequently of a very marked character. This is sometimes the case to such a degree, that she may almost be said to live two lives; one while she is pregnant, and one while she is not.

Some women experience a greatly improved state of health during pregnancy, both bodily and mentally. They feel uncommonly active, strong, gay, and happy. This is, however, not common. It is much more usual for the mother to be subject to loss of appetite, nausea, and to other disturbances of the stomach and other internal organs; to be annoyed by low spirits, fancies, and "longings;" to be nervous and irritable; and sometimes to be seriously disordered in mind for the time being.

Many women experience a good deal of discomfort from their fears of the pain of childbirth, and even from an apprehension that they will not survive it. Such apprehensions are, of course, not wholly to be avoided; yet, unless the assertions and reasonings of the present work are thoroughly wrong, it is true that both the ailments of pregnancy and the danger and pain of parturition can be, in all ordinary cases, almost entirely done away with. And as for the danger, even in the present ordinary condition of affairs, where no efficient means are used to prepare the patient for labour or to carry her comfortably through it—even now, the actual danger of childbirth is so small, that there is no more need of being terrified about it than about any common attack of illness. How trifling is the real risk from child-bearing is forcibly shown in some laboriously compiled tables in Duncan's *Mortality of Childbed Hospitals*, which show that it is one hundred and twenty to one, even in hospital, that the child-bearing woman will recover. Her chances are better than this in private practice, because health, attendance, and comfort average better in private families.

Indeed, it would be a strange self-contradiction of the divinely established order of things, if child-bearing were such as to be actually a danger to the mother. It is hardly possible to conceive of a wise and kind Creator ordaining death or danger as constant companions in the individual to a process which is the very life of the species—to suppose him regularly imperilling the life of that very mother whose existence is all but indispensable to her helpless infant.

There is no more need of apprehension about a painful or difficult labour than of the loss of life; for even under the ordinary regimen such cases are really uncommon, and almost every one passes through the ordeal without more suffering than she can well endure. Moreover, it is a well-known fact that even where the pain of childbirth is great at the immediate occasion, yet, owing to some wisely bestowed provision of nature, the impression of it vanishes almost with the pain itself, not leaving the nervous weakness and dread which often make the memory of physical suffering a serious burden long after the reality is over.

Further, setting aside these general considerations, others, which it is a principal object of this book to explain, are additional reasons for confidence. One of these is, the extraordinary facilitation of the process of labour by the Fruit Diet system explained in the preceding chapter; and another, the hardly less assistance which can be derived, where it is deemed necessary by the medical adviser, from the use of anæsthetics, as will be shown in a following chapter.

These brief suggestions must suffice for the topic of anticipated sufferings.

Happiness, or at least content, or if not, at any rate good humour, is, it may almost be said, a duty during pregnancy. At any rate, all the best authorities, ancient and modern, agree in saying that the cheerful or sorrowful state of the mother is often gradually, quietly, and indelibly transferred to the disposition of the child while yet unborn. Thus Mrs. Gleason, in her *Talks to My Patients*, observes: " Many times, in the care of chronic invalids, I find some peculiar tendency to irritability or mental depression which I cannot explain, and ask if there was anything unfortunate in their mother's constitution previous to their birth, and often receive for reply, 'I was an unwelcome child, and my mother was very unhappy in the prospect of another baby, and I, too, wish I had never been born.' "

A moderately active and hygienically correct way of living, according to the directions in this book, will very greatly promote mental ease and comfort, and additional help can be derived from sensible self-control. This, however, must be a habit previously acquired. It cannot be taken up at a moment's notice by one previously in habits of peevishness, or anger, or grief; and this fact lends additional force to the considerations suggested in Chapter IV., as to the influence of the whole previous life on the maternal functions.

In discussing this point, Dr. Dewees says, " The physical treatment of children should begin, as far as may be practicable, with the earliest formation of the embryo; it will therefore necessarily involve the conduct of the mother, *even before her marriage*, as well as during the period of pregnancy." Again, the same high authority remarks : " How especially essential and proper are certain observances of the mother during pregnancy, *that she may insure desirable dispositions to her infant.*"

Dr. Dewees thus enumerates the possible evils of indulging a bad temper during pregnancy:

"The immediate evils which may result from yielding to temper are convulsions, nervous inquietudes, uterine hæmorrhage, and perhaps abortion. Should this last not occur, the fœtus may yet receive such injury as shall impair its natural stamina, and thus entail upon it a feebleness of constitution so long as it may live. It is a remark long since made, and we believe it to be in perfect conformity with fact, that passionate and irritable women are more prone to abortion than those of an opposite temperament....

"Nothing contributes more certainly to the safety and future good health of the child than cheerfulness of mind, or at least equanimity on the part of the mother."

A well-known belief respecting both the mental and physical condition of women during gestation is, that they are subject to what is called "longings," viz., desires for some article, usually of diet, which desires must be gratified, or else the child when born will be found "marked" with a spot in the similitude of the things longed for. This notion is mostly nonsense. Considering that the process of gestation renders the mother peculiarly liable to both bodily and mental disturbances, she is justly entitled to additional care and kindness, exactly as any person is who is similarly affected from whatever cause. Therefore, her wishes should be gratified, as far as practicable, even though they may seem unreasonable. Where they are obviously wrong they should not be gratified; and there need be no fear of any really dangerous consequences from a refusal. "Ungratified longings," observes Dewees, "may cause sickness at the stomach, temporary loss of appetite, sometimes vomiting; *but here the evil ceases, so far as we have observed.*"

On these same points of self-control, of reasonable indulgence, and effects of temper and of "longing," Dr. Verdi says:

It will do no harm to avoid what is repugnant to you but it may be detrimental to your health to satisfy the longing for slate-pencil, chalk, or other deletericus substances which sometimes women in your condition crave.

"But above all, keep a cheerful mind and do not yield to grief, jealousy, hatred, discontent, or any perversion of disposition. It is true that your very condition makes you more sensitive and irritable; still, knowing this, control your feelings with all your moral strength.

"Your husband should be aware also, that this unusual nervous irritablity is a physical consequence of your condition, and would therefore be more indulgent and patient, unless he is a brute.

"If you believe that strong impressions upon the mother's mind may communicate themselves to the fœtus, producing marks, deformity, etc., how much more should you believe that irritability, anger, repinings, spiritual disorders, may be impressed upon your child's moral and mental nature, rendering it weakly or nervous, passionate or morose, or in some sad way a reproduction of your own evil feelings. And, indeed, this is more frequently found to be the case than is physical marking of a child by its mother's impressions."

With regard to the belief that sudden frights or painful or startling impressions of any kind upon the mother produce corresponding results upon her unborn child, there is a conflict of evidence, but it is believed, with a decided preponderance against the existence of such liability. The case stands somewhat thus:

There are many accounts, very detailed and circumstantial, of the birth of children with marks corresponding to the painful impressions upon the mother during pregnancy. These cases are to the same extent proved as are cases of modern miracles by images of the Virgin Mary, many spiritualist phenomena, etc. That is, many perfectly honest and respectable people have believed in their occurrence.

But, in the first place, there is no nervous connection between the mother and her unborn child; and, therefore, the only means known to physiology by which sudden impressions can be transmitted are absent. Gradual modification, derived from the continued circulation of the same supply of blood through both bodies, are on a very different footing. Moreover, there are many recorded cases of the occurrence of terrible experiences during pregnancy without any ill results on the child. Cases even are recorded of the death of the mother and the subsequent birth (though of course in a very short period) of a healthy child. And again, physicians have more than once instituted systematic and extensive inquiries for authentic instances of "mother's marks" without finding even one. Such was the well-known investigation of the celebrated English surgeon, Mr. William Hunter, who carried his observations through *two thousand consecutive cases* of childbirth at a lying-in hospital to which he was attached. In every one of these, as soon as the woman was delivered, he asked if she had been disappointed of anything she had longed for, if so, what it was; also, if she had been suddenly shocked or surprised in any way, and how; or frightened by any unsightly or horrid object, and what. The answer in each case he regularly noted down, and he then inspected the child; and he never in any single instance met with a coincidence. He found blemishes where no cause was acknowledged, and found none where some cause was given; but absolutely nothing to support the belief.

Dr. Dewees, who quotes Mr. Hunter's experiments and other authorities, states his conclusion thus:

"Nor do we believe in the influence of the 'imagination' upon either the form, colour, or future destiny of the child, however powerfully this faculty may have been exerted during gestation. We entirely reject all the reasoning, as well as the appeals to facts supposed to be illustrative of this wonderful influence. We have, ever since our commencement in business, been attentive to this subject, and we can most conscientiously declare we have never, in a single instance, had reason to believe the imagination had exerted the slightest control, *though contrary to our early belief upon this subject.*"

It is comfortable, where there is evidence on both sides, to find that the most agreeable doctrine is at any rate well enough supported to justify a belief in it by anybody who prefers it.

The most extreme views thus far put forth respecting the mental perversions resulting from pregnancy are those of Dr. Storer, in his *Reflex Insanity in Women*. In this work Dr. Storer shows the well-known, intimate, and powerfully sympathetic connection between the uterus and its associated organs, and the brain; and he proceeds to arrange many of the phenomena of pregnancy in a manner admitting of a scale of intensity or importance, from headache, irritability, low spirits, and difficulty of self-control, through such phenomena as a morbidly extravagant love of pets, longings, etc., up to such manifestations as an irresistible impulse to steal (kleptomania), and even to actual temporary insanity; and he even argues that women ought not to be punished for crimes committed during pregnancy. This may be just, but if so, it is equally unavoidable that women during pregnancy must be so kept that they cannot commit crimes.

Dr. Storer's discussion is even painfully interesting, though the limitations which would be applied by a full handling of the question would remove the first unqualified impression of terror; for to argue that insanity, or at least irresistible immoral impulse, is a condition of pregnancy, is little better than arguing that death is a condition of it. No such consequences ensue except in exceptional cases; and those where real and important danger exists are still fewer.

Yet the undoubted existence of such extreme cases, notwithstanding their fewness, lends great force to the views expressed in this chapter upon the existence of a disturbed condition of the mind, or at least of a liability to such disturbance, during gestation, and to the suggestions made for controlling such disturbance.

To recapitulate and complete the suggestions of this chapter:

Be even-tempered and good-natured; remember that the transfer of your *habitual states* of mind or body to your child is substantially certain.

Avoid horrid and uncomfortable sights and stories. It does no harm to avoid them, and it avoids discomfort if not danger. If they are encountered, however, remember that they have millions of times been encountered without harm; that there is not the least certainty of their doing harm; that there is much more evidence, indeed, that they cannot do harm than that they can.

Have whatever you can get that is harmless, that you want. If it is harmful, go without it; if you cannot get it, do the same, and think of something else.

Understand that your unreasonable fancies and impulses are temporary; superficial, so to speak, and not real; and use the same good sense and self-control about them that you should do in managing your temper and impulses at times. It is a received truth that even actual lunatics are capable of a great degree of self-control, and that its exercise is an important element in their cure. Much more will it be found efficient in the government of such mental irregularities as arise from a condition which is in its own nature perfectly natural and perfectly healthful.

Enlist the sympathy and aid of your husband, of your physician, and of such other close and confidential friends as you may possess.

Let your love for your own baby reinforce your resolution to adhere to such a line of behaviour as is best.

Lastly, reflect that philosophy may teach you that it is useless and foolish to torment yourself over whatever you find you cannot help; that not only selfishness, but justice and decency and love call on you to act as is sensible and right, for your own sake, for the sake of your husband and your friends, and for the sake of your own baby; and if you are so happy as to possess a living religious faith, use that. It is given you for the express purpose of helping out your lower motives where they are feeble, and, where they disappear, of affording you a clear and practical path for thought and action.

Make a proper use of that set of motives, and no place is left for the mental disturbances of pregnancy to do any great harm.

CHAPTER IX.

THE AILMENTS OF PREGNANCY.

THOSE ailments to which pregnant women are liable are, most of them, inconveniences rather than diseases, although they may sometimes be aggravated to a degree of real danger. Arising as they do from the temporary physical condition of the organism, what they require is not such medical treatment as may be needed for a true disease, but rather a general hygienic regimen; and for a similar reason, while on one hand it may not be possible to remove them entirely, yet on the other they can almost always be greatly alleviated.

In general, therefore, it may be first observed that such a way of living as shall maintain and elevate the standard of general physical and mental health will of course increase the power of resisting and surmounting all ailments whatever. Accordingly, the two chief instrumentalities toward that end which are urged in this book, namely, the judicious use of baths, and the fruit diet system, may be confidently relied upon to greatly diminish the discomforts incident to the period of pregnancy.

It may, however, be useful to briefly enumerate the difficulties, not which every pregnant woman must have, by any means, but one or more of which different women are liable to experience. What has been before recommended on general principles in the previous chapters is here implied of course. The suggestions in this chapter are not intended to furnish a substitute for the advice of a physician, but to give directions for cases that do not require his attendance. As is repeatedly remarked under the various heads that follow, he should be called in promptly where the case is at all serious; and, under the peculiar circumstances of pregnancy, it is probably good sense to call him too often rather than too seldom. By a good understanding with your physician you can almost always induce him to prescribe for you only hygienic remedies rather than poisonous drugs. There are multitudes of doctors who would give very few medicines did not their patients demand them.

Sickness at the stomach at rising in the morning or at eating.—This is usually most annoying in the first months of pregnancy. After quickening, it usually disappears or diminishes. Sometimes it only happens during the latter months, or reappears at that time, and then continues until delivery or a few days before it. In this last case, viz., of the latter months, it will be best to consult a physician if there be vomiting to such an extent as to be troublesome.

In the first case, much is to be expected from the general regimen herein prescribed for body and mind. In case of nausea on getting out of bed, the evil may sometimes be cheated by lying comfortably in bed while you eat breakfast. Swallowing a very little pounded ice will sometimes give relief, and so will a cold wet compress over the stomach. If these fail, try hot fomentations over the same region, continue for ten or fifteen minutes, and to be followed by wearing a wet girdle.

If any particular kind of food is "longed" for, it is more likely to be retained. So is an *unexpected* article of food. Where the retention of food is particularly difficult, some concentrated form of nourishment may be used, as beef-tea, calf's-foot jelly, etc., as its small bulk is less liable to excite the irritability of the stomach.

There is much reason for believing that this "morning-sickness" is not a necessary accompaniment of healthful pregnancy, but due, in great measure at least, to such conditions of modern civilized life as may be effectively varied in such a way as to escape it. If, however, the decisive change of regimen which would happen to most women by the adoption of the fruit diet and bath method be not adopted, the nausea must be put up with.

Deranged appetite.—"Longings" have been discussed Where the appetite fails, let the patient go without eating for a little while, say for two or three meals. If, however the strength begins to go, try the offering of some unexpected delicacy; or give small quantities of nourishing food, as directed **in case of nausea.**

Flatulence and colic.—Eat in small quantities and often, instead of rarely and largely; and eat nothing for three or four hours before bedtime. Chew thoroughly. These directions are because these ailments usually come from bad digestion. Sometimes drinking a tumbler of warm water will bring on vomiting and relief from wind if in the lower bowels, an injection of warm water may relieve.

Heartburn.—To be prevented by right living. In particular, let magnesia, chalk, or other alkalies *be avoided* and try a day's fasting, and another day's very small eating. A very severe heartburn will often be relieved by drinking rapidly several tumblers of blood-warm soft water, so as to vomit easily. Those, however, who adopt a proper regimen are not likely to have heartburn.

Constipation.—For this common and troublesome disorder of pregnancy, the fruit diet and healthy exercise are the best preventives. Injections of tepid water will often facilitate evacuation. A physician should always be consulted before the case becomes serious. The fruit diet and exercising regimen may sometimes be reinforced by drinking a glass of water just before going to bed, or by eating an orange before breakfast. The difficulty is much more easily prevented than cured; and it is the more indispensable to provide against it, since it tends directly and powerfully to bring on a train of painful and dangerous consequences, resulting in headache, palpitation, and perhaps piles, inflammation of the bowels, **and even miscarriage.**

Diarrhœa.—This may be a result of constipation, the watery discharge being secreted by the lining of the bowels in the effort to discharge the compacted waste matter. The tepid sitz-bath, with injections of small quantities of cool water, together with lying quietly on the back, will generally remove the difficulty. This, with a proper regimen, will in all probability either prevent it or cure it. Care should be taken to keep the abdomen warm by proper clothing.

Piles.—For cases of significance consult a physician. As with constipation, so with piles, its frequent result: fruit diet, exercise, and sitz-bath regimen will do much to prevent the trouble. Frequent local applications of a cold compress, and even of ice, and tepid water injections, are of great service. Walking or standing aggravate this complaint; lying down alleviates it. Dr. Shew says, "There is nothing in the world that will produce so great relief in piles as fasting. If the fit is severe, live a whole day, or even two, if necessary, upon pure, soft cold water alone. Give then very lightly of vegetable food."

Toothache.—There is a sort of proverb that a woman loses one tooth every time she has a child. Neuralgic toothache during pregnancy is, at any rate, extremely common, and often has to be endured. It is generally thought not best to have teeth extracted during pregnancy, as the shock to the nervous system has sometimes caused miscarriage. To wash out the mouth morning and night with cold or lukewarm water and salt is often of use. If the teeth are decayed, consult a good dentist in the early stages of pregnancy, and have the offending teeth properly dressed. Good dentists, in the present state of the science, extract very few teeth, but save them.

Salivation.—Excessive secretion of the saliva has usually been reckoned substantially incurable. Fasting, cold water treatment, exercise and fruit diet may be relied on to prevent, cure, or alleviate it, where this is possible, as it frequently is.

Headache.—This is, perhaps, almost as common in cases of pregnancy as "morning sickness." It may be from determination of blood to the head, from constipation or indigestion, constitutional "sick headache," from neuralgia, from a cold, from rheumatism. Correct living will prevent much headache trouble; and where this does not answer the purpose, rubbing and making magnetic passes over the head by the hand of some healthy magnetic person will often prove of great service.

Jaundice.—See the doctor.

"*Liver spots.*"—These, on the face, must probably be endured, as no trustworthy way of driving them off is known.

Itching.—A wash, or injection, of castile soap and water, of borax and water, or of water containing aromatic spirits of ammonia, at two teaspoonfuls to a tumbler, or of water containing say fifteen grains of benzoic acid to half-a-pint, will commonly be effective. Solicitous cleanliness is the first requisite, and this, with no other treatment except cold hip-baths, and if necessary even ice, would probably answer the purpose.

Pain on the right side.—This is liable to occur from about the fifth to the eighth month, and is attributed to the pressure of the enlarging womb upon the liver. Proper living is most likely to alleviate it. Wearing a wet girdle in daytime or a wet compress at night, sitz-baths, and friction with the wet hand, may also be tried. If the pain is severe a mustard poultice may be used. Exercise should be carefully moderated if found to increase the pain. If there is fever and inflammation with it, consult a physician. It is usually not dangerous, but uncomfortable only.

Palpitation of the heart.—To be prevented by healthy living and calm good humour. Lying down will often gradually relieve it, so will a compress wet with water as hot as can be borne placed over the heart and renewed as often as it gets cool.

Fainting.—Most likely to be caused by "quickening," or else by tight dress, bad air, over-exertion, or other unhealthy living. It is not often dangerous. Lay the patient in an easy posture, the head rather low than high, and where cool air may blow across the face; loosen the dress if tight; sprinkle cold water on the face and hands.

Sleeplessness.—Most likely to be caused by incorrect living, and to be prevented and cured by the opposite. A glass or two of cold water drank deliberately on going to bed often helps one to go to sleep; so does bathing the face and hands and the feet in cold water. A short nap in the latter part of the forenoon can sometimes be had, and is of use. Such a nap ought not to be too long, or it leaves a heavy feeling; it should be sought with the mind in a calm state, in a well-ventilated though darkened room, and with the clothing removed, as at night. A similar nap in the afternoon is not so good, but is better than nothing. The tepid sitz-bath on going to bed will often produce sleep, and so will gentle percussion given by an attendant with the palms of the hand over the back for a few minutes on retiring. To secure sound sleep do not read, write, or severely tax the mind in the evening.

Abortion.—This has been discussed, as far as space permitted, in Chapter II.

Swelled feet and hands.—Correct living, washing with cold water, and frequent lying down, are palliatives for this difficulty. It is not dangerous, and it usually ceases with childbirth. If there are symptoms of its spreading to the whole system, consult a physician. Friction upon the limbs, applied upward, while they are lifted upon a chair or couch, is sometimes of use, and the skin may be rubbed with sweet-oil or glycerine if it becomes painfully distended. Relief has been given by the use of a roller or broad bandage round the limbs affected.

Swelling or pain in the breast.—See that the dress is loose so as to allow the natural enlargement of the bosom.

Wear a wet bandage; if there be pain of a spasmodic kind foment with warm water.

Cramps.—If in the legs, to rise and walk about will often quickly remove them. Friction with the hand is of use.

Varicose Veins.—Wear a laced or elastic stocking. If this is not to be had, apply carefully and snugly a roller or broad bandage of cotton cloth, from the toes upward, swathing and compressing the leg to a point above the distended veins. Keep the legs horizontal as much as possible. Cold water, wet bandages, and hand friction may be tried.

Rigidity of the skin.—This sometimes occasions a good deal of distress in the region of the abdomen. Rubbing with sweet-oil or glycerine is useful. If the skin over the abdomen is made tough and healthy by proper gentle friction before pregnancy has far advanced, most of the suffering will be avoided.

Mental disturbances.—These include nervous irritability, despondency, hysteria, and, in rare and extreme cases, loss of mental balance, and even actual temporary insanity. Enough has been said on these subjects in Chapter VIII. It is believed that the suggestions there given afford satisfactory means of preventing any avoidable trouble from this source.

Leucorrhœa.—Frequent washings, and injections of blood-warm suds of castile soap are useful. Allay itching by washing with water in which one grain of carbolic acid to an ounce of water has been dissolved.

Miscarriage.—See Chapter II. on this subject.

False pains, neuralgic and other pains.—Pains somewhat like labour-pains sometimes occur during the last one or two months of pregnancy. They may be distinguished from the real ones, however, by laying the hand on the abdomen. In the false pain, the womb does not contract and grow hard under the hand.

Similar pains may occur from rheumatism of the womb.

This may be known by the excessive sensitiveness of the abdomen, which becomes unable to endure the least pressure of the hand, or even the weight of the clothes. Consult a physician in this case. A silk wrapper next the body is often a great relief.

Various temporary or wandering pains are often felt in the back, abdomen, or legs. These are the result of nervous irritability, or perhaps of colic, and are only troublesome, not dangerous.

Womb displacements.—For such occurrences, and in case of the discharge known as "false waters," be quiet, and send for your physician.

Paralysis, amaurosis, deafness.—Pregnant women are sometimes seized with partial paralysis, with amaurosis, or loss of sight from paralytic affection of the optic nerve, and with deafness of a similar kind. As the physician will say, they are temporary affections, and may be expected to disappear after childbirth.

Convulsions.—Call your physician. In the mean time, the application of cold water to the head, and of hot water to the legs, is all that need be tried.

Mechanical inconveniences.—The inconvenience arising from the enlargement of the abdominal region may sometimes be eased to some extent by wearing a broad belt with an adjustable lacing behind. It should be next the skin, and taken off at night.

Retention or incontinence of urine will be guarded against as far as possible by a correct way of living. Consult a physician at once, especially in case of retention, which quickly becomes dangerous. Great care should be taken to secure the natural evacuations regularly, and at any other time when the desire is felt.

CHAPTER X.

ANÆSTHETICS; FEMALE PHYSICIANS.

ON the question of preventing the pains of childbirth by the administration of anæsthetics, there is a conflict of evidence, but it is believed, with a great preponderance in favour of the practice where the pain is likely to do more harm to the nervous system than the anæsthetic could possibly do. In cases where the patient is robust, the labour likely to be short, and the suffering light, it is of course advisable to avoid the use of anæsthetics.

The chief objection urged is in substance that the effect of chloroform (the only anæsthetic which is meant in this chapter; as the others, mixtures of chloroform with ether or other substances, and also nitrous oxide, hydrate of chloral, etc., are not recommended in the present state of medical experience of them) is to so modify the constituents of the blood as to impede recovery and increase the liability to various bad sequences of labour. A theological objection has been made, viz., that God meant childbirth to be painful, and that it is wicked to try to ease it. To this it is sufficient to reply that no woman is known to have made this objection, and that any *man* who chooses to undergo the agony that has heretofore too often accompanied childbirth without anæsthetics, should be made welcome to do so.

In the mean while, all that it is necessary to remark here is, that Sir James Y. Simpson, the celebrated Edinburgh surgeon who discovered the anæsthetic use of chloroform, and many other eminent surgeons after him, have used it literally in hundreds of thousands of cases of surgical operations and childbirth, with at least as little harm as for instance attends a similar number of cases of travelling by railroad and steamboat. A few quotations from medical authorities will serve to show what conclusions physicians come to from their own experience and observation of the use of chloroform.

As regards the safety of its administration in surgical cases, the following remarks by Dr. J. A. Otis embody statistics of immense significance:

"You know well the history of the use of chloroform in the Crimean and Italian campaigns, where it was employed without a single disaster; and I am informed by Langenbeck and Stromeyer that a similar result attended the seven weeks' Austro-Prussian war. In our own unhappy struggle chloroform was administered in more than one hundred and twenty thousand cases, and I am unable to learn of more than eight cases in which a fatal result can be fairly traceable to its use."

Dr. Tilt says, of the use of chloroform in labour:

"In our own time the sting has been taken from the curse (of pain) by the discovery of chloroform, for which one of our greatest men will ever rank next to, if not before, the discoverer of vaccination."

Dr. W. P. Johnston says, in speaking of Sir J. Y. Simpson:

"Throughout the length and breadth of this great American Union there is not a single well-educated physician, I will venture to assert, who is not prepared to unite with me in the declaration that this branch (obstetrics) of the healing art is immensely indebted to that great discoverer of the anæsthetic properties of chloroform, for the evidence he afforded of its safety and beneficial effects in many cases of natural labour, but especially for its inestimable value in obstetrical operations."

Dr. H. R. Storer, until he relinquished midwifery practice, "made it his rule always to administer chloroform to parturient patients, and this, no matter whether the labour was a rapid one or no, or whether the patient had or had not organic disease of the heart or lungs; believing, as he did, that not only was it the physician's duty to relieve pain, here ordinarily so exquisite, and to lessen the risk both to mother and child, as was done by the relaxation of voluntary muscles effected by the anæsthetic, but that for certain manifest reasons chloroform was preferable for obstetric use to ether."

Dr. Beatty, in his *Contributions to Medicine and Midwifery* says:

"Its employment, *when properly conducted*" (Dr. Beatty's italics), " is not attended with any injurious effects upon either mother or child. I have never seen any unpleasant result from it, and I believe that out of the many thousand cases in which this agent has been employed in parturition, not a single case of death has occurred from its use."

In a subsequent paper, two years afterward, Dr. B. said, referring to the above statement:

"Since that time I have continued to use chloroform very extensively, and with the happiest results. I have given it to every patient who desired to have it, unless I saw some good reason to refuse. I have not pressed it upon any, and rejoice, at the end of two years' additional experience, to be able to state that in all cases its use has been productive of the greatest relief and happiness, and that in no case has anything unpleasant occurred to either mother or child during its administration, or subsequent to delivery. . . . It will be easily imagined that my confidence in the power of the agent has increased with my experience, and I now feel distressed when obliged to witness the sufferings of a patient, prolonged, perhaps, in a first case for hours, when I have the power to alleviate her agony, and (without for a moment interfering with her consciousness) to render her labour a 'pleasure,' 'happiness,' or 'heaven'—phrases which have been frequently made use of to me by patients to whom chloroform has been administered."

The following details, given by Dr. Beatty of a case where the patient was during four hours under the influence of chloroform, will be found interesting:

"The nurse (the delivery being accomplished) was sitting at the fire with the infant in her arms, without the mother being in the slightest degree conscious of what had taken place; and in about five minutes afterward the lady turned round in bed and said to me 'Do you think that it will soon be over?' I replied: 'Don't you know that the child is born?' and I will never forget the expression of her countenance when she said: 'Now, don't deceive me, but tell me truly, shall I soon be well?' In short, it was not until the child was placed in the bed with her that she could be made to believe that her delivery had been accomplished, and she then declared most solemnly that she had not the slightest idea till that moment of what had taken place."

It is true that thorough precautions must be employed in the use of this medical agent. Dr. Beatty insists emphatically upon the necessity of using a pure article, of its being taken upon an empty stomach, and in a horizontal attitude. He doubtless thought it superfluous to add what is the chief requisite of all for non-professional persons—it should never be taken except when a thoroughly competent physician superintends the whole administration and all the effects of it.

Lastly, the fruit diet and the accompanying regimen recommended in this book will be found in most cases to do away with the necessity of any anæsthetic, by the prevention of the pain.

As regards the employment of female physicians, it is apprehended that few will deny that, *other things being equal*, a female physician should deal with female patients.

There can be no doubt that the introduction of the employment of professional obstetric surgeons instead of uneducated midwives, between two and three centuries ago, was a great advance in the medical art. But the employment of skilled female assistance is another great advance; and reason and public opinion both point toward the conclusion here stated. Only, it should be remembered, *other things should be equal.* The female physician should be as thoroughly trained, as skilful, and as competent, as the male physician. That being the case, it is impossible not to perceive how immense a relief to the feelings it must be—*and therefore to the physical condition*—to be able to depend upon a person of the patient's own sex.

SUMMARY.

PAINLESS parturition may be secured by attention to the following points during pregnancy (besides correct previous bringing up, moral, mental, and physical):

Moderate healthful exercise, and avoidance of shocks, fatigue, and over-exertion.

Comfortable, or at least quiet and patient, mental condition, avoiding all bad tempers.

Amusement and agreeable occupation as far as possible.

Judicious use of bathing, particularly of the sitz-bath.

The Fruit Diet, and avoidance of unsuitable food, and of alcoholic, narcotic, and other stimulants.

Watchfulness and prompt treatment of the various ailments of the situation, should they appear.

Kindness and indulgence by the patient's husband and friends.

The use of chloroform, if required, at delivery; but only if administered and watched by a professional attendant.

APPENDIX.

THE HUSBAND'S DUTY.—It is very necessary that the wife, who is pregnant, should have the co-operation and sympathy of her husband in carrying out all the details of the mode of life laid down in this book. Few women are strong enough to go alone through the months and years of child-bearing without the moral help of him on whom she looks for support. Indeed, it will often fall to the husband to decide for the wife what course it is best to pursue. He should see that she has such books to read as will be of service to her; should often read them to her. He should see that she is properly informed on all those topics that are essential to her well-being and that of the child; that proper food is provided; that means for bathing, recreation, etc., are not wanting; that care and perplexity are not bearing her down. The wise stock-breeder tenderly looks after the wants of pregnant animals. The wise man should not do less for the wife whom he has sacredly promised to love and protect. He ought rather to do for her a great deal more.

SMALL FAMILIES.—It is the fashion of those who marry nowadays to have few children, often none. Of course this is a matter which married people must decide for themselves. As was stated in an early chapter, sometimes this policy is the wisest that can be pursued. Diseased people, who are likely to beget only sickly offspring, may follow this course, and so may thieves, rascals, vagabonds, insane and drunken persons, and all those who are likely to bring into the world beings that ought not to be here. But why so many well-to-do folks should pursue a policy adapted only to paupers and criminals, is not so easy to explain. Why marry at all if not to found a family that shall live to bless and make glad the earth after father and mother are gone? It is not wise to rear too many children, nor is it wise to have too few. Properly brought up, they will make home a delight and parents happy.

Galton, in his great work on hereditary genius, observes that "The time may hereafter arrive, in far distant years, when the population of the earth shall be kept as strictly within bounds of number and suitability of race, as the sheep of a well-ordered moor, or the plants in an orchard-house; in the meantime, let us do what we can to encourage the multiplication of the races best fitted to invent and conform to a high and generous civilization, and not, out of a mistaken instinct of giving support to the weak, prevent the incoming of strong and hearty individuals."

BEST AGE FOR PROCREATION.—The best age for begetting children is those years in which there is the highest vigour and maturity of body and mind. These are, for man, from twenty-five to forty or forty-five, and for woman from twenty to forty. Even healthy women lose the power of procreation between forty and forty-five. Men who take proper care of their bodies retain it much longer, though dissipated men become impotent very early in life. There are thousands of men who are *impotent* before forty. It is a shame to them that it is so, but nature is inexorable in her laws, and punishes all her children for disobeying them.

SHALL SICKLY PEOPLE RAISE CHILDREN?—The question whether sickly people should marry and propagate their kind, is briefly alluded to in an early chapter of this work. Where father and mother are both consumptive, the chances are that the children will inherit physical weakness, which will result in the same disease unless

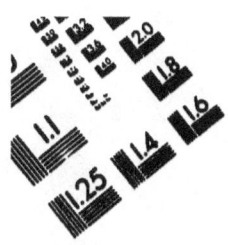

**IMAGE EVALUATION
TEST TARGET (MT-3)**

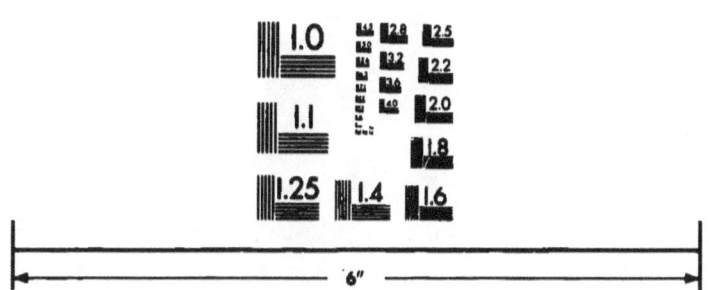

Photographic
Sciences

23 WEST MAIN STREET
WEBSTER, N.Y. 14580
(716) 872-4503

great pains are taken to give them a good physical education, and even then the probabilities are that they will find life a burden hardly worth having. Where one parent is consumptive and the other vigorous, the chances are just half as great. If there is a scrofulous or consumptive taint in the blood beware! Sickly children are no comfort to their parents, no real blessing. If such people marry, they had better, in most cases, avoid parentage.

IMPORTANCE OF PHYSIOLOGICAL ADAPTATION.—Before two persons "fall in love" with each other they should try and decide if the union is the best one by which to produce healthy, well-bred offspring. People should never marry without love; but all who love should not marry. The object of marriage is not love, but to carry out the family relation, especially to rear and educate children, and while love is absolutely essential to a true marriage, so also is physiological adaptation. There are those who think if two persons love each other they are justified in marrying, but no marriage is a good one that takes this alone into account.

Mr. Darwin, in his great work on The Descent of Man, says: "Man scans with scrupulous care the character and pedigree of his horses, cattle, and dogs before he matches them; but when it comes to his own marriage, he rarely or never takes such care. He is impelled by nearly the same motives as are the lower animals when left to their own free choice, though he is in so far superior to them that he highly values mental charms and virtues. On the other hand, he is strongly attracted by mere wealth or rank. Yet he might by selection do something not only for the bodily constitution and frame of his offspring, but for their intellectual and moral qualities. Both sexes ought to refrain from marriage if in any marked degree inferior in body or mind; but such hopes are utopian, and will never even be partially realized until the laws of inheritance are thoroughly known. All do good service who aid toward this end. When the principles of good breeding and of inheritance are better understood, we shall not hear ignorant members of our legislature rejecting with scorn a plan for ascertaining by an easy method whether or not consanguineous marriages are injurious to man.

"The advancement of the welfare of mankind is a most intricate problem: all ought to refrain from marriage who *cannot avoid abject poverty* for their children; for poverty is not only a great evil, but tends to its own increase by leading to recklessness in marriage. On the other hand, as Mr. Galton has remarked, if the prudent avoid marriage, while the reckless marry, the inferior members will tend to supplant the better members of society. Man, like every other animal, has no doubt advanced to his present high condition through a struggle for existence consequent on his rapid multiplication; and, if he is to advance still higher, he must remain subject to a severe struggle. Otherwise, he would soon sink into indolence, and the more highly-gifted men would not be more successful in the battle of life than the less-gifted. Hence our natural rate of increase, though leading to many and obvious evils, must not be greatly diminished by any means. There should be open competition for all men; and the most able should not be prevented by law or customs from succeeding best and rearing the largest number of offspring."

CELIBACY.—The following paragraph from Mr. Galton is very significant, and, though the same policy is not likely to be again repeated, in the same way, it may be in other forms which will be quite as unfortunate. He says: "The long period of the dark ages under which Europe has lain, is due, I believe, in a very considerable degree to the celibacy enjoined by religious orders on their votaries. Whenever a man or woman was possessed of a gentle nature, that fitted him or her to deeds of charity, to meditation, to literature, or to art, the social condition of the time was such that they had no refuge elsewhere than in the bosom of the Church. But the Church chose to preach and exact celibacy. The consequence was, that these gentle natures had no continuance, and thus, by a policy so singularly unwise and suicidal that I am hardly able to speak of it without impatience, the Church (Catholic) brutalized the breed of our forefathers. She practised the arts which breeders would use who aimed at creating ferocious, currish, and stupid natures. No wonder that club-law prevailed for centuries over Europe. The wonder rather is, that good enough remained in the veins of Europeans to enable their race to rise to its present very moderate level of natural morality."

TOBACCO AND ALCOHOL.—The effects of tobacco on offspring are now known to be serious. Of course those who use but little of it may not see the direful consequences in their children, but it hardly needs the eye of a physiologist to trace many serious cases of nervous disorders, including idiocy, to the direct excessive use of this loathsome and disgusting weed. Dr. Pidduck, a London surgeon of extensive operation, says: "In no instance is the sin of the father more directly visited on the children than in tobacco-using. It produces in the offspring an enervated and unsound constitution, deformities, and often an early death." The writer of these lines has seen the most fearful effects produced upon children begotten by those whose nervous systems had been shattered by its use. A potent cause of impotency is found in the use of tobacco. Let women beware how they mate themselves with those addicted either to smoking or chewing. Not less disastrous is the use of alcoholic beverages. Dr. Napheys says: "Not only does the abuse of alcoholic beverages shorten virility, but it transmits the same tendency to the male descendants, even when no intemperance can be charged, yet the peculiarly American habit of taking strong liquors on an empty stomach is most destructive to nervous force, and most certain to prevent healthy children." Darwin, than whom there are few higher authorities, tells us that intemperance, persisted in for a few generations by any family, is likely to lead to its extinction. Nature does not find it profitable to keep them on the earth—they cannot contend with the more temperate in the struggle for existence. Morel mentions a family where the father was a drunkard, the son inherited his father's habits, the grandson had suicidal tendencies, and the great-grandson, the last of the race, was stupid and idiotic.

DETERMINING THE SEX OF CHILDREN.—There are many persons who would give a great deal to know the law for determining the sex of offspring at will, and there are many respectable physiologists who, no doubt honestly, believe that they have discovered this law. Surely effort enough has been made in this field of inquiry; but with what success? The theory now more generally accepted than any other is that of Prof. Thury, of the Academy, Geneva, and his experiments seem to have been perfectly satisfactory. His theory is, that if impregnation takes place immediately or very soon after menstruation, the child will be a female; but if impregnation does not take place until some days after, the child will be a male. Darwin, however, states in his latest works that recent experiments discountenance Thury's theory as incorrect. If this be true, our men of science will turn their attention in other directions to discover this law. Certain it is, that every false theory disproved, by negation at least, brings us one nearer the true one.

FATHER'S vs. MOTHER'S INFLUENCE.—It has been a question of much interest and no little importance, to decide whether the father or mother influences the character of the offspring most. Many have contended that the mother's influence by far exceeds the father's, for the reason that the child is for months nourished by her blood, and made better or worse by her state of mind. Some writers have gone so far as to maintain, that a woman, by living right during the months of pregnancy, can make the unborn child bear almost any character she pleases, and many facts bearing on this point have been adduced. Mrs. Farnham believed this, and maintained it strongly in her "Woman and her Era." "To the masculine," said this thoughtful writer, "parentage is an incident;" and then she adds, "To the feminine it is being set apart by nature to a sacred trust which can be violated only at tremendous peril; peril to the moral and physical welfare, both of herself and the coming life; peril proportioned to the awful magnitude of the responsibility, and to the divine demands it makes upon nature in whose innermost depths of soul and body, a life is deposited, to draw thence support, form, and expression." Galton has probably done more to settle this question than any other man; and, as his views are the most recent and not generally known, a brief statement of them will not be out of place. He carefully traced the biographies of a large number of illustrious men in different walks of life, and found that among judges, statesmen, commanders, men of literature, and men of science, in one hundred cases 70 of them would be found to have derived their talent mainly from their fathers, and 30 mainly from their mothers. In the case of poets and artists, the influence of the female line is enormously less than the male, being 94 to 6 in the former, and 85 to 15 in the latter. Eminent divines, however, he finds inherit their talent very largely from their mothers, the relation being 73 to 27 in their favour. Mr. Galton, however, admits that the apparent incapacity of the female line for transmitting peculiar forms of ability may be due to the fact that the daughters of eminent men do not marry so frequently as other women. He makes an exception in the case of the daughters of eminent divines, they being quite as likely to marry as the women of any class. If we admit the truth of these investigations, the conclusions we must arrive at are, that the intellectual faculties are most likely to be inherited from the father, and the moral nature from the mother. And this is no doubt near the truth. Each sex gives to the offspring what it has the most of.

In regard to bodily conformation, the same general principle seems to hold good, the male transmitting the bony frame-work and the muscular system, lungs and heart, and the female the vital organs, especially the organs of digestion and assimilation. It is well to bear these points in mind, as they may often aid in deciding the physiological adaptation of two persons who may wish to marry.

On the whole we may infer that the influence of the different sexes on offspring is about equal, and it is probably well that this is so. It gives to each an equal right in them, and imposes, if not the same, at least equal duties, and this is what all children need. A child should never be brought up under the exclusive influence of either sex; there are many things a mother only can do for it, and quite as many things a father only can do.

SHALL PREGNANT WOMEN WORK ?—Some years ago, a thoughtful mother wrote an article for a leading American magazine, from which the following sentence is taken:— "Children born of over-worked mothers, are liable to be a dwarfed and puny race. I am inclined to think, however, that their chances are better than those of the children of inactive, dependent, indolent mothers who have neither brain nor muscle to transmit to son or daughter. The truth seems to be that excessive labour, with either body or mind, is alike injurious to both man and woman; and herein lies the sting of that old curse." This paragraph suggests all that need be said on the question whether pregnant women should or should not labour. At least it is certain they should not be foolishly idle; and on the other hand, it is equally certain that they should be relieved from painful laborious occupations that exhaust and unfit them for happiness. Pleasant and useful physical and intellectual occupation, however, will not only not do harm, but positive good.

INTELLECTUAL ACTIVITY AND PARENTAGE.—Another question of interest is, whether great intellectual activity is favourable to maternity, or the reverse. There is probably but one answer to this question, and that is—"the more personal expenditure of nervous energy, the less maternal vigour." If all the life-force is used up on the brain and nerves, little is left for the processes of procreation. Great and constant nervous exertion involves a costly outlay of life.

E. Ray Lankester, in his excellent Prize Essay on Comparative Longevity, says: "It is noteworthy that the generative expenditure is lessened in women when the personal expenditure is increased, as is distinctly observed in the United States of America, where the women are intellectually far more active than elsewhere, and suffer, so far, from the relatively enormous costliness of nervous outlay. Thus the material of generation serves as a store which is drawn upon before the general powers involving longevity are affected in women." The reader, however, must not misunderstand this quotation. It does not teach that women may not become cultivated and intellectual without loss of procreative power, but they must not use up too much of their energy in intellectual activity if they wish to become mothers. Engrossing literary pursuits, no less than anxiety, care, and an overtaxed physical system, interferes with procreation. There are those who spurn child-bearing as ignoble compared with intellectual labour, but the successful rearing of noble boys and girls, is the greatest work that has ever been accomplished on this planet. Literature, art, science, all pale before it. In it all culture and discipline, all goodness and beauty combine. "The woman's womanliness and the man's manliness find full expression here in the quality of offspring." James Parton says: "The best man is he who can rear the best child, and the best woman is she who can rear the best child." We very properly extol to the skies Harriet Hosmer, the artist, for cutting in marble the statue of a Zenobia; how much more should we sing praises to the man and the woman who bring into the world a noble boy or girl. The one is a piece of lifeless beauty, the other a piece of life including all beauty, all possibilities.

Mrs. Stanton's Testimony.

Elizabeth Cady Stanton, in a lecture to ladies, delivered after most of this work was in print, thus strongly states her views regarding maternity, and painless parturition:—

"We must educate our daughters to think that motherhood is grand, and that God never cursed it. And the curse, if it be a curse, may be rolled off, as man has rolled away the curse of labour; as the curse has been rolled from the descendants of Ham. My mission among women is to preach this new gospel. If you suffer, it is not because you are cursed of God, but because you violate His laws. What an incubus it would take from woman could she be educated to know that the pains of maternity are no curse upon her kind. We know that among Indians the squaws do not suffer in childbirth. They will step aside from the ranks, even on the march, and return in a short time bearing with them the new-born child. What an absurdity, then, to suppose that only enlightened Christian women are cursed. But one word of fact is worth a volume of philosophy: let me give you some of my own experience. I am the mother of seven children. My girlhood was spent mostly in the open air. I early imbibed the idea that a girl was just as good as a boy, and I earried it out. I would walk five miles before breakfast or ride ten on horseback. After I was married I wore my clothing sensibly. Their weight hung entirely on my shoulders. I never compressed my body out of its natural shape. When my first four children were born, I suffered very little. I then made up my mind that it was totally unnecessary for me to suffer at all; so I dressed lightly, walked every day, lived as much as possible in the open air, eat no condiments or spices, kept quiet, listened to music, looked at pictures, and took proper care of myself. The night before the birth of the child I walked three miles. The child was born without a particle of pain. I bathed it and dressed it, and it weighed ten and one-half pounds. That same day I dined with the family. Everybody said I would surely die, but I never had a relapse or a moment's inconvenience from it. I know this is not being delicate and refined, but if you would be vigorous and healthy, in spite of the diseases of your ancestors, and your own disregard of nature's laws, try it."

www.ingramcontent.com/pod-product-compliance
Lightning Source LLC
Chambersburg PA
CBHW032015220426
43664CB00006B/258